110
90
62
262

225
163
62

289
163
46

90

A HISTORY OF PORTUGAL

By CHARLES E. NOWELL

D. VAN NOSTRAND COMPANY · INC.

PRINCETON, NEW JERSEY
NEW YORK · London · Toronto

D. VAN NOSTRAND COMPANY, INC.
120 Alexander St., Princeton, New Jersey (*Principal office*)
257 Fourth Avenue, New York 10, New York

D. VAN NOSTRAND COMPANY, LTD.
358, Kensington High Street, London, W.14, England

D. VAN NOSTRAND COMPANY (Canada), LTD.
25 Hollinger Road, Toronto 16, Canada

First Published August 1952

Reprinted September 1958

Designed by Lewis F. White

Library of Congress Catalog No. 52-6387

Printed in the United States of America

Dedicated to

HERBERT EUGENE BOLTON

Entre historiadores meu amigo mais velho e mais prezado

FOREWORD

VERY few Americans—and in general the scholars are no exceptions—have ever read a book on Portuguese history. The available reading matter in English is limited, and only the largest collections and libraries have much to offer in Portuguese. Textbooks and general histories almost ritualistically award a few paragraphs to Prince Henry, Vasco da Gama, and Afonso de Albuquerque, usually in a chapter bearing some such title as "The Great Discoveries." The same books, several centuries and several hundred pages later, often record that Portugal became a republic in 1910 and even now manages to hold a large colonial empire. The hows and whys of all these interesting phenomena are left to the reader's imagination.

If a country must today enjoy great power status in order to justify the study of its past, contemporary historiography will have to be limited virtually to Russia and the United States. On such a basis, attention to the Hellenic past can hardly be warranted from the present world position of the kingdom of Greece, nor can the status of contemporary Italy justify the continued study of Rome. Fortunately, none but the shallowest minds will insist on this criterion alone. A nation and people are important quite as much for what they have been as for what they now are, and on this basis there is plenty to be said for Portugal and the Portuguese.

Although Portugal at present does not figure prominently in world affairs, there is no truth in the glib and familiar charge that it is a "decadent" country. The nation is small and poor; it has had many misfortunes; it is no longer a great power and probably never will be one again. But all this has nothing to do with decadence. The people of Portugal are hard working, have good minds, and possess a culture that is worth anyone's favorable consideration. Above all, their geographical position is important, a fact which nothing can change. It is easy to imagine a situation arising in the near future that would turn the thoughts of Americans, as never before, to Portugal.

As an avowed and unashamed enthusiast for Portuguese history, I can only hope that I have transferred some of my enthusiasm to the printed page.

CHARLES E. NOWELL

Urbana, Illinois
January 1952

TABLE OF CONTENTS

LIST OF ILLUSTRATIONS

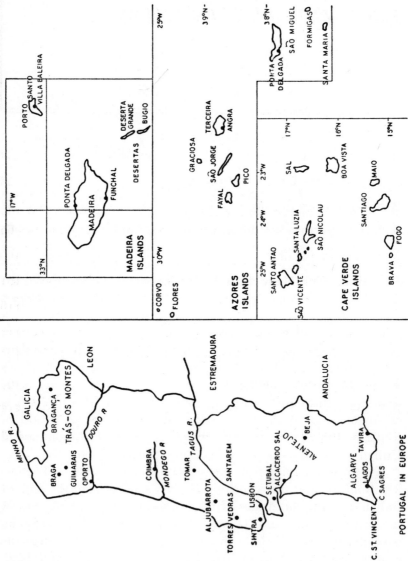

MADEIRA ISLANDS

CORVO
FLORES

AZORES ISLANDS

CAPE VERDE ISLANDS

PORTO SANTO
VILLA BALEIRA

PONTA DELGADA
MADEIRA
FUNCHAL

DESERTA GRANDE
BUGIO
DESERTAS

GRACIOSA
TERCEIRA
ANGRA
SÃO JORGE
PICO
FAYAL

PONTA DELGADA
SÃO MIGUEL
FORMIGAS
SANTA MARIA

SAL
BOA VISTA
MAIO
SANTIAGO
FOGO
BRAVA

SANTO ANTÃO
SÃO VICENTE
SANTA LUZIA
SÃO NICOLAU

GALICIA
MINHO R.
BRAGA
GUIMARÃIS
OPORTO
BRAGANÇA
TRÁS-OS MONTES
LEON
DOURO R.
COIMBRA
MONDEGO R.
TOMAR
TAGUS R.
ESTREMADURA
ALJUBARROTA
TORRES VEDRAS
SINTRA
SANTAREM
LISBON
SETUBAL
ALCACERDO SAL
ALENTEJO
BEJA
ANDALUCIA
ALGARVE
TAVIRA
LAGOS
C. ST. VINCENT
C. SAGRES

PORTUGAL IN EUROPE

33°N
17°W
30°W
25°W
39°N
38°N
17°N
16°N
15°N
23°W
24°W
25°W

INTRODUCTION

THE LAND AND THE PEOPLE

*P*ORTUGAL today lies almost forgotten in its corner of southwestern Europe. In the fast moving history of the twentieth century, amid the conflicts of mighty powers, nearly everyone has forgotten that this small nation a few centuries ago produced the greatest explorers and some of the greatest conquerors and colonizers the world has ever seen. Many also forget that the Portuguese language is still one of the world's leading tongues. A linguistic map of the earth will easily prove this. Such a chart, showing the places where Portuguese is either the mother tongue or the second language, would touch all the continents except Australia and would include many islands in the various oceans. Important spots on this map would represent large areas still under Portuguese control, such as the vast African districts of Angola and Mozambique. The largest spot of all would of course be Brazil, with an area greater than that of the continental United States and a population of about fifty million.

Portugal occupies just over 34,000 square miles in Europe, which means that the country is slightly smaller than the state of Indiana. Facing the Atlantic, it takes up most of the west coast of the Iberian Peninsula. The land frontiers, which all touch Spain, have changed very little in the last seven centuries. Although the country is a rather narrow coastal strip without much hinterland, it is drained by several important rivers, especially the Tagus, the Mondego, the Douro, and the Minho. For hundreds of years the metropolis of Portugal has been Lisbon, near the mouth of the

Tagus, and the second city is Oporto, farther north at the mouth of the Douro. Other places worth noting are Guimarães, once the leading city of the country, and Braga, far to the north, which is the oldest religious center of the nation. Coimbra, on the Mondego, is the university city, where many of Portugal's most brilliant men, including the literary hero, Camões, went to school. Although Portugal has some severe mountain regions, especially that of the Trás-os-Montes in the northeast corner, the climate is generally temperate and permits the growing of wheat, grapes, and olives. In this area now live about eight million people, devoted almost entirely to peaceful occupations. Their ancestors, four hundred years ago, could have come closer than any other nation to qualifying as the "master race," had that expression then been in use.

Geographically, Portugal has no sharp line of cleavage from the rest of the Spanish Peninsula. Therefore, it is rather difficult to find an historical explanation for the emergence, eight centuries ago, of an independent Portugal, except on the basis of events that seem to have been largely accidental. In classical times the geographical writers gave the name Lusitania to the western part of Spain, but the territorial correlation between this ancient region and the modern Portugal is only a rough one. The Portuguese sometimes call their country Lusitania, but such usage is entirely literary and means scarcely more than "Columbia" does when applied to the United States. Portugal, on the west coast of the peninsula, is less isolated from Castile in the center than is Catalonia lying on the east coast. The Portuguese language has more resemblance to Castilian than has Catalan. Yet Castile and Catalonia have long been united, while Portugal has fiercely guarded its independence. From this the logical conclusion seems to be that history and sentiment are more powerful forces than geography and language in molding a nationality. No one who knows the Portuguese can deny that they are among the most nationalistic peoples in the world.

Chapter I

BEFORE THE BEGINNING

*P*ORTUGAL made its appearance as a separate nation in the twelfth century. But long before that time events had been at work to give color and character to the nationality that would presently emerge.

Lusitania, like the rest of coastwise Spain, received visits in ancient times from the Phoenicians and probably from the Greeks. The primitive inhabitants learned a few things from these civilized travelers and traders, but not enough to change them materially from the healthy barbarians they were. The southern part of Lusitania passed briefly under the control of Carthage in the time of Hamilcar and Hannibal, during the third century before Christ. Rome next crushed Carthage in the Second Punic War (218-202 B.C.), and when the fighting ended the legions had a foothold in eastern Spain, though as yet they had not made contact with Lusitania. But the Romans had now eliminated any organized opposition to their control of the peninsula and could proceed to conquer it all at their leisure. They made this conquest rather slowly, because the Iberian natives, including the Lusitanians, resisted the legions bravely. But by the reign of Emperor Augustus, a few years before the birth of Christ, the last resistance to Roman power had been broken.

During the centuries in which the territory of the future Portugal belonged to Rome great changes took place, and some of the effects have lasted until now.[1] The whole peninsula, Lusitania

[1] Roman rule in the peninsula is well summarized by Rafael Altamira, *A History of Spain*, transl. by Muna Lee (D. Van Nostrand Co., Inc., New York, 1949), Ch. III.

included, adopted the style of civilization that is called "classical."
Roman merchants and colonists from Italy followed on the heels
of the legions. They built cities, often on the old sites once occupied by the Iberian villages, and they pierced the mountains and
lined the valleys with the famous Roman aqueducts and roads.
They taught the provincials better methods of farming, and with
an increased food supply the peninsula became able to support a
greater population. Another importation was the Roman law,
which with many modifications is still basic for Portugal and
Brazil. Of even greater importance was the Latin language, which
in a simplified form gradually became the everyday speech of the
people and replaced the older dialects. The Portuguese language
which finally emerged departed less in some respects from the
original Latin than did any other Romance tongue. Architecturally Portugal became a fair imitation of Roman Italy, since numerous surviving ruins show that the building style the Romans
introduced was the same as they had used at home. The name of
many a Portuguese city and town reveals its Latin origin. Good
examples of the transition made over the centuries are *Olisipo*
(Lisboa), *Portus* (Pôrto), *Conimbriga* (Coimbra), and *Ebora*
(Évora). Finally, as the Roman Empire changed from pagan to
Christian, Lusitania changed with the rest of the provinces. During the earlier persecutions, Lisbon, Braga, and Évora had given
martyrs to the faith.[2]

By the opening of the fifth century the Roman Empire in the
west was approaching the end. The sack of the imperial city itself
by Alaric the Visigoth in 410 was the signal for the provinces to
begin falling away, although the fiction of Roman unity was maintained until nearly the end of the century. The Spanish Peninsula,
whose inhabitants had lost their warlike qualities during the long
protection furnished by the legions, became the prey of several
tribes of German invaders in quick succession. The Vandals plundered the country for several years before moving on to Africa
and lived in southern Spain long enough to give their name to
Andalucia (Vandalusia). A people called the Suevi roamed
through the peninsula and were presently driven by the Visigoths
into the northwest, where they set up a kingdom which included
Galicia and the northern part of Portugal. The Visigoths, mean-

[2] Fortunato de Almeida, *História de Portugal*, 6 vols. (Coimbra, 1922-1929), I, 77.

while, took the rest of the peninsula and gradually pressed on the less numerous Suevi, whom they conquered during the sixth century and wholly absorbed. Visigothic domination of Spain was now complete and lasted until the year 711.

During the three centuries that the Visigoths ruled, we still do not find much basis for distinguishing the Portuguese part of Spain from the rest. Certainly the people of that time failed to make any important distinction. The Gothic chieftains became nobles and divided the land, each becoming an hereditary lord in his own domain. There was a king who lived at Toledo, but he had no great power, and the Visigothic aristocracy weakened him still further by keeping their monarchy elective and refusing to let it become hereditary. In a few cases a father was succeeded on the throne by his son, but the customary procedure of election often brought civil war and prevented any effective unification of the country.

Although the Visigoths at first belonged to the Arian faith, which was a schismatic form of Christianity somewhat different from the orthodox Roman form, they made no headway in propagating their doctrines among their Iberian subjects and ended by adopting the Roman creed themselves. Roman civilization, in a debased form, went on. Instead of destroying the ancient culture, the German conquerors made an effort to keep it alive and gradually absorbed as much of it as they were capable of appreciating. Nearly all writing was done in Latin, which had always been the language of the church. To some extent the conquerors continued the Roman custom of building, and to this day in Portugal there are several architectural monuments dating back to Gothic times, but having nothing to do with the style commonly called Gothic, which was a north European invention of later centuries. Although intermarriage between Goths and Romanized Iberians was never encouraged, race mixture nevertheless went on, and as a result some modern Portuguese by their blondness reveal a Germanic ancestry.

The Visigothic kingdom fell in the year 711, when Spain was invaded and conquered by the Moslem Arabs. The followers of Mohammed, then at the height of their conquering career, had previously swept across northern Africa and conquered Morocco. The Emir Musa, encouraged by the visible weakness of the Visi-

gothic monarchy, sent a small army across the strait from Ceuta
to Gibraltar, and the Arabs routed Roderick, last of the Visigothic
kings, who probably fell in the battle. Without much further opposition the Moslems overran eastern Spain to the Pyrenees and
the western part to the River Douro. A little later they passed
into France, where Charles Martel finally halted them at the
Battle of Tours in 732. Not long after this, the Arabs of Spain
broke away from the main Moslem Empire, or Caliphate, and
became independent under a ruler of their own. Many Moors
from northern Africa had by this time migrated to the peninsula,
and these probably outnumbered the original Arab contingent
from the Near East.

The Moslem influence on the Portuguese land and people was
much greater than the Visigothic. Place names still exist showing
Arabic origin, and words of the Portuguese language are based on
Arabic. Customs, traditions, styles of dress, folk music, and architecture, to mention only a few examples, show the influence of Africa or Arabia. Although the Portuguese territory was somewhat
remote from the center of Arab power at Córdoba, important
buildings and archaeological remains show that the conquerors
gave the western districts some attention. Except at rare intervals
the Moslems did not proselytize fiercely, but there were such obvious advantages in belonging to the faith of the ruling caste that
many Christians, both in Portugal and Spain, forsook their religion for Islam. Great numbers of Jews entered the peninsula in
Arab times, for there they enjoyed more freedom and protection
than they received in most places. They long outlasted the Arabs,
and remained in Christian Spain and Portugal after their original
masters had been expelled.

In the course of time the Spanish Arabs built a brilliant civilization, which in most ways far outshone that of Christian Europe.
In literature, mathematics, medicine, and most of the arts, the
Anglo-Saxons, Franks, Germans, and even the Italians, seemed
crude by comparison. Portugal, lying on the fringe of this Islamic
glory, shared rather modestly in the benefits.

For all this, the Spanish Arabic state rested on unstable foundations. Even though Arabs and Africans settled in considerable
numbers in the peninsula, they remained always a conquering
minority, whose supremacy depended on the maintenance of

unity. They developed feuds among themselves and seemed to relish waging these bloody vendettas more than they enjoyed defending the frontiers against their Christian neighbors. They made some show of holding together until the death of their great minister Al-Mansur in 1002, when they broke into a group of minor warring principalities and never reunited.

As events ultimately proved, the Arabs had made their gravest mistake immediately after their overthrow of the Visigoths. The error lay in having failed to crush at once a small band of Gothic refugees who assembled in the mountains of Asturias under a chief named Pelágio (in Spanish Pelayo), whom they elected king. In 718 Pelágio won a skirmish with a small Moslem force, and the victory, exaggerated out of all resemblance to the truth, furnished a great inspiration to the Christians. The failure of the Arabs to avenge their defeat and wipe out the small Christian nucleus, when they could easily have done so, allowed Pelágio's successors time to build the Kingdom of Asturias, which was soon too strong to be crushed without a major effort. The Arabs declined to make the effort, and soon the Christians were raiding deeply into Moslem territory, on plundering forays at first, but presently in larger numbers with an eye to conquest.

In the ninth century, Alfonso III of Asturias expanded his kingdom southward to the Douro River in the west, by the capture of several cities lying in the present territory of Portugal. More time passed, and the original kingdom of Asturias, now greatly enlarged, became known as León. It had a satellite state in Galicia to the west and another called Castile to the east.

By the eleventh century, Moslem unity in Spain had been broken. Divisions among the Arabs gave the Christian monarchies a splendid opportunity which they were not long in seizing. During the second half of the century they all made a somewhat coordinated southward drive against the Arabs. As a result of this expansion, Portugal, in its modern form, began to take shape.

Alfonso VI of León, the feudal overlord of all Spanish Christian states and the most powerful ruler Christian Spain had seen since the Arab conquest, took the lead against the infidels. He seemed on the verge of conquering them entirely. They checked him for the moment by calling in the fanatical Almoravides from Africa, but soon Alfonso was on the march again. In the west, along the Atlantic coast, he pushed his conquests southward until he had captured Lisbon, Sintra, and Santarem on the Tagus. Even before this, the territory farther north, on both sides of the Douro River, had begun to be known as *Terra Portucalense,* the name being derived from that of the town of *Portucale,* which is the modern Oporto, at the mouth of the Douro.[3] Administratively this region had been made into a county, belonging on feudal terms to the Crown of León. Immediately south of the *Terra Portucalense* lay the County of Coimbra, a separate jurisdiction but also attached to the Leonese crown. When Alfonso made his push to the Tagus he established a third county there, with one of his nobles in charge. Under the feudal conditions of medieval Europe, to subdivide in this way was the normal way of providing for feudal defense, because it gave the exposed region a local ruler immediately responsible. But such solutions, though necessary, often cost a king dearly, because it was almost a foregone conclusion that the *locum tenens* would sooner or later strike for independence. These Portuguese districts ultimately ran quite true to form.

During the long wars of conquest waged by Alfonso VI, many foreign knights came to enter his service, attracted by prospects of plunder and land. One such adventurer was Henry, a relative of the Duke of Burgundy. He served so well and so gained the esteem of Alfonso that the king entrusted him with the County of Portugal, meaning the old *Terra Portucalense.* With the land went the hand of Alfonso's illegitimate daughter, Teresa, in marriage. Henry, now having a territorial jurisdiction of his own, proceeded to make the most of it. He soon managed to annex his southern neighbor, the County of Coimbra, and proved very successful in campaigning against the Moslems and in administering his area. He died about 1112, leaving his widow, Teresa, and a small son, Afonso Henriques, not more than three years old.

Young Afonso Henriques grew up in a hectic environment. Over in León, the heirs of his grandfather, Alfonso VI, fought for the kingdom and seemed bent on pulling it to pieces. To the south the Moors, quickly sensing their opportunity, passed to the offensive again and retook Lisbon and other places on the Tagus. Meanwhile, the boy's mother, the still-youthful Teresa,

---

[3] Fortunato de Almeida, *História de Portugal,* 6 vols. (Coimbra, 1922-1929), I, 125.

seemed inclined to make her widowhood a merry one and took as a lover the Galician nobleman Fernando Peres. As her son grew older, the Peres influence outweighed maternal devotion, and Teresa seemed bent on excluding the young Afonso from his inheritance. But this stripling was not a person to be jostled aside. Knowing that he had partisans, he gathered them; and in 1128 he led a successful revolution against his mother and Peres, who then both decided to leave the country.

Afonso Henriques took undisputed possession of Portugal.[4] He is the first character in history who can truly be called a Portuguese, for he was born in the country, ruled it until his death, and devoted his whole career to its interests. Before long he would give independence and a sense of nationality to its people.

[4] Damião Peres, *Como nasceu Portugal* (Portucalense Editora, Oporto, 1942), p. 100.

Chapter II

THE BUILDING OF THE PORTUGUESE NATION

*T*HE modern Portuguese are quite right in feeling that their national history begins with Afonso Henriques. He ruled for nearly sixty years and left the state on a firm basis. Living in the twelfth century, he was contemporary with such famous monarchs as Henry II of England, Philip Augustus of France, and Emperor Frederick Barbarossa. If his fame is eclipsed by theirs, it is only because he reigned in an out-of-the-way corner of Europe. Beginning with almost nothing, in contrast to the larger resources of his famous contemporaries, he built more solidly and enduringly than any of them.

Afonso's most important achievement was that of throwing off all allegiance to the Spaniards and assuming the title of King of Portugal. With his prestige raised by a victory over the Moors, he felt strong enough to promote himself to royal rank. The King of Castile, which had succeeded León as the paramount power in Spain, agreed to this elevation because at the moment he could not prevent it. Some understanding between the two rulers was reached in 1143 [1] in spite of the fact that Afonso evidently did not feel inclined to trust his Castilian neighbor very far. In order, therefore, to protect himself and his infant kingdom, he appealed to the pope and placed Portugal under the Holy See as a feudal fief. Lucius, the reigning pontiff, accepted his allegiance and

[1] Afonso Henriques began to use the royal title in 1140, but the ruler of Castile did not recognize it until 1143. Fortunato de Almeida, *História de Portugal* (Coimbra, 1922-1929), I, 145.

8

tribute at once but delayed recognizing the royal title. Not until 1179, in fact, did Pope Alexander III finally address Afonso as king.

Afonso Henriques is best remembered as a warrior and conqueror. By his expansion against the Moors to the south, he clearly marked out the future shape of Portugal. In spite of his ability and his success, it would be wrong to say that he had any over-all plan in the beginning. His main interest lay in conquest regardless of the direction in which it took him. He extended his boundaries against both the Spanish Christians and the Moslem Moors and fought against both with the utmost impartiality. But, since progress proved easiest against the weakening Moors, Afonso followed the line of least resistance.

Then, too, anyone could see the advantage of striking southward to the Tagus, where Lisbon and other good seaports lay. Lisbon had once been in Christian hands for a short time, and Afonso decided to make it permanently his. After overrunning the intervening territory, the king laid siege to Lisbon in 1147. Here he had the unusual good fortune to gain the help of a large force of English, French, German, and Flemish crusaders, who had left home bound for the Holy Land to take part in the Second Crusade. Touching at Portugal on their way, they were persuaded by Afonso to remain long enough to help him take Lisbon from the Moors, his plausible argument being that here was as good a crusading objective as any. For three months the allied forces besieged the city, and, running true to form for such joint enterprises, they ended by hating each other as cordially as they did the common enemy. But at least they persevered with the long and bloody siege, and Lisbon fell in October, 1147, to remain a Portuguese city forever after.[2]

When his allies had gone their way, Afonso divided his time between clearing out the main pockets of Moslem resistance north of the Tagus and invading the Alentejo, which is the name of the land south of the river. Large areas of his new territories had been left devastated and almost depopulated as the result of generations of war between Moslems and Christians. Afonso brought in colo-

[2] The capture of Lisbon is described in *De Expungatione Lyxbonensi* (The Conquest of Lisbon), transl. and ed. by Charles Wendell David (Columbia University Press, New York, 1936).

nists to repopulate and rehabilitate these empty zones. He founded towns and monasteries, encouraged agriculture and stock raising, and built roads and bridges. Further conquest was never out of his mind for long, however, and with this end in view he persuaded the great religious orders, the Knights Templar and Knights Hospitaler, to establish branches in Portugal. At the same time, he introduced the two local Spanish orders of Calatrava and Santiago. These military monks usually received land and castles close to the Moslem frontiers. They furnished the surest kind of border defense and were also the best shock troops for offensive operations.

When Afonso Henriques died in 1185, he had not extended the Portuguese frontier far beyond the Tagus; but the expansion he had started was sure to go on, because he left a sturdy little kingdom, military in structure, with a warlike aristocracy and a rugged peasantry. The kingdom, even though rather poor due to incessant fighting, had the resources to attain a modest prosperity should peace ever come.

The history of Portugal in the two centuries that followed the death of Afonso Henriques is largely the history of its rulers. While the royal line produced no genius, the succeeding kings were all men of some ability and judgment, at least until the end of the fourteenth century. Each was identified in a remarkable way with the spirit of his people and the times. Whether the kings shaped the situations or the situations shaped the kings would be difficult to say; each was probably true in some degree.

For example, Sancho I (1185-1211), the son and successor of Afonso Henriques, is remembered as *O Povoador,* or the colonizer. He won this name by his energy in placing settlers in his father's conquests, as well as in the new ones he made himself. Some of the colonists came from the older parts of Portugal, but many were foreigners. Especially important here were the Flemings, who immigrated in some numbers into southern Portugal with a clergyman from Flanders to whom Sancho awarded a benefice.

Although King Sancho did not equal his father's record as a conqueror, he continued the southern expansion in a modest way. His own successors carried on the work until there was nothing left for them to conquer. Expansion proved rather easy after 1212, because in that year the Castilians won the great victory of Las

Navas de Tolosa over the African Almohades, who had come into Spain in the wake of the earlier Almoravides. This Christian triumph brought Moslem military power so low that the Portuguese had little trouble in surmounting the few obstacles left in their conquering path. The process was completed in 1249, in the reign of Afonso III (1245-1279) when the Portuguese army, spearheaded by the knights of Calatrava and Santiago, overran the last of the Algarve in the extreme south and came face to face with the sea. The first act in the Portuguese national drama, the establishment of permanent boundaries, had now come to an end. Thereafter, the only change of a territorial nature was a minor frontier adjustment with Castile to the east.

Portugal, during these early years, was a land of nobles, peasants, and clergy. Because the cities were small, there had been scarcely time for the growth of any sizable middle class, although Lisbon and Oporto did have some prosperity and a little trade. National exports were few, since the famous Portuguese wine trade had not yet developed. Most of the land belonged to the nobles, who still bore the primitive Portuguese titles of *Fidalgo* or *Rico Homen*. The latter meant simply "rich man," there being no better way as yet to designate the aristocracy. Portugal later adopted a graded scale of rank with differing titles for the nobles, copying the idea from England.

During the thirteenth century, the Portuguese cortes began to be important in the life of the nation. This cortes was fairly typical of European institutions in the middle ages and had equivalents in several other countries, the best example being the states general of France. It consisted mainly of selected members of the two major classes of the realm—the clergy and the nobles. From the very beginning it had some representation from the burgers of the towns, but, because this class was still small and insignificant, the merchants and craftsmen carried very little weight. Considerable time had still to elapse before these groups could speak loudly and decisively.

The cortes met, whenever the king chose to summon it, to discuss the affairs of the realm, make provision for the welfare of the church, and advise the ruler on sundry matters. To compare it with a modern legislature is to miss the point completely, because the cortes was not elective, did not pass laws, and did not convene according to any set schedule. Those persons whom the king invited to attend were summoned because of their individual importance. If they represented anything it was their own classes, or estates, and their chief concern in the cortes was to protect class interests. Nevertheless, there was another side to the picture. The cortes, although not a progressive body and completely alien to any democratic concept, insisted on the maintenance of the *forais,* meaning the laws and customs that prevailed locally in the various districts of Portugal. The king had a natural tendency to override these when he could, in the interest of establishing more efficient administrative machinery. Thus, the *forais* existed largely to bolster up local customs and privileges, often quite antiquated, and the cortes, by its devotion to these sometimes archaic institutions, served as a useful check on royal absolutism. Although the cortes members had no thought of acting as champions of popular rights, there were times when, by their stubborn resistance to executive usurpation, they did play some such role.

The modern languages and dialects of the Spanish Peninsula made their appearance side by side. They were all based on Latin, enriched by words from the Arabic, with a few added from the Visigothic. Local variations naturally appeared, and by the thirteenth century Portugal had a clearly developed speech of its own. This bore a close resemblance to the Galician spoken immediately to the north, being somewhat more liquid and nasal than the sharper and clearer-cut Castilian. It was King Dinís (1279-1325) who decided that in the future all official documents should be written in the Portuguese vernacular instead of in the Latin that had been customary up to then.[3] This gave a great stimulus to the improvement and perfection of the national language.

A Portuguese literary movement appeared about the same time, largely the work of troubadours and ballad makers, who developed the language into a more adequate instrument for the expression of abstract ideas. In keeping with the troubadour spirit, most of the work composed was love poetry, and two general types of verse were predominant. In the *Cantares de Amigo,* or songs of friendship, the speaker or narrator was always supposedly a woman, and the composition developed from the feminine point

[3] Fortunato de Almeida, *História de Portugal* (Coimbra, 1922-1929), I, 241.

of view, even though the actual composer was usually a man. In the male counterparts, or *Cantares de Amor,* the theme was more avowedly love, and here of course a man presumably did the talking. The Portuguese language proved to be so well adapted to the expression of romantic sentiment that its reputation spread. Some Castilian versifiers preferred to use Portuguese, which they regarded, for this purpose, as superior to their own language. The highest born people in the country did not disdain to be composers of verse. King Dinís himself won a merited reputation as a poet, and over a hundred works are attributed to him.[4]

Dinís did not neglect the practical side of life, however, and in his reign Portugal began to grow more important economically. This ruler is sometimes called *O Lavrador,* or the farmer, because he was a great fomenter of agriculture, interested in breaking up some of the feudal and church holdings and placing them in the hands of smaller proprietors who would work them more effectively. He did so well as a patron of agriculture that, for the first time in its history, Portugal produced more cereals than were needed for home consumption and began to export a surplus.[5] In a modest way, Dinís also stimulated industry, and Portugal started the production of excellent linen cloth, some of it for sale abroad. Markets and fairs had been held before this time, but Dinís gave them a new stimulus. The Portuguese now also had a merchant marine, and traded in their own ships to Catalonia, Biscay, Brittany, England, and Flanders. Foreign merchants, especially Genoese, came to settle in Lisbon. So economically minded was Dinís that his wealth, which was certainly much exaggerated, became a matter for comment and even for versification by foreigners. A bit of early English doggerel ran

> Good King Dinís
> Doth just as he please
> For a king with such gold
> May do as he wold

The remote beginnings of overseas expansion may also be traced to the farmer king, who was responsible for attracting able

[4] Fidelino de Figueiredo, *Literatura portuguesa* (Editora a Noite, Rio de Janeiro, 1940), p. 49.
[5] Fortunato de Almeida, *História de Portugal* (Coimbra, 1922-1929), I, 250.

seafaring men to Portugal to teach his subjects the newest developments in the technique of navigation. Among those who came was the Genoese Emmanuele Pessagno, who became the first Admiral of Portugal, being succeeded in office by his son. Their descendants, with the name slightly altered in spelling, became the famous Portuguese and Brazilian family of Peçanha. The original Emmanuele is believed to have started a series of explorations in the Atlantic that resulted in the first discovery of the Azores—the first, it must be emphasized, because the islands were straightway all but forgotten.

In the reign of Dinís's successor, Afonso IV (1325-1357), the Portuguese sent an expedition commanded by another Genoese to explore the Canary Islands, which had been known in ancient times but virtually forgotten during the middle ages. Portugal thus early established a national claim to this important island group, although in the course of time the Castilians won the Canaries by conquest.

There is probably no European country with a history richer in romantic episodes than Portugal. In the fourteenth century, several amorous escapades went past the limits of private intrigue and exerted a decided influence on the course of events. The most famous of these romances is the one between Pedro, son and heir of Afonso IV, and Dona Inês de Castro.

Pedro, at the time the story begins, was no callow youth but a widower past thirty, who was already the father of the heir presumptive to the Portuguese throne. His late wife, a Spanish princess, had had as one of her ladies-in-waiting the *formosa donzela* (fair damsel), Inês de Castro, with whom Pedro straightway fell in love. The princess had tried by every means in her power to end the romance, but her headstrong husband continued to pay court to Inês, and his love was returned. After his wife died, Pedro openly installed Inês as his mistress, she being considered too low in rank to share his future throne. They had several children, who later, on growing up, considerably complicated the matter of royal succession. The *donzela* herself apparently lacked personal ambition and cared only to make her royal lover happy.

Meanwhile, there were those at court who hated Inês and feared that she would use her influence over Pedro to further family ambitions. They had some reason for uneasiness, because her brothers were ambitious men who might some day try to dominate Portugal through their sister. A group of nobles began to insinuate to the old king that Inês and her brood of children offered a grave danger to the life and succession prospects of his legitimate grandson, Fernando. Afonso himself had been worried by the situation and repeatedly had urged Pedro to marry again, which the prince refused to do. At last, most reluctantly, since he was no hard-hearted parent by nature, the elderly king gave his consent to the murder of Inês, believing that he acted in the interest of the state. Afonso even accompanied the bloodthirsty nobles to Coimbra where Inês resided, Pedro being absent at the time. On learning that they had come to kill her, she made a pathetic appeal to Afonso for her life, an appeal that has been immortalized in the poetry of Portugal's greatest literary figure, Camões. The king, who had a merited reputation for gallantry and chivalry, was sufficiently moved to change his mind and leave the place. But once out of the lady's presence, the courtiers renewed their arguments, saying that Portugal would be lost on account of this woman. Afonso, again won over, told his companions that they might do as they wished, whereupon they returned and cruelly stabbed Inês to death.

When Pedro learned of the murder he at once broke into rebellion. Later he realized that his father had acted on the advice of others and a reconciliation took place. In 1357 Afonso died and Pedro became king. He straightway commenced a campaign of vengeance against those responsible for the death of Inês. The chief culprits fled to Castile, but Pedro arranged for their extradition, and when they were delivered to him he showed them no mercy. One or two of the lesser conspirators managed to elude him and escape to more distant countries.

As Pedro I (1357-1367), Inês's lover devoted much of his short reign to exalting the memory of his departed mistress. He insisted that he and Inês had been properly married but was never able to furnish satisfactory proof. He also tried to have their children legitimatized; the Portuguese public, however, felt dissatisfied on this score and never regarded them as royal. A story to the effect that Pedro had the skeleton of Inês exhumed and crowned Queen of Portugal is evidently fictitious, for it implies that Pedro became a madman. This was never the case, because, even though his private tragedy made him moody and morose, he ruled the nation with some ability.

Pedro's nickname, *O Justiceiro,* or the impartial, is a reflection of the rigor with which he governed Portugal. He traveled through the land, intervening personally in the administration of justice. Enforcing the laws to the letter, he could also inflict rough and ready justice when he deemed the case warranted special treatment. He became an especial terror to those in positions of administrative authority who abused their power for private gain or pleasure. Particularly noteworthy was his order for the execution of two of his own servants for robbing and killing a Jew, saying that "what they had learnt on Jews they would practice on Christians." [6] Pedro was restrained from horsewhipping a bishop convicted of adultery, and he punished a lesser person guilty of the same offense with castration.

At death, Pedro was succeeded by his son Fernando I (1357-1383), the last of the Burgundian dynasty. This sovereign, who was in general a weak ruler, has left a sad place in Portuguese history, but he deserves to be remembered for a few important acts. Chief among these was the law of the *sesmarias,* passed in 1375, by which Fernando ruled that all lands uncultivated by their owners should be taken and bestowed upon agriculturalists who would till them. Subsidiary parts of the law stated that vagrant persons should be seized and put to work, whether vagabonds, beggars who faked physical disability, false hermits, or merely lazy individuals. Other clauses ordered that all farm lands have suitable livestock, with the provision that such draft animals must be bought and sold at reasonable prices.

Portuguese commerce prospered in Fernando's time, and Lisbon, already an important Atlantic seaport, grew steadily. To encourage seaborne trade further, the king passed laws in favor of shippers, exempting them from various duties and enabling them to build their vessels with timber cut in the royal woods. Shipowners of Lisbon and Oporto were banded into companies with common treasuries to which all contributed. Loss of ships, through wreck or piracy, could thus be made good out of company

[6] H. V. Livermore, *A History of Portugal* (Cambridge University Press, Cambridge, England, 1947), p. 162.

funds, and the national merchant marine in this way was kept from dwindling.

In the main, however, Fernando's reign proved unfortunate and almost led to a national calamity. Showing the same amorous traits as his father, the king loved not wisely but too well and, by so doing, produced the gravest crisis that had arisen thus far in Portuguese history. Against the general wish of his nobles, he insisted on marrying the beautiful Leonor Teles, who was not of royal blood and who furthermore had to be separated from an earlier husband to make her available for the king. Dying in 1383, Fernando left this fair widow and a daughter, Beatriz, who had been married at a tender age to Juan I of Castile. After her husband's death, Leonor tried to hold the throne, ostensibly as regent for her young daughter but with the main ambition of ruling Portugal indefinitely herself. She apparently differed from Inês de Castro both in her greater catholicity of taste where men were concerned and in her desire for political power. It was almost inevitable, under the circumstances, that Leonor should have a lover, who in this case was João Fernandes Andeiro, Count of Ourém. This favorite, who lacked any real ability or judgment, behaved like the conceited fool he was and earned the hatred of the Portuguese nobles and the general public.

Popular hopes now began to be centered in João, Master of the Order of Avís, who was one of Pedro's illegitimate children by a mistress other than Inês de Castro. The Master of Avís at first felt timid about heading a party of his own, but the nobles, by their repeated arguments, at last managed to raise his courage. He then led a band of armed aristocrats, who assassinated the Count of Ourém in the very presence of Queen Leonor. Public opinion in Lisbon applauded this deed so highly that the queen's partisans did not try to avenge the death of Ourém.

Leonor realized that she must act quickly or else lose Portugal. Her main hope was her son-in-law, Juan of Castile, to whom she now wrote, urging him to invade Portugal to uphold the rights of his child bride and his mother-in-law. The idea pleased Juan, who scarcely needed an invitation. Castile and León had long been united, and the Spaniards had never been fully reconciled to the existence of an independent Portugal. Juan, therefore, prepared to attack his small western neighbor, and meanwhile the

Master of Avís took charge of the defensive preparations. He made
the important move of sending envoys to England, then ruled by
Richard II, to ask for help and an alliance. John of Gaunt, Duke
of Lancaster, who was the English king's uncle, showed especial
interest in the Portuguese situation. He saw to it that the mission
bore fruit, and the Master of Avís did receive help from England
before his final showdown with Castile. The aid consisted mostly
of a force of those magnificent longbowmen who were accustomed
to mow down the French knights in the Hundred Years' War,
then temporarily halted by a truce.

João of Avís had already taken the throne in everything but
name. He had not yet been officially hailed as king, however, and
there was still the Castilian enemy to face. Two men were indispensable in managing João's ascent to full regal power. One was
the learned doctor, João das Regras, who knew more than any
man living about the *forais,* laws, and history of Portugal. His part
lay in convincing his own nation that the Master of Avís was the
rightful king. The other was Nuno Álvares Pereira, a heroic soldier and able general, who was soon to be constable of the kingdom. His part was to command the Portuguese armies in the field,
because, while the Master was a splendid individual fighter, he
lacked the qualities necessary for higher command.

After the Castilians had made a preliminary invasion of Portugal and had besieged Lisbon once unsuccessfully, a national cortes
was called at Coimbra in 1385. There João das Regras took full
charge. He addressed the members learnedly and eloquently, and
he proved to his satisfaction and theirs that no claimant other than
the Master of Avís had any legitimate pretension to the Portuguese throne. The cortes for the most part desired to be convinced;
but, for the benefit of those with ultra-legal consciences, João das
Regras argued with sublime patience and incomparable erudition.
The cortes ended by applauding his argument and by acclaiming
the Master as João I, King of Portugal.[7]

João das Regras had performed his assignment brilliantly; now
came the turn of Nuno Álvares. Later in the same year, 1385, he
met the Castilians on the field of Aljubarrota, north of Lisbon.
The new king nominally commanded the Portuguese army, but

[7] João Ameal, *História de Portugal* (Livraria Tavares Martins, Oporto, 1940), pp.
173-176.

since his idea of generalship consisted of plunging into the thickest of the fray and letting the battle tactics take care of themselves, the real responsibility rested with Nuno Álvares, now constable.

Tactically, the battle of Aljubarrota somewhat resembled Bannockburn, fought between the Scots and the English seventy-one years earlier, with the Portuguese playing much the same role as Robert the Bruce's Scots. The Castilians had great superiority in numbers, and most of their strength lay in heavily armored mounted men. Nuno Álvares, on the other hand, had to depend mostly on infantry, supported by the English archers and some Portuguese crossbowmen. This situation was forced on the constable because many of the Portuguese nobles, who normally would have provided the heavy cavalry, hung back from the battle, expecting a Castilian victory and wishing not to antagonize Juan, who might soon be master of the country. But Nuno Álvares surprised his faint-hearted countrymen, not altogether pleasantly, by winning a smashing victory. His infantry phalanx held firm, he threw the Spanish horsemen into disorder, and an impetuous Portuguese onset at the right moment sent the Castilians into disorganized flight. Their king, who was ill at the time of the battle, a fact which no doubt aided Nuno Álvares, barely managed to reach his own country in safety. The routed Spanish army made its way back across the frontier in fragments.[8]

The battle of Aljubarrota decided the war. Formal peace was years in coming, and in the meantime Nuno Álvares invaded Castile and won another victory on enemy soil. But Portugal had proved itself in the moment of crisis, and João I, founder of the House of Avís, now sat securely on his throne.

Portuguese nationalism had shown itself strong in a century when national sentiment was only dimly awakening in most European states. By 1385 the little kingdom had had too much history of its own to be willing to undergo a tame incorporation into Castile, which would have happened in case of defeat. Brilliant lawyer and pleader that João das Regras was, his complicated arguments and convenient conclusions were merely an expression of the national determination to keep Portugal independent. Brilliant soldier that Nuno Álvares was, his ability would have gone

---

[8] The whole Aljubarrota campaign is brilliantly described by Joaquim Pedro de Oliveira Martins, *A vida de Nun'Alvares*, 6th ed. (A. M. Pereira, Lisbon, 1944).

for nothing without the courage of the Portuguese yeomen who made up his rank and file at Aljubarrota—men who felt that they were fighting and dying for a cause worth all their sacrifices. Attractive and likable though he was, the king would have lived and died obscure if the hopes of the nation had not happened to center in his person. More than two centuries earlier, Afonso Henriques had sired the infant Portugal. In those two hundred years the child had grown strong and self-reliant, determined to keep the place in the world that had been won with so much toil and bloodshed.

Chapter III

THE EARLY HOUSE OF AVÍS

*T*HE Portuguese had won their victory at Aljubarrota partly with the help sent from England by John of Gaunt,
Duke of Lancaster. The duke had allied with the Master of Avís
for very practical reasons: having married a daughter of Pedro
the Cruel, a former king of Castile, he himself had a claim to the
Castilian throne. John of Gaunt now meant to press this claim,
and it was up to João, as king of Portugal, to help in any way he
could.

The first step was to make a formal alliance between Portugal
and England. This was signed at Windsor, on May 9, 1386, and by
it the two kingdoms agreed to be firm allies forever.[1] Although the
later ups and downs of Portuguese history caused several temporary lapses in the agreement, it is still considered to be in
existence and is now the oldest alliance in the world.

Next, John of Gaunt arrived in Portugal with 5,000 English
soldiers to fight for his coveted Castilian throne. He overran
Galicia without much opposition, and João of Portugal prepared
to take the field to support his ally in a serious invasion of Spain.
Before the allied operations began, João was married to the Duke
of Lancaster's daughter, Philippa, who was destined to become the
ancestress of many generations of Portuguese kings.

However, the joint invasion which followed broke down completely after a promising start. No one in Castile showed any par-

---

[1] Marques Guedes, *A aliança inglesa* (Editorial Enciclopédica, Lisbon, 1943), pp.
88-92.

ticular enthusiasm for John of Gaunt, whose soldiers, who were used to the very different climate of their island home, sickened and died off rapidly from the diseases they contracted in the peninsula. Before the summer of 1387, both English and Portuguese realized that the whole thing had better be called off.[2] So, when the king of Castile offered to pay all John of Gaunt's expenses in return for peace, the duke decided to accept the offer and retire what was left of his army to English-held Bayonne in southern France.

Between Portugal and Castile the war dragged nominally on for years, and formal peace did not come until 1411. But there was no more serious fighting, and in its later stages the war degenerated to a series of border raids.

Freed from outside interference, João I, almost from the beginning of his reign, could work to stabilize his throne and give Portugal the overhauling it needed. Numerous factors were in his favor, ranging all the way from his private household situation to the general temper of the country. In place of the beautiful but overly-amorous Leonor Teles, there was now the plain but virtuous Philippa, and the Portuguese considered the new queen a great improvement. She proved an excellent manager of the royal household, maintained a model court, and gave careful attention to the education of the *infantes,* or royal children. Hers had been a marriage of state, not love, but the king respected the queen highly and they lived very comfortably together. Although João had started life as the head of a religious order, he lacked any vocation for a monkish career. He had had his private intrigues, which were considered the privilege of a high-born man, and no one thought the worse of him. Philippa was perfectly aware of what went on, but she handled matters so discreetly that her husband had no cause for complaint and finally resigned himself to complete domestication.

For years João continued to lean heavily for support upon João das Regras, whom he made chancellor, and upon Nuno Álvares, who was now constable, meaning commander of the armies. Since a part of the nobility had decamped to the side of Leonor Teles and Castile during the war, João did not place a great deal of trust in this class. With the João das Regras influence now

[2] Fortunato de Almeida, *História de Portugal* (Coimbra, 1922-1929), II, 20.

paramount, the king preferred to use middle-class doctors of law for administrative work and found them much superior in efficiency to the nobility.

Circumstances now made it possible to commence a rather thorough revamping of the nobility itself. Those who had lost their lives or estates through upholding Leonor Teles were replaced by a new group raised from bourgeoise rank, chiefly because of their loyalty to the Avís cause in the recent crisis. This rather wholesale substitution of one nobility by another was followed by an important change in the whole nature and theory of Portuguese aristocracy.

The terms *rico-homem* and *fidalgo* had gone side-by-side in early Portugal to mean men of high rank. Specifically, the word *fidalgo,* meaning *filho de algo* (son of somebody), referred to the individual's nobility of blood, and *rico-homem* referred to the administrative duties usually entrusted to a man of proud station. In short, a *fidalgo* who was also an administrator became in addition a *rico-homem.*

With the creation of the new fifteenth-century Portuguese nobility the old terms soon lost their meaning. *Rico-homem* continued to be used in João's time and somewhat later, but no longer did it imply the exercise of any public duties. At the same time, *fidalgo* lost a great deal of its earlier meaning and finally came to have about the same significance as "gentleman." Lesser persons in the past had been *cavaleiros,* meaning literally "horsemen," which made them as a class about equal to the knights of England and France. These too took a drop in prestige, although in the fifteenth century a man might still be made a *cavaleiro* for some brave feat of arms.

The new nobility of Portugal was modeled definitely and consciously on the English plan, which João had studied and approved at the time of Lancaster's peninsular campaign. The title duke, just as in England, came to be reserved largely for the sons and close relatives of the king. It was bestowed, for the first time, just after the capture of Ceuta in 1415, when King João I made his sons Pedro and Henrique the Dukes of Coimbra and Viseu, respectively.[3] Marquis, as a noble rank, did not come into use

[3] Fortunato de Almeida, *História de Portugal* (Coimbra, 1922-1929), III, 169.

until 1451, when Afonso V created a Marquis of Valença.[4] The title "count" was not completely new to Portugal, since in very early times it had been used by the protector of a *condado,* or county, and had been the original rank of Afonso Henriques, founder of the nation. But now, considerably diminished in importance, it was spread about freely among the new nobles of the country.[5] In England and elsewhere, the word "viscount" meant the deputy or eldest son of an earl or count and came to be used with the same meaning in Portugal, although the crown distributed this rank sparingly.[6] Baron, the lowest grade in the titled nobility, was another late importation, and appeared for the first time in Portugal in 1475.[7]

The coming of the House of Avís meant a definite swing toward royal absolutism. The cortes continued to be very important and was called many times in the reign of João I and frequently by his successors. But it is possible to note a slight decline in its influence, setting in almost as soon as the new dynasty had firmly grasped the throne. It had met almost constantly in João's early years, but then the intervals between meetings began to lengthen, and once, from 1418 to 1427, Portugal went nine years with no cortes.[8] Later kings, as the record shows, ordinarily assembled the cortes frequently near the beginning of their reigns and after that dispensed with it as much as possible. Shortly after the death of João I, the cortes lost an important fight when it demanded and failed to gain the right to be summoned every year. More than this, the kings gradually succeeded in having cortes business limited to an agenda prepared by themselves, and in this way eventually drew most of the august body's teeth. Although the time was still far distant, the Portuguese cortes was destined ultimately for the oblivion suffered by the states-general of France in the generations before the French revolution.

This did not mean any decline in the power and influence of the Portuguese middle class, for the reverse was actually true. Not that the Portuguese bourgeoisie ever became great, as the same

[4] Fortunato de Almeida, *História de Portugal* (Coimbra, 1922-1929), III, 169.
[5] *Ibid.,* p. 170.
[6] *Ibid.*
[7] *Ibid.,* p. 171.
[8] *Ibid.,* p. 75.

class did in the Netherlands and England; for indeed the failure to do so later contributed to cutting Portugal's imperial career dramatically short. But at the opening of the fifteenth century this class was definitely on the rise, a fact the monarch noted and approved. The corporations of the *mesteres,* or master craftsmen, already organized in Lisbon before 1385, had been among the principal supports of João of Avís during his ascent of the throne. In return for this, he gave them concessions and privileges, and they continued to receive favors from the crown for almost a century.

The story of the organization of the guilds (*grêmios*) in the Portuguese cities is very much the same as the story elsewhere in Europe. They were located by streets (*ruas*), each street belonging to the craftsmen of a particular guild. The guilds selected saints as their patrons, particularly those whose lives had been associated in some way with their particular craft. When the masters assembled for deliberation in the guildhall they flew the banner of their saint. These banners were gay and colorful, made of damask or brocade, with gold trimmings, and from them the guilds were often known in popular speech as *bandeiras* (banners). Masters had complete control of guild policy and set standards for quality of work. They gave examinations to apprentices deemed ready to pass to the journeyman stage and to journeymen ready to graduate to mastership. The whole guild arrangement in each city came finally to be topped by a *Casa dos Vinte e Quatro* (House of twenty-four), so named because there were twelve *bandeiras* and each one had the right to elect two representatives to a supreme council to look out for bourgeoisie rights in the city. The members of the *Casa* were all required to be over forty years of age and to have been elected by the votes of two-thirds of the masters of their respective guilds. It was understood that they should always have the ear of the king whenever matters within their scope arose needing his attention.

The years went by, and João and Philippa found that they had a most interesting and talented group of sons, several of whom were already approaching manhood. The heir to the throne had been given the English name Duarte (Edward) in honor of his mother's ancestors. He was a young man of chivalrous and knightly ideals. The book he later wrote, called the *Leal Conselheiro*

(Loyal Counselor), reveals his character well. Although in it Duarte shows himself a bit of a preacher, there is no denying his devotion to the highest ideals of kingship. The second prince, Pedro, was possibly the real genius of the group. He had great imagination and love of scholarship. Travel appealed to him, and he indulged this craving when the opportunity came. He certainly had more to do with encouraging the geographical discoveries sponsored by his younger brother than is commonly supposed.[9] Henrique, the third son, was the renowned Henry the Navigator, father of all modern discovery. His character is well summed up by the French motto he took for himself, *Talent de bien faire* (Devotion to duty). The fifth prince, Fernando, years younger than his brothers,* was the saintly one of the family, whose later martyrdom in Morocco plunged all Portugal into mourning.

Europe was then passing out of the age of chivalry, but devotion to its ideals was never stronger than in Portugal during the time of João I, where the saintly and now aging Nuno Álvares represented to the younger generation the beau-ideal of a warrior. From their own mother the princes could, and probably did, learn the tales of King Arthur and the Round Table which she brought from her native England. It was their century, too, that saw the birth and finest flowering of the novel of chivalry, that odd literary movement devoted to the over-idealization of an age gone forever. It is no wonder, then, that João's three eldest sons, on growing up, regretted living in such quiet times, with no war going on to give them an opportunity to win their spurs. Since a war seemed unlikely to come spontaneously to their country, the next best thing was to create one. The question was where, and also how to get their father's consent, since the old king did not conspicuously share their knightly dreams, having seen plenty of hard fighting in his youth. However, he did see a point in giving his sons some military seasoning, and the campaign he presently was persuaded to undertake had a direct connection with the princes' coming of age. Moreover, João had once enjoyed wielding

[9] Charles E. Nowell, "Prince Henry the Navigator and his Brother Dom Pedro," *Hispanic American Historical Review*, XXVIII (1948), 62-67.

* Between Henrique and Fernando came Prince João, who did not play much of a role in history.

a lance himself and, as he thought it over, rather relished the idea of one more fight before his battling days were forever past.

After some discussion and debate, the king decided to invade Morocco and capture the city of Ceuta. This seemed to him a sane and reasonable objective, for it would not interfere with his general policy of peace in Europe and might do Portugal some good. Ceuta commanded the western entrance to the Mediterranean, and possession of it would be helpful in stopping those Moslem corsairs who often raided the coasts of Spain and Portugal and preyed on Christian ships. The city was reported rich with a valuable trade, which promised both plunder and the possibility that some of this commerce could be diverted into Portuguese hands. Also, the religious motive was never completely absent, and taking Ceuta meant striking a blow at Moslem power. For Portugal, this would be a logical continuation of the crusade that had thrown the unbelievers out of the home country over a century and a half before.

After studying the situation from all angles, João began to mobilize troops and collect ships. Ordinarily, raising money for a war meant consulting the cortes, but that would endanger success by giving the purpose away. So João undertook the financing privately and got together money enough to pay the costs, which must have been heavy. Infantes Pedro and Henrique and their illegitimate half-brother, the Count of Barcelos, collected contingents of men in widely separated parts of the country. It was arranged that Henrique and the count could quickly embark their fighters at Oporto and Pedro's could take ship at Lisbon. Cattle in great numbers were driven down to the coast from interior Portugal and slaughtered near the shore, the meat being salted and placed aboard ship. Armorers, carpenters, shipwrights, sailmakers, and butchers turned Lisbon and Oporto into mobilization camps. The whole nation worked furiously, for the most part ignorant of the reason, since the best chance of success lay in secrecy and only a few people knew where the expedition would go. Neighboring Christian states took alarm at these preparations and sent embassies to João, who assured them that they had nothing to fear.

With the fleet nearly ready to sail, in the spring of 1415, a plague struck Lisbon. The death toll was high, Queen Philippa being among the victims. But she died urging her husband and sons to go on with the crusade, and they left Lisbon on June 23, before the disease had run its course. Even as the ships swept out of the Tagus the watchers on shore and most of the crew members and soldiers aboard still did not know the real destination.

João took his fleet southward by easy stages, for he planned to assault the objective about mid-August. Unfavorable winds delayed the Portuguese in the vicinity of Gibraltar, and it was not until August 20, 1415, that the vessels suddenly shot across the strait and made a quick landing by Ceuta. Resistance was not very heavy, for the Moslems had learned the Christian plans only shortly before and had not had time to assemble much of a force. Prince Henrique had the honor of fighting with the first contingent into the town and of personally hoisting the standard from the walls. Much booty awaited the Portuguese, for Ceuta had been in touch commercially with the whole Moslem world and even with the East Indies beyond it. The rough soldiers from the poor European land reveled in the luxury of their first African plunder.[10]

As soon as João had restored order following the looting, he embarked most of the army for home, leaving Dom Pedro de Meneses with 3,000 men for a garrison. Three years later the Moroccans tried to recapture their stronghold but revealed their plans in advance and gave Portugal time to act. A quickly-levied army was thrown across the strait in time to forestall the assault that might have made the town change hands again.

To King João and the greybeards of his council table, this conquest represented a successful military climax to a reign already crowned with laurels. To the young generation, and especially to Prince Henrique, it was the beginning and not the end of an era. Possession of Ceuta merely emphasized the boundless further possibilities that existed. So, at an early age, Henrique became a man with a mission. He renounced all thought of marriage and family life for himself, in order to devote his undivided time to solving the great riddle of Africa. In short, he became

[10] An excellent description of the expedition to Ceuta is given by Oliveira Martins, *The Golden Age of Prince Henry the Navigator*, transl. by J. J. Abraham and W. E. Reynolds (Chapman and Hall, London, 1914), pp. 30-60.

Henry the Navigator, whose place in history will be assured forever.

Just what Henry's plan was at the start is a question that can never be answered. Whether the motive was primarily religious or primarily economic can be debated interminably; it was most likely some of both.[11] Before his time the great international crusade had failed, leaving the eastern Christian frontier weaker than ever before. The Byzantine empire was tottering, and during Henry's lifetime was to go down in utter ruin before the rising power of the Ottoman Turks. The church itself was in danger, having been rent for years by the Great Schism, as rival popes at Rome and Avignon had made the papacy, once so mighty, lose caste in European eyes. Although the election of Pope Martin V ended the schism in 1417, two years after Ceuta fell, the flagging energies of Christendom needed to be revived. For an ineffectual international crusade, backed by an impotent church, Henry would substitute the national effort of loyal, religious Portugal.

On the economic side, there was every reason for action southward in Africa. Europe in general and Portugal in particular then suffered from a gold shortage that threatened to become a famine. The principal cause was the steady drain via the Isthmus of Suez eastward to India and beyond, where Europe paid heavily for the spices and luxuries it had imported from the Orient since the crusades. Venice, allied with the Sultan of Egypt, had almost a monopoly of this trade and profiteered, although most of the gold found its way farther east. In Portugal the shortage, combined with a past government policy of debasing the coinage, had caused both a scarcity of good coins and a lack of confidence in the bad ones. Prices rose, and no law the government passed would keep them down to any arbitrary level. Europe had few gold mines, and most of its slender supply of the metal came across the Sahara in caravans, from the region of the Upper Volta, near Timbuktu. The Europeans did not know the exact location of the source but knew the general direction. Nearly a century before Henry's time, ships from Europe had occasionally sailed down Africa seeking a

[11] The motives are discussed at length by Charles R. Beazley in two articles, "Prince Henry of Portugal and the African Crusade of the Fifteenth Century," *American Historical Review,* XVI (1911), 11-23, and "Prince Henry of Portugal and His Political, Commercial and Colonizing Work," *ibid.,* XVII (1912), 252-267.

"river of gold," supposed to flow into the Atlantic from the aurif-
erous country.[12] A few maps even showed the river, largely imaginary but based on vague reports of the Senegal.

Closely related to the gold search was the quest for Prester
John, the mysterious eastern prince of Christian faith whom Europeans for over two centuries had sought as an ally against the
hated Moslems.[13] By now the Prester was fairly well identified
with the Christian Negus of Abyssinia-Ethiopia. But a little before
Henry's time there had been a large though short-lived African
empire existing in the western Sahara. Reports of this empire of
Meli caused Henry and the Portuguese to confuse it with Prester
John's and thus to believe they could find the Prester not far
from the west coast of Africa.

Prince Henry, then, thought at first in terms of limited goals,
which, as he imagined them, were not far away. But allowance
must be made for development during his long career, and by his
death in 1460 the aims were not the same as they had been at the
start.

Besides Henry's personal motive and the European need for
gold, natural forces impelled Portugal to the sea. The country,
being a narrow coastal strip, lacked any substantial hinterland.
The national boundaries had long since been rounded out, and
powerful Castile to the east blocked any expansion by land. The
small Portuguese population had abundant energy to spare, and
the most pressing home questions of national organization and security had been at least temporarily solved. All the larger European states had grave internal problems to fight through in the
fifteenth century. Portugal alone was ready for the next step, to
discovery and empire.

Yet Prince Henry was not an imperialist in the modern sense
of the word. Except in Morocco, with its dangerous and implaca-
ble Moslem population, he showed no wish to spread conquest
by the sword. Time and again he sent his captains out with orders
to "make peace" with the natives they might find.[14] His only an-

[12] E. G. R. Taylor, "Pactolus: River of Gold," *Scottish Geographical Magazine*,
XLIV (1928), 138.
[13] L. Denison Ross, "Prester John and the Empire of Ethiopia," *Travel and Travellers of the Middle Ages*, ed. A. P. Newton (London, 1930), pp. 174-194.
[14] This statement occurs many times in Gomes Eanes de Azurara's *The Chronicle*

nexations to Portugal were the Madeira, Azores, and Cape Verde islands, all uninhabited when discovered and hence open to peaceful colonization. In trade and profit he certainly had an interest, and naturally so, because these voyages had to be paid for somehow and if possible should finance themselves. Henry was Grand Master of the Portuguese Order of Christ and dipped liberally into its treasury for funds. But this money would not go far unless eked out by profits along the way.

Nor was Henry a great enthusiast for discovery merely for the sake of advancing knowledge. That quality belonged more to his brother, Pedro the traveler, and the best proof of this lies in the fact that the main Portuguese progress along Africa came while Pedro was regent of the kingdom and stopped at the time of his death.

Henry never sailed with his voyagers, so his surname "Navigator" is something of a misnomer. Indeed the Portuguese themselves have never used it, foreigners having coined the title. His actual work was even more important than sailing, and consisted of planning, directing, raising money, and determining the next objectives.

Henry built a residence and settled on the Sagres Peninsula near Cape St. Vincent at the southwest tip of Portugal, and tradition says that he founded there a school of cosmography and navigational science. The idea of a "school" is greatly exaggerated, although the prince did attract some distinguished scholars to his service. His ships generally made use of the nearby port of Lagos. This removal from Lisbon and the center of Portuguese affairs is a tribute to his fixity of purpose and his determination to concentrate on the great effort.

The first voyages were devoted to rediscovery rather than pioneering. In the previous century, Genoese ships had discovered the Canaries, the Madeiras, and probably the Azores. The Catalans, seeking the river of gold, had gone down the African coast, certainly past Cape Bojador, which in Henry's time was popularly supposed to mark the limit of the known world. The prince knew at least vaguely of these voyages, and the knowledge helped him

of the Discovery and Conquest of Guinea, transl. and ed. by C. R. Beazley and E. Prestage, 2 vols. (Hakluyt Society, London, 1896-1899).

form his plans. As recently as 1402, a pair of Norman adventurers,
Gadifer de la Salle and Jean de Bethencourt, had commenced the
conquest of the inhabited Canary Islands in the name of Juan III
of Castile. Portugal had claimed the Canaries since the time of
Afonso IV; and the question of ownership was to arise again in
Henry's lifetime.

The first of the rediscoveries came in 1418, when two of
Henry's captains, João Gonçalves Zarco and Tristão Vaz Teixeira,
found the island of Porto Santo in the Madeira group. The prince,
delighted when they brought the news home, sent them back the
next year and they discovered Madeira itself, which the Genoese
had found and forgotten generations earlier. Henry divided the
island between his two discoverers on feudal terms, and they soon
moved there with colonists and livestock. Madeira flourished
from the start, for it had a rich soil and a fine climate. Soon it
began to produce sugar and wine and, even before Henry's death,
paid a substantial revenue.

No discoveries are recorded for the Portuguese in the 1420's,
and Henry seems not to have pushed matters very hard just then.
If he tried to send ships past Cape Bojador, his captains certainly
had no success in rounding it. Just possibly old King João, who
was still living, looked unfavorably on these distant and outlandish
ventures. But two things did happen in that decade to affect
Henry's future work. The first was the arrival in Portugal of
Jafuda Cresques, a renowned Jewish cartographer from the island
of Majorca. Jafuda and his father Abraham before him had collected almost all the known data about the earth, and this included
a little about the briefly discovered and almost forgotten Azores.*
The second was Prince Pedro's return to Portugal, after several
years of traveling that took him over much of Europe and perhaps
to parts of the Near East. He had picked up a great deal of geographical data, especially in Venice where he received as gifts a
world map and a copy of Marco Polo's famous travel narrative.

The next effort by Henry shows the Jafuda Cresques influence
clearly. At a date impossible to determine exactly, but very likely
1431, one of the prince's captains named Gonçalo Velho Cabral
discovered the Formigas Rocks, which are the easternmost Azores,

* The world map made about 1375 by Abraham Cresques is known as the Catalan
Atlas and shows the Azores.

and a year later found Santa Maria, one of the larger islands.[15] Henry at once stocked the island with cattle in preparation for the colonists that Gonçalo Velho presently took out to populate the place. The discovery of the rest of the Azores followed within a few years.

In 1433, on the anniversary of the battle of Aljubarrota, King João I died after a prosperous reign of forty-eight years. He had far outlived his contemporaries, João das Regras and Nuno Álvares being long since gone. Prince Duarte, now a man in the early forties, ascended the throne. Duarte had not altogether lived up to his earlier promise and evidently reached kingship a little too late in life. A man of scholarly tastes, as shown by his *Leal Conselheiro*, one of the more learned books of the time, he combined learning with too reflective a turn of mind to be a person of great will power or decision. Added to this, his health had already begun to fail, and he gave Portugal a kindly but rather weak administration during the five remaining years he lived. Not long before his ascension to the throne, when already a man of mature years, he had married Dona Leonor, sister of King Alfonso V of Aragon. Of their numerous children, only a few lived past infancy.

During the brief reign of his brother, Prince Henry's discovery projects went ahead rapidly, certainly with King Duarte's blessing. In 1434, Gil Eanes rounded Cape Bojador and dispelled whatever terrors may have existed about the unsavory nature of the lands and coasts beyond. Making use of this brave captain and others, Henry rapidly pushed the discoveries several hundred miles beyond the cape. The ships occasionally brought him back a little profit in the cargoes of fish they caught and the seals they were able to slaughter and skin. Finally they reached and named the *Rio do Ouro*, which they took for the river of gold that the prince had been seeking all along. Insofar as there was really a river of gold, it was the Senegal much farther south, and it is ironic that the Portuguese should have bestowed the golden appellation for all time upon a worthless place that was not even a river but merely an indentation of the sea. It was at *Rio do Ouro* that the Portuguese encountered their first African natives south of Mo-

[15] Jules Mees, *Histoire de la découverte des Îles Açores* (Librairie Vuylsteke, Ghent, 1901).

rocco, but they turned out to be a poverty-stricken lot, not Negroes but the dark whites of the western Sahara.

Now that the Portuguese were regularly sailing south of Bojador, they constantly passed close to the Canary Islands, several of which had been continuously occupied since 1402 in the name of the King of Castile. Portugal, with an old title to the Canaries dating back to Afonso IV's reign, had already protested and claimed these islands, but the Castilians had paid no attention. Prince Henry several times thought of colonizing one or more of the Canaries, but never got around to it. Meanwhile the Castilians continued to spread their rule from island to island, until at last Portugal recognized an accomplished fact and abandoned the claim.

Just before the end of Duarte's short reign, Portugal experienced a tragic sequel to the capture of Ceuta over twenty years before. Ceuta, though a strategic asset, had become an economic liability. It cost Portugal heavily to hold the place, and the trade once expected from Africa had never flowed in, either because the importance of this trade had been exaggerated or because Moslem merchants took to shunning Ceuta after the Portuguese conquered it. Without Tangier, the important city close by, Ceuta would always be a drain on the national exchequer. Moreover, Castile, as a part of the Canary Islands dispute, showed a tendency to claim all of Morocco, which Portugal could never allow. Since the central Moroccan government at Fez had been weak for generations, it seemed that the Portuguese might now capture Tangier rather easily and thus both forestall Castile and add enormously to the value of what they already had. Another factor also counted. Prince Fernando, the younger brother of Duarte, Pedro, and Henry, had been too young to fight at the capture of Ceuta and wished an opportunity to distinguish himself.

The House of Avís held a family council, where Queen Leonor and Henry strongly backed Fernando's wish to go against Tangier. Pedro opposed, since he thought all spare resources should be concentrated on the African voyages. Duarte yielded to the majority opinion and summoned the cortes, which very grudgingly voted money for the expedition. Ships had to be rented from Asturias, Biscay, Flanders, and England, since the Portuguese merchant marine was inadequate. Henry and Fernando gained the right to lead the army and left in August, 1437. They took a force known to be too small for their purpose, because Portugal as a whole had not favored the enterprise and the volunteers had been few.

Henry and Fernando landed their men at Ceuta and the small army marched across country to Tangier, the fleet preceding it along the coast. On finding the city fully prepared for the attack, the *infantes* made the mistake of camping their army inland, beyond reach of help from the ships. The fighting went on for thirty-seven days, and ended by turning the besiegers into the besieged, when they were surrounded by a larger Moroccan army and forced to surrender. The princes accepted the enemy's terms, whereby all Portuguese lives should be spared, but in return the old conquest, Ceuta, should be surrendered. Fernando remained in Moorish hands as a pledge that the agreement would be fulfilled.

News of the disaster reached Portugal, where Duarte at once called another cortes to advise him. Should Ceuta be handed over? Would the Moroccans possibly accept a ransom for Fernando instead, and if so would the cortes stand for another financial levy? Opinions clashed sharply. Pedro and the Count of Barcelos spoke for carrying out the treaty terms to the limit. But the Count of Arraiolos, who had taken part in the Tangier disaster, thought that reasons of state called for holding Ceuta and should have priority over even a prince's safety. In the meantime a pathetic letter arrived from Fernando, describing the hardships of his prison life. In the cortes, business interests spoke for keeping Ceuta, and agricultural interests favored saving the prince. Duarte could decide nothing for himself. Henry, after reaching Portugal, suggested trying every means of ransoming his brother short of giving up Ceuta.

In the midst of all the agonizing debate, King Duarte fell ill and died on September 9, 1438, without having decided. His six-year old son, Afonso V, ascended the throne. The boy counted for nothing in the situation as yet, and the regency question at once took precedence over that of Fernando. Portugal solved this problem by doing nothing about it, and the poor prince, loved by his brothers and everyone else for his goodness and generosity, suffered for years in a Moroccan prison until he died of hardships.

Pedro took the regency, against the wishes of his sister-in-law, Queen-Mother Leonor, and also against the desires of a large part of the Portuguese nobility, who knew he would rule too firmly to suit them. Pedro had never been on good terms with Leonor, who considered him an enemy from the start, and who believed, or pretended to believe, that her young son was in danger from his supposedly ambitious uncle. Afonso, Count of Barcelos, an illegitimate son of old João I, now began to take a prominent hand in politics, and his intrigues against Pedro showed that he had always resented his inferior position in the family. The rights and wrongs of all this are still very hard to assess; certainly Pedro proved overbearing at times, but certainly also the charges made against him were severer than the case would warrant. The queen-mother finally went to Spain, where she soon died, and the malicious rumor spread that Pedro had arranged for her to be poisoned. The young king grew older and, as this and many other stories were pumped into his ear, he began to hate his uncle. Although he married Pedro's young daughter and loved the girl dearly, this did not lessen the tension between the now elderly regent and the maturing young king.

Prince Henry was one man who had every reason to be satisfied with his brother's government. This enabled him to return to Sagres and carry on the real work of his life. During the few years Pedro ruled the country, the Portuguese voyagers made a great spurt down the African coast and carried their explorations well into the Guinea Negro country.

The voyages, interrupted by the Tangier fiasco and by Duarte's death, recommenced in 1441. Antão Gonçalves and Nuno Tristão went below the *Rio do Ouro* and returned with a cargo of seal oil and skins as well as ten Moorish captives. Learning that it was a Moslem country, Henry thought in terms of a crusade and appealed to Pope Eugenius IV for support. The pope offered spiritual inducements to all Christians who would help the prince battle the infidels in this region. A little later, Regent Pedro gave his brother a complete monopoly on all voyages south of Cape Bojador and exempted him from paying any part of his profits to the crown. At this point, the search for Prester John came prominently into Henry's plans. On sending out Antão Gonçalves again, the prince told him to gain all possible information about the Prester's kingdom. Henry obviously thought it could be reached by turning up one of the large west African rivers.

Gonçalves returned from his voyage still hazy about Prester John, but bringing some gold which he had gained in trade with the natives at *Rio do Ouro*. This was indeed encouraging and had to be followed up at once. Soon the Portuguese had swept past Cape Branco, discovering Arguim Island and Arguim Gulf, where they found an excellent harbor and a good sized Moorish population with whom trade could be started.

Feeling that he was finding something important at last, Henry now sent his voyagers out in greater numbers. A whole fleet went in 1444 and came back with several hundred slaves, predominantly Moorish in blood. But in 1445 Dinís Dias made contact with the Senegal region, the first true Negro country, where he discovered the great promontory of Cape Verde.

Now the real slave trade began and cargoes were regularly brought back to Portugal. This trade did not become extremely important, because there was very little to do with slaves in the kingdom. According to Azurara, Prince Henry's main chronicler, the Negroes were looked upon more as curiosities than as valuable property and became something more akin to pets than laborers. After they had been converted to Christianity, the tendency was to teach them useful trades and to allow them virtual freedom, even to the extent of marrying Portuguese if they wished.

News of the trade opportunities in Guinea soon spread and many Portuguese shippers flocked there to violate Prince Henry's monopoly. In 1446 alone, fifty-one caravels went to Guinea, and it was presumably these profit-hungry traders who broke down the good relations at first established with the natives due to Henry's careful policy. There began to be incidents of bloodshed and tragedy. Nuno Tristão and most of his crew perished in a hail of poisoned arrows while exploring a river sixty leagues south of Cape Verde. In 1448, a Dane, whom the Portuguese called Valarte (Wollaert?) and who had been entrusted with the command of one of Henry's caravels, ventured ashore with a small party and was attacked. Those on the ship could not tell whether Valarte was killed or made prisoner, since they had to hoist sail and depart to save their own lives.

Henry, as was usual after one of his discovery spurts, had

to halt because of pressure of home events. The friction between his brother Pedro and his nephew Afonso had steadily grown. The young king had been declared of age by the cortes in 1446, and the regent, reluctantly bowing to this verdict, had handed over the government. Henry, who always tried to be a peacemaker in the family, considered his brother's complete retirement in favor of a fourteen-year old king a trifle premature and managed to secure an understanding whereby Pedro would still remain in an advisory capacity. But those interested in fomenting trouble would not let matters rest here. The ringleader was old Afonso of Barcelos, now promoted to the dukedom of Bragança. One by one he had Pedro's official appointments annulled, which meant the dropping of all the former regent's friends from the government. Early in 1448, Pedro received his own final dismissal and retired to his private estate, thoroughly disgruntled, while the newly created Duke of Bragança and his son, the Count of Ourém, in effect took over the government. These two poured all the old anti-Pedro stories into the ear of the king, who believed them. Afonso's young queen, Isabel, was devoted to her famous father, Pedro, but appears to have been a timid girl. She never realized that she had the power to influence her husband more than the dour old Duke of Bragança possibly could.

Matters came to the breaking point late in 1448, when the king asked Bragança to appear at court, suggesting that he come with a well-armed following since he would have to pass through Pedro's lands on the way. Bragança prepared to make the journey, and Pedro resolved that his bastard and now-hated brother should under no circumstances cross his holdings. Stern orders from Afonso to allow Bragança a free passage meant nothing now to Pedro, who had collected a small army of his own. Bragança finally avoided a battle by taking a long way around, but this did not satisfy King Afonso, who felt that he had been flouted in his own kingdom. Proclaiming Pedro a rebel, he raised an army to crush him. Henry again tried to be a peacemaker, but it was now too late. Pedro had an adviser of his own, the reckless Count of Avranches, a fearless fighter who declared that it would be disgraceful to submit to these insults, and that he personally would sustain Pedro to the last and would not survive him if worst came to worst.

Pedro's small army and the king's large one came face to face by the small Alfarrobeira River early in 1449, still not quite certain that they meant to fight. When a wild cannon shot from Pedro's side fell near King Afonso's tent, the battle was on. The large royal army overwhelmed the ex-regent's, although for a short time there was desperate fighting and Pedro defended himself and led his troops bravely. An arrow through the heart instantly killed him, and a few minutes later Avranches fulfilled his oath by attacking a group of adversaries single-handed and dying. The body of Pedro lay for a day abandoned on the field, until some peasants carried it to a poor hut, and from there it was taken from place to place until finally given a decent burial in the castle of Abrantes.

So ended Pedro, in many respects the ablest man of his time. His death was regretted all over Europe, where there was a general tendency to blame young Afonso for what had happened. However this scarcely seems the right verdict. The great prince failed to realize that his own generation was fast passing off the scene and that it was hopeless to try to cling to power too long. His last actions bordered perilously on treason, and even his devoted brother Henry had to abandon him before the end.

This left Henry as the last prince of his generation. He remained on formally good terms with Afonso V, but naturally missed Pedro greatly. He retired again to Sagres and went on with his main work, a work in which Afonso never showed much interest. But the last voyagers sent out by Henry were not primarily concerned with discovery, although Luigi da Cadamosto did advance as far as the forbidding Lion Mountains (Serra Leoa or Sierra Leone). The prince now thought more of exploring up the great rivers that had been discovered, especially the Gambia, in search of Prester John and the gold country. His last two famous captains, the Venetian Cadamosto and the Portuguese Diogo Gomes, were chiefly engaged in this quest. Each went a good way up the Gambia, and although no Prester John was forthcoming, prosperous Negro kingdoms were found with reports of even greater ones beyond. Both Cadamosto and Gomes claimed to have discovered the Cape Verde Islands, and the explanation seems to be that both had visited the archipelago, although separately and at different times.[16] Cadamosto's discovery was made in company with another Italian, the Genoese Antonio de Noli, when the two sighted four or five of the group in 1457. Gomes, while returning from the Gambia, also visited the islands, but evidently did so a year or two after Prince Henry's death, which gives the Italians a clear priority. It was Antonio de Noli and not Cadamosto who was presently awarded Santiago in the Cape Verde group, with colonization rights.

Henry made one more trip to Morocco before his death. In 1458, his nephew Afonso decided on an African expedition, with the modest objective of capturing the little city of Alcácer Ceguer, near Tangier. Because of Henry's experience in Morocco, the old prince was taken along on what proved to be a quick and easy campaign. Alcácer surrendered in a short time, and Henry arranged the terms, which were for peaceful evacuation by the Moors with their families and goods, leaving behind all Christian captives in the city.

Late in 1460 Henry fell ill, and on November 13 he died at his Sagres home. The prince had passed his sixty-sixth birthday and, since the capture of Ceuta in 1415, had given most of his time and attention to sponsoring voyages. Although not the most brilliant son of João and Philippa, he was the stablest and the most capable of a relentlessly sustained effort. The importance of his life and career is so great as to make overestimation simply impossible. Probably he did not realize the enormous significance of his life work to Portugal and Europe, but it is not too much to say that every discoverer by land or sea since his time has, in a measure, followed in his footsteps.

The conventional picture of Henry that has come to us is that of an austere, monkish individual, setting aside all personal passions and desires as too trivial to occupy his intensely valuable time. Yet it may be that friends and admirers carved too granite a portrait of the great prince, because one imprudent contemporary blurted the information that he had an illegitimate daughter to whom he was greatly attached.[17]

[16] The discovery of the Cape Verdes is discussed in detail by Richard Hennig, *Terrae Incognitae*, 4 vols. (Leyden, 1936-1939), IV, 147-168, 191-195.
[17] Gomes Eanes de Azurara, *Crónica do descobrimento e conquista da Guiné*, ed. José de Bragança, 2 vols. (Lisbon, 1937), I, xxi.

Diogo Gomes, who was with Henry at the last, takes leave of him thus:

Then the king commanded his brother D. Fernando Duke of Beja, and various bishops and counts, to carry the body to the monastery of Batalha, where the king awaited the corpse of the deceased. And the infante's body was buried in a large and most beautiful chapel, that his father King João had commanded to have made, where the king himself lies, and his wife Queen Philippa mother of the infante, and his five brothers, all of whose memories will be lauded forever. And there they rest in holy peace. Amen.[18]

[18] Fortunato de Almeida, *História de Portugal* (Coimbra, 1922-1929), II, 107.

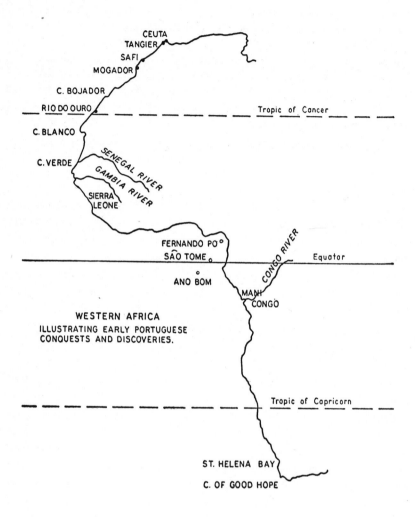

CEUTA
TANGIER
SAFI
MOGADOR
C. BOJADOR
RIO DO OURO   Tropic of Cancer
C. BLANCO
C. VERDE   SENEGAL RIVER
                  GAMBIA RIVER
          SIERRA
          LEONE
                  FERNANDO PO
                  SÃO TOME   Equator
                                    CONGO RIVER
          ANO BOM
                              MANI
                              CONGO

WESTERN AFRICA
ILLUSTRATING EARLY PORTUGUESE
CONQUESTS AND DISCOVERIES.

                                            Tropic of Capricorn

          ST. HELENA BAY
          C. OF GOOD HOPE

Chapter IV

THE BEGINNINGS OF NATIONAL GREATNESS

*I*N Portugal, as anywhere else in Europe during the late middle ages, a great deal depended on the personality and ability of the kings. The major trend in all countries was toward the building of royal power and the slow grinding away and reduction of the privileges of the nobility. But there could be fluctuations within this main cycle, and the coming of a ruler too young or too weak to hold a tight rein invariably meant a reaction with the nobles temporarily regaining some lost ground. Portugal combined both misfortunes in Afonso V, who was successively a boy and a weak man.

The quarrel between young Afonso and his uncle Pedro had had a bearing on the rivalry between the crown and the nobility. Although most of the noble titles were recent and had been granted by the Portuguese kings, their holders came quickly to react in the typical feudal way. They had disliked Pedro because he meant strong government and preferred Afonso who showed signs of giving a weak one. The middle class town councils had seen clearly where their interest lay and, accordingly, had favored the regent. But not being a military group they had been helpless when Pedro went down at Alfarrobeira. The nobility now had young Afonso in their grasp, and never let go as long as he lived. The result was several decades of weak rule, in which the crown temporarily lost many of its recent gains.

There is much to be said for Afonso on the personal side. He was affable and generous and cared for literature and the arts. He had high ambitions and was brave as a soldier. But the generosity took the form of giving titles, revenues, and privileges away with too lavish a hand. The ambitions consisted largely of chasing political phantoms and of trying to be a knight errant in a coldly practical age. The bravery was at the expense of generalship, and his son, João, when only twenty-one, was a much better commander than he. Afonso also failed to appreciate Portugal's greatest achievement of the time—the start that had been made toward the circumnavigation of Africa.

Although Afonso was surnamed "the African," this was entirely with reference to Morocco, where he garnered the few successes of his reign. He had captured the town of Alcácer Ceguer when accompanied by Henry the Navigator in 1458. His romantic spirit, lifted by this success, pressed him to try further conquests nearby. He attempted to take Tangier in 1464, but the assault failed, and Afonso did not try Africa again until 1471. By then a civil war had broken out in the interior of Morocco, and most of the best fighting men had been gathered around Fez. Afonso seized the chance and crossed the strait again with an overwhelming force. He stormed Arzila, in spite of a fierce resistance by the Moors. News soon came that the Moroccans were evacuating and burning Tangier, not many miles away. Afonso rushed a column there, which arrived in time to save most of the city. Counting Ceuta, Portugal now owned four Moroccan strongholds, all on the peninsula facing the Strait of Gibraltar. The Avís dynasty seemed to be on the verge of building a North African empire, because Azemmour and Safi, some distance away, now recognized the sovereignty of Afonso and asked to be taken under his protection. To complete the king's triumph, he was able to exchange several noble Moroccan captives for the remains of the martyred Prince Fernando, which were brought back to Portugal in state and laid in the Batalha monastery.

However, Afonso was soon pursuing bigger game than an empire in Morocco, for he next aspired to become king of Castile and thus to unite most of the peninsula under his rule. His sister, Joana, had been married to Enrique IV of Castile, who died in 1474. Twelve years before this, Joana had given birth to a daughter bearing the Castilian equivalent of her name, Juana. Most people thought this girl was not the king's child but the offspring of illicit amours between the queen and one Beltrán de la Cueva, a noble of the Castilian court. For this reason she was popularly known as Juana la Beltraneja, as a delicate tribute to her supposed paternity.[1] Enrique IV, before dying, had chosen to declare the child his own and the heiress to his throne. But the king had a half-sister, Isabel—the same Isabella who years later became the patron of Columbus. Isabel being years senior to Juana la Beltraneja, a Castilian party formed about the older girl and proclaimed her queen, having earlier married her to Fernando, heir to the throne of Aragon. But the Beltraneja had a party too, and this naturally called on Afonso of Portugal, her mother's brother, for help.

Here was a situation exactly to Afonso's liking. It would permit him to shine as a soldier and protector of defenseless womanhood and, incidentally, might mean picking up a kingdom. Being now a widower, he offered his heart and hand to the Beltraneja, despite their close relationship and an age difference of thirty years. The nobles of Portugal encouraged him, doubtless somewhat with the idea that this would take him away from ordinary kingly duties and make him more than ever dependent upon them. Louis XI of France had a score to settle with Aragon, which was now tied up in this embroglio through Isabel's husband, Fernando. Louis therefore made an alliance with Afonso and promised to create a diversion along the Pyrenees.

Leaving his son João to govern Portugal, Afonso crossed the frontier with an army in May, 1475. He joined his niece at Placencia, and the two went through a marriage ceremony, which, however, they could not consummate until the pope had given a dispensation for this union of uncle and niece. Afonso passed the rest of the year in futile maneuvering against Isabel's husband, Fernando, who commanded the Castilian army.

Meanwhile, Prince João at home had worked loyally to give the king every support. Calling the cortes, he was able to get both money and reinforcements. He decided to go to Castile in person with these soldiers, and joined his father at Touro, not far inside the Castilian frontier. Near there, in March, 1476, they fought a pitched battle with the Castilian army. The king behaved with

[1] Rafael Altamira, *A History of Spain*, transl. by Muna Lee (D. Van Nostrand Co., Inc., New York, 1949), p. 239.

his usual personal gallantry and lack of generalship, and his own forces were swept off the field. Where João commanded, things went much better, and before nightfall the prince had rallied much of the Portuguese army and had made the engagement scarcely worse than a draw. But the battle of Touro was as good as a victory for Fernando and Isabel, since most of the Castilian partisans of Afonso and the Beltraneja, seeing no victory in sight, became discouraged and sought peace.

João at once withdrew to Portugal to resume charge of the government, while Afonso remained for awhile in Castile, raiding the country and refusing to admit that the cause was lost. Meanwhile, Louis of France had provided more encouragement than help, and the Portuguese king decided to appeal to him personally for assistance. So his next move was to bring the Beltraneja to Portugal and place her in safety while he went off to confer with Louis XI at Tours. Once in France, Afonso slowly realized that he had been made a catspaw and that no real help would ever come from Louis. He turned next to the Duke of Burgundy, to whom he was related, only to learn that Burgundian plans did not involve mixing in a distant Castilian war.

Afonso next talked of renouncing the world and retiring to Jerusalem. He sent word to João to have himself crowned king of Portugal, and the young man obeyed. But presently the father changed his mind about Jerusalem and arrived back in Portugal in 1477, saying that in the future he would reign over the Algarve and that João might have the rest of the kingdom. The prince paid no attention to this paternal nonsense and handed over the crown, so that Afonso was called king for the remaining four years of his life. But he gave up the government almost completely, and João carried on as he had been doing for several years. Juana la Beltraneja continued to live a retired life, for the pope had refused to bless her marriage to Afonso. Ultimately, the *Excelente Senhora,* as she was called, retired to a nunnery where she lived until 1530, long surviving most of those who remembered her brief burst into fame.

Afonso as a king had been something of a comic opera monarch—impetuous, vain, and extremely gullible. But, even though he was a political failure, there was another side to his character. He had a real and unfeigned love of the arts, and Nuno Gonsalves, his court painter, was one of the finest artists of the Renaissance. The contemporary historian, Ruy de Pina, says that Afonso was the first king to collect books and to create a library in the palace. Although not a musician, as some have thought, he nevertheless liked and encouraged the art.

Afonso gets credit by name for the Afonsine Ordinances; a really important codification of laws and a contribution to the development of Portuguese jurisprudence. But it turns out that the code was made in 1446, during his boyhood, and that it was really the work of Regent Pedro.[2] The ordinances show the hand of an administrator, which Afonso certainly was not.

From the death of Prince Henry in 1460 to that of Afonso in 1481, Portuguese African exploration did not exactly languish but clearly showed the lack of powerful sponsorship. Afonso, who cared little for anything in Africa south of Morocco, leased out the whole Guinea coast as a concession to one Fernão Gomes on condition that he pay the crown a yearly rental of 200,000 *reis* and explore 500 leagues beyond Sierra Leone. Gomes presumably could make back his expenses and more from the trade along the coast. When the Portuguese encountered malagueta pepper a little later, this made the concession more valuable and an extra 100,000 *reis* was charged Gomes annually. The proprietor carried out the exploration part of the bargain. His voyagers pushed eastward from Sierra Leone along the Guinea coast and rounded the southward bend at the Bight of Biafra. João de Santarem and Pero Escobar discovered the island of São Tomé in 1471 and sighted Santo Antão and Ano Bom on the same voyage. Fernão do Pó, a year later, found the island which still bears his name, slightly distorted to Fernando Pó. Lopo Gonçalves and Rui Sequeira, finding that Africa bent southward again at the Bight of Biafra, carried the exploration down to a point not far above the Congo River.[3]

Meanwhile the trade had grown profitable. Not only was there pepper, but there were also slaves and ivory. Gold also was now coming from Guinea in substantial amounts. Apparently it proved difficult for a private party to maintain such a monopoly. Indi-

[2] Fortunato de Almedia, *História de Portugal* (Coimbra, 1922-1929), III, 18-22.
[3] Portuguese African activity as managed by Gomes is well summarized by John W. Blake, *Europeans in West Africa*, 2 vols. (Hakluyt Society, London, 1942), vol. I.

vidual Portuguese took chances and broke the law. A Frenchman named Eustache de la Fosse was on the Guinea coast as early as 1473, and various stray references show that Castilians also went there.

Probably at the wish of Prince João, King Afonso transferred the Guinea concession to him in 1474. There is not much record of further exploration until João became king, which is explained by the Castilian war and the heavy home duties that fell to the young prince.

In 1481 Afonso put an end to his own shadowy kingship by dying. This brought his son to the throne as João II, doubtless the ablest king ever to rule Portugal, and possibly too the ablest ruler of his generation in Europe. But João found a bad situation confronting him at the start. Although in effect he had governed the kingdom for years, there was a difference between this and being full sovereign, and he had not been ready before 1481 to take strict measures for putting his house in order.

It was high time to do so now. In the lax reign of Afonso the nobility had run amuck. They had overstepped the rights and privileges which legally belonged to them; going so far as to withdraw large districts of the country from the royal jurisdiction and operating their own courts, where they dealt out whatever justice best suited them.[4] The people complained through the cortes, but Afonso had been too indifferent or too weak to stop the aristocratic usurpations. The nobles steadily encroached on the jurisdictions and holdings of the cities, and insisted on meddling in municipal affairs that were no rightful concern of theirs. The bishops, who in secular matters were essentially a part of the nobility, had been able to push relatives or retainers into the civil services of the towns, and of course these individuals did the will of their masters, regardless of law. Nobles and clergymen considered it their right to give asylum on their estates to any criminal or fugitive from justice when it pleased them to do so. With respect to the peasants, they had taken to "borrowing" such items as livestock, farm produce, and even money. A noble never considered it necessary to repay such a "loan," since he had the power to imprison and torture a peasant who complained. A favorite trick had become that of seizing and storing a large part of the grain of a countryside.

[4] Fortunato de Almeida, *História de Portugal* (Coimbra, 1922-1929), II, 139-140.

until the inevitable shortage was created. The noble would then open his cellars and warehouses, to sell to the public at extortionate prices.[5]

Portugal thus badly needed a king and a real one. When João summoned his first cortes at Évora, the members complained bitterly of all these abuses. The king decided to work thoroughly and get to fundamentals, rather than deal with one local grievance at a time. He first ordered his nobles to take a rigid oath of allegiance, involving a great number of items, which they must swear to and undertake to fulfill. The Duke of Bragança, grandson of old Afonso of Barcelos, was now the greatest nobleman in the country and the spokesman for the group as a whole. Backed by many of these lordly persons, he declared that this oath was incompatible with their dignity as nobles, and that he for one did not propose to submit to it. He said that previous donations to his family confirmed him in every privilege he was enjoying as he would presently show. So Bragança sent to his estate at Vila Viçosa and ordered the *vedor* (overseer) to get out the documents proving his rights. Being busy at the time, the *vedor* entrusted his young son with the search, and the boy was helped by Lope de Figueiredo, one of the duke's secretaries. They found the box containing the documents, but during the search Lope de Figueiredo found something else. It was a file of correspondence between Bragança and Fernando of Castile, which had a definitely treasonable look. The secretary, realizing that he had stumbled upon something important, secretly took the letters and handed them over to the king. João had copies made and told Figueiredo to place the originals where he had found them.[6]

Meanwhile, as the cortes at Évora continued to give him evidence of the noble's arrogance, João announced that a wholesale examination would be made of the titles and privileges pertaining to all estates where the owners excluded royal justice officers and maintained their own courts. He also began an investigation of all such courts and ordered his own judges to assume jurisdiction in the meantime.

[5] Fortunato de Almeida, *História de Portugal* (Coimbra, 1922-1929), II, 141.
[6] The contemporary Portuguese chronicler Ruy de Pina describes this operation in detail. *Chronica d'El Rei Dom João II*, in *Ineditos de história portugueza*. II (Academia Real das Sciencias, Lisbon, 1792), 21.

This was bringing matters to a showdown, and João was now armed with the guilty correspondence between Bragança and Castile. The evidence was as damning as he could have wished. In 1480, even before João ascended the throne, the duke, who knew the kind of man he would presently have to deal with, had written to Fernando, offering to come to his aid with a large party should he invade Portugal. Collaborating with Bragança now was his brother, the Marquis of Montemôr, whose pride still smarted from a dressing-down João had recently given him for appearing gaily clad while the Portuguese court mourned Afonso V. The king had told the marquis that he of all people should respect the memory of the sovereign who had given him his title, with the plain implication that Montemôr did not deserve it. The irritated marquis had written to Fernando saying that 4,000 lancers would be enough to take over the country, with the help that Portuguese noblemen would furnish. As the plan took form, it was agreed that when war broke out again between Portugal and Castile, the Braganças would righteously proclaim João to be in the wrong, refuse to help him, and side with Fernando.[7]

The king did not rush matters but let the plot unfold. He knew everything his enemies did and planned. The messengers to Castile even reported to his agents along the way, and he learned the contents of all their letters.

When João was quite ready, he suddenly arrested Bragança. Scarcely anyone, least of all the powerful duke, thought at first that the prosecution would go the limit. Amazement followed when João's court began the trial and twenty-two charges of the gravest nature were read. Many still could scarcely believe that the king would execute his powerful relative, who owned fifty castles, towns, and cities, and who could put a force of 13,000 men in the field. But the legal machine rolled relentlessly on, and the prisoner three times was called on to defend himself. Twice he spoke, but by the third invitation he realized the hopelessness of the situation, and said that his only further interest lay in making his peace with God. The verdict of the king's judges was unanimous, and on June 20, 1483, the mighty duke was beheaded on a scaffold at Évora.[8]

[7] Ruy de Pina, *Chronica d'El Rei Dom João II*, in *Ineditos de história portugueza*, II (Academia Real *das Sciencias*, Lisbon, 1792), 36.   [8] *Ibid.*, p. 50.

Montemôr saved his own life by fleeing from Portugal, but his estates were confiscated, as were those of the duke and several other Bragança relatives.

A wave of terror ran through the Portuguese nobility. The king had showed himself unafraid to strike down his most powerful subject, and obviously meant to be complete master. The nobles now felt they had but one hope left, and so they planned to assassinate João.

Among those involved in the Bragança conspiracy had been the youthful Diogo, Duke of Viseu, brother of Leonor of Lencastre, the queen. Since João and Leonor were cousins, Viseu was both cousin and brother-in-law to the king. Soon after Bragança's death, João called the youth to an interview in the presence of the queen. He frankly told the duke that he knew of his guilt, but that for Leonor's sake, Viseu's youth, and their close kinship, the matter would be forgotten provided he behaved himself in the future. Viseu seemed so overcome by this generosity that he could say nothing, merely reaching for the king's hand and kissing it before backing out of the royal presence.

The king and queen both believed him a reformed character and thought of marrying him to Juana la Beltraneja, who had not been very long in the religious life and who might be willing to return to the world. But they had misjudged this young man, for Viseu was soon at the head of an aristocratic conspiracy to kill João. Many nobles entered the plot, and their intention was to declare the king's young son, Afonso, ruler for the moment, but presently to do away with him and place the crown on Viseu's head. The greater nobles would then divide Portugal to suit themselves.

Their difficulty was how and where to kill the king. They thought of several places where it might be feasible to do so, and it was agreed that Viseu should strike the blow himself. So many conspirators were involved that secrecy for long was out of the question, yet they proceeded as though they had years at their disposal. One of the plotters was Garcia de Meneses, bishop of Évora. The bishop had a mistress, Margarida Tinoco, to whom he confided the secret. Margarida straightway told her brother, Diogo Tinoco, who was a servant of the king and who at once told João everything. Further confirmation came almost immediately, because another of the plotters had informed his brother, who went straight to the king with the story.

João as before let the matter go for a short time, but took due precautions. He wore a shirt of mail beneath his clothes and never rode out without a strong armed guard.

The plotters thought their chance had come when the king planned to travel by boat from Alcácer do Sal to Setúbal. They lined up at the Setúbal water front, intending to help Viseu perform his cousinly act just as João stepped ashore. But the king, having learned of this plan, surprised them by arriving by land on horseback, with a strong bodyguard. The next day João sent for Viseu who came and was ushered into a private room where the king awaited with three witnesses. Wasting no words, João straightway stabbed the young duke to death.[9]

There was a wholesale running down of conspirators this time. Three were arrested and beheaded. The bishop and a few others were placed in prison, and matters were arranged so that they all died within a short time. Some got away, to Castile and even to England, but never dared to return. Needless to say, the estates were forfeited, and enormous holdings reverted to the crown.

The duel between the king and the nobility had been short and grim, with the monarchy winning a total victory. The peers of the realm had learned their lesson and were thoroughly cowed. João could proceed now in utter tranquillity with the work of abolishing the relics of feudalism in his kingdom.

Through all this trouble with his nobility, João had found time to devote to the matter nearest his heart, which was the pushing of Portuguese discovery both by land and by sea. His first thought was to stabilize the country's position on the Guinea coast and strengthen the hold by building a fortified settlement there. In the first year of his reign he prepared an elaborate expedition equipped with all the necessities for such a settlement and placed it under the command of a faithful officer, Diogo de Azambuja. The ships started in December, 1481, and before the end of January reached a site on the Gold Coast which the Portuguese called São Jorge da Mina (St. George of the Mine). This was the present Elmina, now a British possession. Azambuja made an agreement

[9] Ruy de Pina's words are "E sem muitas palavras que precedessem, ElRey ho matou per sy aas punheladas." *ibid.,* p. 59.

A medieval representation of the Battle of Aljubarrota. From *História da expansão portuguesa no mundo.*

A portion of the *Painel do Infante,* painted by Nuno Gonsalves in
the fifteenth century. The central figure, although representing St.
Vincent, is possibly an idealization of the martyred Prince Fernando.
King Afonso V kneels before the saint, and the elderly man just above
him, to the right of the saint, is Prince Henry. From *História da colonizacão portuguesa do Brasil.*

with Casamansa, the local Negro potentate, and got permission to establish a fort. The Portuguese then built a castle, almost entirely with materials hauled from Lisbon. The commander sent most of the ships and crews back to Portugal, remaining himself with a group of picked men to act as a garrison.[10]

São Jorge da Mina served a triple purpose. It was a bastion of Portuguese power and possession on that remote African coast. It soon began to do a thriving trade with the natives, and every year shipped home articles of value. Most important of all, it helped with further expeditions into the unknown. The next Portuguese discoveries were made much easier by having Mina as an advanced base. Some years earlier another post had been established at Arguim, a little south of *Rio do Ouro,* but this lay too far north to help much with the later and more distant voyages.

While Diogo de Azambuja worked at Mina, João sent out his next voyager, Diogo Cão, to carry the *quinas* * of Portugal still farther to the south. Cão took with him a number of markers or *padrões* (singular *padrão*) to erect at various vantage points along the coast as a tangible sign of Portuguese priority and possession. In Prince Henry's time the voyagers had sometimes marked their discoveries with wooden crosses or carvings on trees, but these were perishable monuments. Diogo Cão's *padrões* were made of *lioz,* a kind of limestone marble quarried near Lisbon. A cross surmounted the pillar, but the most important part was the shaft, because on it would be found carved the discoverer's name, the date of the discovery, and the name of the king sending out the expedition. Much of the *padrão* could be prepared before leaving home, but a few details, such as the date, had to be left until the time of erecting the pillar. Needless to say, it was planted firmly enough to withstand all foreseeable weather conditions.

Cão sailed from Portugal in 1482,** and, after making a short stop at Mina, proceeded on around the Bight of Biafra and past the farthest point reached by Rui Sequeira in 1475. As he went

[10] The expedition to build Mina is described in detail by Luciano Cordeiro "Diogo de Azambuja," *Boletim da Sociedade de Geografia de Lisboa,* XI (1892), 173-249.
* This refers to the royal standard of Portugal which consisted of five shields or *quinas,* one in the middle surrounded by the other four. In modern Portuguese, *quinas* can mean the five spots on playing cards.
** João de Barros gives the date erroneously as 1484. The finding in recent years of Cão's own *padrão,* with its date, enables us to make the correction.

south, the amount of sediment in the water revealed that a great river must be nearby. Next, though far out to sea, the Portuguese found themselves sailing in fresh water. They turned in and came to a great estuary, inhabited by peaceful Negroes, who said they were subjects of a mighty ruler who lived some way up the river. They called this river the Zaire, but it is now known as the Congo in all countries except Portugal, which clings to the old name. The powerful monarch bore the title Mani Congo, and Cão decided to make his acquaintance through emissaries at first. Planting his first *padrão* on the left bank of the river's mouth, the commander sent several men to greet the emperor and persuade him if possible to turn Christian. He, meanwhile, proceeded to explore the coast further down and sailed as far as Cape Saint Mary in Angola. There, before turning back, he planted a second *padrão* to mark his southern limit of progress. The inscription on the pillar, now back in Portugal and the property of the Lisbon Geographical Society, reads as follows:

Year of the creation of the world six thousand 681, year of the birth of Our Lord Jesus Christ one thousand four hundred 82, the very high, very excellent and powerful prince King João second of Portugal sent to have this land discovered and these *padrões* placed by Diogo Cão, squire of his household.[11]

On returning to the river, Cão found that his messengers to the Mani Congo had not returned. So he seized a few Negroes, whom he had enticed on board, and sailed for Portugal, explaining to their friends on shore that they were being kidnapped in the friendliest spirit and would presently be returned in good condition. When Cão reached Lisbon, the king was so pleased with his work that he conceded him a pension for life and made him a noble with a coat of arms. But he had further services to request of his voyager. The Negroes brought from the Congo fast learned Portuguese and the elements of the Christian faith. João wished to repatriate them as soon as possible and use them as an entering wedge with the Mani Congo.

Cão sailed with several ships from the Tagus in April, 1484, with his Christianized Negroes and a valuable present for their ruler. There was another brief stop at Mina, after which the

[11] Cordeiro, "Diogo Cão," *Bol. Soc. Geog. de Lisboa,* XI (1892), 103-105.

Portuguese soon reached the great Congo River. Cão landed his Negroes at their home and sailed southward, this time going much farther than before. He planted another *padrão* at Cape Negro, near Port Alexander in Angola, and set up the last one at his final point of progress, Cape Cross in Southwest Africa. There is some reason to think that the commander died here, although the evidence is vague. What is certain is that the Portuguese, on their way back, ascended the Congo, at least as far as its junction with the Mpozo and the Yellala Falls. They then visited the Mani Congo, who received them with joy, and they found their first emissaries alive and well. There was feasting and general good will, the king promising that he and all his subjects would become Christians and good ones at that.[12]

When the Portuguese at last returned to Lisbon, they took an ambassador, Caçuta by name, and various young *fidalgos*, from the Mani Congo, to request that priests and friars be sent at once to bring the "waters of baptism" to their home. They also asked for masons and carpenters to build churches in their land, in order to make it as much like Portugal as possible. João of course was delighted at this and ultimately did his best to comply with the native wishes.

The Portuguese king's next moves show the large scale on which his thoughts then operated. Africa surely ended somewhere, reasoned João. That being so, his ships would sooner or later enter the Indian Ocean, and it would be well to know just what they would encounter there on arrival. So, for the year 1487 the king prepared both a scouting mission and a sea expedition. The scouts, consisting of two trained Arabists, Pero de Covilhã and Afonso de Paiva, should cross the Mediterranean and proceed down the Red Sea to India and the land of Prester John. The small fleet, commanded by Bartolomeu Dias with Pero de Alenquer as chief pilot, should solve the riddle of Africa by following it on to the end. A combination of the two reports would tell João what to do next.

Covilhã and Paiva traveled by way of Italy and Rhodes to Egypt. There they separated, Paiva going toward Ethiopia and Covilhã across the Indian Ocean to Hindustan. The latter visited

[12] Ruy de Pina, *Chronica d'El Rei Dom João II*, (Academia Real das Sciencias, Lisbon, 1792), p. 148.

the main places of the Indian coast, and even traveled as far south in Africa as Sofala. On returning to Cairo he somehow learned that Paiva had died. At the same time he encountered two Jews from Portugal who bore further instructions from João, which were to reach Ethiopia at all costs. Covilhã wrote a detailed letter to the king carefully outlining what he had learned so far. One Jew carried this back to Portugal, and with the other Covilhã made a second trip to Aden and around to Ormuz, at the mouth of the Persian Gulf. Once back in Cairo he said goodbye to the Jew, his last remaining link with home, and, disguised as usual, set out for Prester John's Ethiopia. Nothing more was heard of him for years, but it must be presumed that his first letter had meanwhile safely reached the king.[13]

In the meantime, Bartolomeu Dias sailed with three small ships in the track of Diogo Cão. After the usual stop at Mina, he went on past the Congo and past Cão's last *padrão* at Cape Cross. He stopped a time or two to place on shore a few African men and women who had been Christianized and given the rudiments of an education. Their careful instructions were to be on the watch for any reports of African Christianity they might hear—in other words, news of the Prester John empire—and to pass these on to the next white men they encountered. João had chosen women as well as men for this purpose, because it would not be possible to land them on their home shores, and he reasoned that strange women would be less likely than strange men to be summarily speared by the first party of Africans they encountered.

After leaving a harbor which he named *Angra das Voltas* (now Lüderitz Bay), Dias encountered a storm, and for thirteen days was blown steadily southward in the Atlantic. When the storm subsided, the Portuguese turned eastward to make contact with the coast again. They could not find land, and the meaning suddenly dawned upon them. They had passed the southern limit of the dark continent. On realizing this, Dias turned north and struck land at Mossel Bay, where he found Negroes herding cattle and accordingly named the place *Angra dos Vaqueiros* (Cowherd anchorage). Turning eastward, the Portuguese sailed far enough

[13] Nearly all that is known of Covilhã's career is related by Francisco Álvares, *Verdadeira informação das terras do Preste João das Indias* (Agencia Geral das Colonias, Lisbon, 1943), first published in 1543, ch. civ.

to perceive clearly the northward bend of the continent, which told them they were getting into the Indian Ocean. Dias would have liked to proceed farther, but the seamen at this point struck, saying that they had gone far enough and wished to sail home. Reluctantly, Dias turned back at the Great Fish River, after planting a *padrão* nearby.

On their way home, the Portuguese rounded the Cape of Good Hope, which they had missed before due to the storm. The story is that they had more rough weather while turning the cape, and that this caused Dias to name it *Cabo Tormentoso* (Stormy Cape). According to the same story, King João insisted in rechristening it *Cabo da Boa Esperança* (Cape of Good Hope), since it gave them good hope that in time they would reach their objective. It is a good story, but can hardly be vouched for, because only one writer mentions it, and he was far from contemporary with the event.[14]

The Cape of Good Hope was discovered some time in 1488, when João still had seven years of his life and reign before him. In view of his previous determination to reach India, it may seem surprising that he did not press matters and reach it at once. But various things delayed. Dias had learned that caravels, which were the standard ships for coasting Africa, should be replaced by a rounder type of vessel for sailing around the cape. The king put Dias himself to work supervising this new construction, which took several years.[15] Since the Portuguese rarely used the same commander twice in succession, João meanwhile picked one Estevão da Gama to direct his next fleet, which, if all went well, should be the one to reach India.

In the meantime João had family griefs, which not only touched him personally but struck the deathblow to the direct line of Avís. The king had only two children, Prince Afonso and an illegitimate son named Jorge. The father had hoped that in Afonso the Avís family would reach the height of power and greatness. He had betrothed him to Isabel, daughter of the Catholic

[14] The sole authority for the details of the Dias voyage is João de Barros, *Da Asia*, decade I, book iii, ch. iii. Among the modern reconstructions of the voyage, the best is that of E. G. Ravenstein, "The Voyages of Diogo Cão and Bartholomew Dias," *Geographical Journal*, XVI (1900), 625-655.

[15] Henry H. Hart, *Sea Road to the Indies*, (The Macmillan Company, New York. 1950), ch. vi.

Rulers, Fernando and Isabel. Since the girl seemed to have an excellent chance of inheriting the thrones of both Castile and Aragon, João had hopes of living to see his grandson in line to inherit the entire peninsula. Isabel did come to Portugal and was married to young Afonso in 1490. Eight months later the prince, while galloping his horse recklessly, was thrown and died without regaining consciousness. King João, although still a young man himself at this time, never quite recovered from the blow, which deprived him both of a son and of any hope that his line would continue. But even while mourning, the wise king realized what many others knew—namely, that Afonso had not been a very promising youth and probably could not have played successfully the historical role planned for him.

João had no great share of the religious intolerance so common in the Iberian peninsula in his time. His yearning to find Prester John and to make contact with India had both a political and economic basis, but there was little of the crusader about him. In his own service he employed Jews as freely as Christians, in both scientific and economic capacities. He would never have taken the step of expelling all Jews, as Fernando and Isabel did from Spain, or as his own successor, Manuel, did from Portugal. But he was a man with a coldly practical mind, certainly not above profiting from the misfortunes of others.

Early in 1492, just after they captured the last Moorish stronghold of Granada, the Spanish rulers ordered all Jews who had not accepted baptism to leave their dominions within four months under pain of death and total confiscation of property. During the short period of grace, they had permission to sell off their belongings in order to raise cash to take with them. They were cheated and gouged by the Christian purchasers, who took advantage of their desperation to buy for a song.

But where were the Jews to go? No nation welcomed them, and the Catholic Monarchs would not grant a minute's delay. João saw here a chance to make a profit for himself and for the country. He called a council at Sintra and urged that Jews from Spain be temporarily admitted to Portugal for a good stiff price. Although some opposition came from persons who feared the Portuguese orthodoxy might be damaged, the king had his way, and the frontiers were opened to the Jews at various points. Each one who entered had to pay a toll of eight *cruzados,* in addition to the regular entry fees. On certain conditions, the Portuguese Government allowed them to stay in the country and several hundred rich families made enough of a financial bargain to be permitted to remain in Lisbon or Oporto. The rest were herded down to the docks and placed aboard ships whose commanders were engaged to take them to stated places, often in Africa, but who thought nothing of breaking the agreement and sailing wherever they pleased. Some Jews, on entering Portugal, had spent all their money and so could not buy passage beyond. These the government seized, if it had any reason to wish to do so, and sold as slaves. The bulk of the Spanish Jews gained very little from being admitted to Portugal. If they went from there to Morocco or Algiers, where a cruel reception generally awaited, they found that they had merely delayed their suffering by a few months. Enough did stay in Portuguese territory, however, to make a substantial increase in the Jewish population.[16]

João is perhaps best known in history for his refusal to back Columbus, who negotiated with him before going to Spain. It was probably in 1484 that the strange and impressive man from Genoa made Portugal the offer to discover Antillia and Cipangu by a direct voyage across the Atlantic. João was interested enough to refer the proposition to a trio of scientists whom he consulted several other times about discovery matters during his reign. The precise terms Columbus proposed and the exact reasons for Portuguese refusal are unknown, but it is certainly true that João and his councilors found the price too high. After all, there seemed little Columbus could do for the king that the king could not do for himself. João had master pilots and experienced navigators, and, from his point of view, why subsidize a foreigner and pay him huge rewards? After this refusal Columbus went straight to Castile and began to plead there for a hearing. By 1488, there seemed some chance that he would be engaged by Fernando and Isabel for the voyage he planned. João then showed interest enough to invite Columbus back to Portugal, but if he came he soon returned to Castile and continued to ask for aid there.[17]

[16] Alexandre Herculano de Carvalho, *História da origem e estabelecimento da inquisição em Portugal,* 3 vols. (Imprensa Nacional, Lisbon, 1854-1859), I, 107.

[17] Evidence concerning the interviews between João and Columbus is reviewed by

It may have been the memory of his dealings with the Genoese, however, that caused João, in 1486, to license Fernão Dulmo, of Terceira in the Azores, to undertake a voyage westward with the privilege of governing and colonizing any islands or *terra firma* he might discover.[18] Dulmo evidently could not finance this by himself, because a few months later the king gave him permission to go in partnership with João Afonso do Estreito of Madeira.[19] It is not certain that they ever sailed; certainly they made no discoveries, but with better luck they might have been the discoverers of America. There is also some rumor that João Fernandes Lavrador, likewise of Terceira, set sail and discovered land in the west by 1492, but whatever concrete evidence exists on the subject points to Lavrador's having made the voyage after the discovery by Columbus.[20]

It seems clear that what kept João from pushing out voyagers to the west was his almost complete absorption in the route around Africa. By this time, thanks largely to his own energy, it could be predicted with reasonable certainty that this would lead the Portuguese to the Indian Ocean.

In March, 1493, Christopher Columbus, whom João had turned away some years earlier, came sailing into the Tagus in the *Niña* on his way to Spain from the West Indies, announcing that he had found Cipangu on behalf of Their Catholic Majesties, Fernando and Isabel. The Portuguese Court scarcely knew whether to take this assertion at its face value or not. Evidently Columbus could not resist doing a little strutting, to which he thought his recent success entitled him. Some of the courtiers were so irked at this that they proposed to João that the upstart be killed. The king vetoed this drastic proposal, but did tell Columbus that in his opinion the new land found westward in the Atlantic belonged not to Spain but to Portugal.

Charles E. Nowell, "The Rejection of Columbus by John of Portugal," *University of Michigan Historical Essays, 1937* (Ann Arbor, 1937), pp. 25-44.

[18] *Alguns documentos do Archivo Nacional da Tôrre do Tombo ácerca das navegações e conquistas portuguezas*, ed. by J. Ramos Coelho and others (Imprensa Nacional, Lisbon, 1892), pp. 58-61.

[19] *Ibid.*, pp. 61-63.

[20] Samuel Eliot Morison, *Portuguese Voyages to America in the Fifteenth Century* (Harvard University Press, Cambridge, Mass., 1940), pp. 51-68. The Morison thesis is that there were no such Portuguese voyages.

In making this brazen sounding claim, João had in mind an article of the Treaty of Alcaçovas that had been ratified in 1481, ending Afonso's profitless war with Castile. At that time, Their Catholic Majesties were about to start the conquest of Granada from the Moors, and felt indifferent to what happened across the water. They insisted on holding the Canary Islands, but guaranteed not to do any exploring or claiming of territory south of Cape Bojador, where they gave Portugal a free hand. Now, in 1493, João thought that Columbus had violated this monopoly and seemed to feel that he had somehow visited Guinea.

Columbus rushed a messenger to Spain warning Fernando and Isabel that João would offer competition, and presently went himself to their court. The Catholic rulers, already alarmed by their admiral's message, now urgently requested Pope Alexander VI, who was a Borja from Aragon and their very good friend, to give Spain a clear title to the lands discovered by Columbus. Alexander obliged with the famous bull, *Inter caetera,* in which he drew an imaginary line from pole to pole passing 100 leagues "west and south" of "any" of the Azores and Cape Verde islands.* He gave Spain complete ownership and discovery rights to all land lying west of this line and did not mention Portugal at all. Later in 1493 Alexander issued another bull, *Dudum siquidem,* by which he and the Catholic rulers intended to forestall Portuguese competition in both hemispheres. In the past, various popes had recognized Portugal's right to claim and hold the territories discovered in Africa. Alexander's bull wiped out all these concessions and in effect reduced Portugal to the parts of Africa she physically occupied, which, except for the Moroccan cities, meant only the posts of Arguim and Mina. There was also an attempt, in this bull, to keep Portugal from making any more voyages toward the East.[21]

João naturally found this unfair arrangement intolerable. He did not bother to protest to the papal court, where his influence was small, but concentrated on Spain, where he let it be known

* Strictly speaking this award was a geographical impossibility, since the Azores and Cape Verdes are not in the same longitude.

[21] Texts of all these papal bulls as well as the Treaty of Tordesillas are translated into English by Frances Gardiner Davenport, *European Treaties bearing on the History of the United States and its Dependencies to 1648,* 4 vols. (Carnegie Institution of Washington, Washington, D. C., 1917-1937), vol. I.

that war would follow unless Portugal obtained a fairer settlement. Although Fernando and Isabel tried to postpone yielding by dragging out negotiations, they ended by agreeing to the Treaty of Tordesillas with João on June 7, 1494. This provided for a real line of demarcation and a clear marking of zones of influence. The line was drawn from pole to pole, passing 370 leagues west of the Cape Verde Islands. West of the line Spain should have a free hand, and east of it the future belonged to Portugal. The two countries guaranteed that neither one would try to seek release from this solemn compact by appeals to the pope or to anyone else.[22]

João considered the Treaty of Tordesillas his crowning diplomatic triumph, and he had reasons for holding that opinion. He had obviously never taken seriously the Columbus-Castilian claim to having discovered Cipangu, meaning Japan. He meant his own seamen to reach the East, and now they could do so, by the one and only feasible route, around the Cape of Good Hope, with no fear of competition from their Castilian rivals. It is no wonder, then, that João feasted and rewarded his envoys when they returned from signing the treaty that gave Portugal so promising a future.

The negotiation of the Tordesillas agreement was the last important act of João's life. In July of the following year, 1495, he fell ill while the court was at Alcaçovas. His physicians could diagnose the complaint as dropsy, but they were unable to cure it. Death did not follow at once, and the king had several months in which to quarrel with his wife, Leonor, over who should inherit the throne. João wished his illegitimate son, Jorge, to be his heir, while Leonor was equally determined that it should be her other brother, Manuel, Duke of Beja, who was then the head of her branch of the family since the death of Viseu. Meanwhile, the royal party traveled about the country, visiting various springs and baths, but none improved the king's health other than momentarily. João died on October 25, 1495, while staying at Alvor.[23]

---

[22] Charles E. Nowell, "The Treaty of Tordesillas and the Diplomatic Background of American History," in *Greater America: Essays in honor of Herbert Eugene Bolton* (Berkeley and Los Angeles, 1945), pp. 1-18.

[23] Ricardo Jorge, a Portuguese professor of medicine, has attempted a diagnosis of the last illness of João II by examining medical evidence over four centuries old. *O óbito de D. João II* (Lisbon, 1922). Jorge pronounces the disease uremia, which

Before the end, he had yielded to his wife and agreed that Manuel of Beja should be king.

João II is known in Portuguese annals as *O Principe Perfeito,* or "The Perfect Prince." This does not mean that he was considered the possessor of every virtue, for the perfection idea refers to his accomplishments in all lines in which a prince is supposed to excel. Machiavelli, had he chosen to cast his eyes beyond the Italian scene, would have found the last of the Avís dynasty a far better person than Césare Borgia to serve as a prototype for his "Prince." João's record speaks for itself. Taking over a run-down kingdom in 1481, with the nobility rampant and the foreign situation grave, he made it in fourteen years a smooth-working absolutism. At the same time he made every preparation for the great Portuguese empire in the East that the next generation was to see. He never beheld the promised land, although unlike Moses of old he did not die at an advanced age, being only forty when the fatal disease struck him down.

-----

is a form of dropsy and cannot be produced by poisoning, thus refuting an ugly story current shortly after the king's death which accused Queen Leonor of removing her husband by this means to make way for her brother Manuel. For a further rehabilitation, somewhat oversentimentalized, of the character of Leonor, see João Ameal, *Dona Leonor, princeza perfeitissima* (Oporto, 1943), especially pp. 214-218.

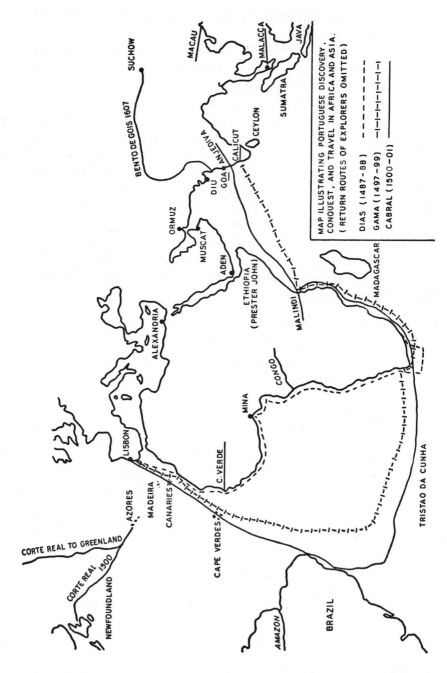

MAP ILLUSTRATING PORTUGUESE DISCOVERY,
CONQUEST, AND TRAVEL IN AFRICA AND ASIA.
(RETURN ROUTES OF EXPLORERS OMITTED)

DIAS (1487-88)
GAMA (1497-99)
CABRAL (1500-01)

SUCHOW

BENTO DE GOIS 1607

MACAU

MALACCA

JAVA

SUMATRA

CEYLON

CALICUT

ANJEDIVA

GOA

DIU

ORMUZ

MUSCAT

ADEN

ETHIOPIA
(PRESTER JOHN)

MADAGASCAR

MALINDI

ALEXANDRIA

CONGO

MINA

LISBON

C. VERDE

TRISTAO DA CUNHA

AZORES

MADEIRA

CANARIES

CORTE REAL TO GREENLAND

CORTE REAL 1500

NEWFOUNDLAND

CAPE VERDES

AMAZON

BRAZIL

Chapter V

THE PORTUGUESE
GOLDEN AGE

WITH the coming of Manuel I in 1495, the House of Beja replaced the direct Avís line on the Portuguese throne. No succession troubles stood in Manuel's way, for matters had been arranged in advance, largely by João II's widow Leonor. In a certain sense the whole reign had been arranged in advance, since it was to consist mostly of reaping the grand harvest of discovery, wealth, and empire that the departed João had sowed. Thus it is difficult to make a reliable estimate of Manuel. The Portuguese have called him *O Venturoso* (The Fortunate), meaning that they regard him as the lucky man who came at exactly the moment to profit from the labor and patience of others. But to say this and nothing more about Manuel is unfair. He inherited a fine role in history, but he understood this and in general played the role well. Although lacking the original genius of João, he showed organizing ability and above all a talent for picking leaders. The king who selected Vasco da Gama, Francisco de Almeida, and Afonso de Albuquerque could scarcely have been a cipher himself.

Yet the first important act of the new reign has earned Manuel much condemnation, for he chose to follow the example of Fernando and Isabel and expel the Jews from his kingdom. While no justification can be offered for this blunder, at least there were reasons other than religious bigotry or sheer caprice.

In one sense the decision to drive out the Jews was a decision of the moment; in another sense it had been foreshadowed for

65

centuries. Jews had lived in the territory of Portugal since Roman times, and the Arab conquest had brought a new influx. Nearly all of them lived in the cities and engaged in the traditional Jewish occupations of commerce, banking, and money-lending. Although their race and religion prevented them from holding the prouder offices of state, they had been useful to past Portuguese rulers in civil-service posts, especially those dealing with money and finance. Some also became scholars, and as mathematicians, astronomers, and cosmographers proved valuable to such patrons as Prince Henry and João II.

The Afonsine Ordinances of 1446 laid down a set of rules for the conduct of Portuguese Jews. They must live in districts *(bairros)* set apart for them in the cities, each *bairro* to be known as a *Judearia*. For dealing among themselves they had special courts and their own judges, although still ultimately subject to royal jurisdiction. Jews had to wear a distinctive costume and, as in many European cities, were literally locked in the *Judearia* early each evening. Severe regulations limited their social contacts with Christians, it being forbidden for a Jew to enter alone the house of an unmarried Christian woman.[1]

In spite of all handicaps they had prospered. Their industry became proverbial, and, since they could hold no high offices, they did not have to spend money on rich clothes and outward show. Moreover, as an underprivileged and sometimes despoiled group, they found it advisable to look as poor as possible, to avoid arousing jealousy.

Every inducement was provided to make a Jew turn Christian. Many did so and became known as *Christãos Novos,* or New Christians, to distinguish them from the *Christãos Velhos,* or Portuguese without taint of Jewish blood. After conversion, however, the *Christão Novo* status would cling to a family for generations and would prevent full acceptance in Christian society. Even so, many a proud house in Portugal, like many in Castile, had Jewish blood, since more than one land-rich, money-poor *fidalgo* married the daughter of a *Christão Novo* for the opulent dowry she brought.

[1] Alexandre Herculano de Carvalho, *História da origem e estabelecimento da inquisição em Portugal* (Imprensa Nacional, Lisbon, 1854-1859), I, 89.

By the end of the fifteenth century, most of the fluid wealth in Portugal was either in Jewish hands or under Jewish or New Christian control. The heads of the state found this alarming, and it is not surprising that they did, since even in the case of New Christians they did not wholly rely on Jewish loyalty.

The church in Portugal had no official stand on the Jewish question. It opposed drastic persecution measures, at the same time making every effort to persuade Jews to change their faith. Meanwhile, irresponsible priests and preaching friars lost no opportunity to stir up anti-Jewish sentiment, which sometimes took violent form.

In the Portuguese middle and lower classes there was much anti-Semitism, based partly, but not entirely, on religion. Scarcely a Christian Portuguese existed who had not at some time in his life received the short end of a business deal from a Jew or been bled, as he considered it, by high interest charges on loans. Therefore, any movement against the unpopular Israelites had always a public and a following ready to hand.

Portugal might have taken no steps had Spain not led the way. Both Aragon and Castile had established the New Inquisition in the fifteenth century, to deal not with Mosaic Jews but with New Christians whose loyalty to the church was suspected with good reason. With Pedro de Arbues acting as Aragonese Inquisitor, and with Tomás de Torquemada later doing the same in Castile, a reign of terror began in some Spanish cities. And after Fernando and Isabel had conquered Granada from the Moors, they took the further step of banishing from Spain all Jews who refused Christian baptism. Some of the exiles received a temporary and dearly-bought refuge in Portugal from João II. Although he enslaved those who could not pay high transportation charges, what small leniency he did show was taken with bad grace by Fernando and Isabel.

At this point Manuel came to the Portuguese throne, and he gave some reason at first to think that he would be a more lenient master. He released the Jews already enslaved, and this earned him such gratitude that the Portuguese Jews, and those from Castile who still had money, offered to make the king a *grande serviço,* meaning a large donation to the royal treasury. Manuel declined the gift, saying he would be content with what the Jews regularly paid.[2]

The king next negotiated for marriage with the Castilian princess Isabel. She was the girl who had been married briefly to young Afonso, one-time heir of João II, and widowed by the prince's accidental death in 1491. Like a true daughter of her parents, Isabel was a hater and baiter of the Jews. She consented to be Queen of Portugal only if all Jews left the country before she entered it.

Before Manuel took final action he discussed the matter with his council, where some opposition developed. It was pointed out that most of Europe tolerated Jews and that they were allowed to live in the Papal State around Rome. Their banishment would mean great loss to Portugal, since Jews were indispensable to some businesses, which they monopolized. Most of the exiles, moreover, would go to Moslem Africa, where the chance of making them Christians would be lost forever.

Manuel, however, thought of the marriage which in time might bring him the throne of Fernando and Isabel. Other countries, notably England and Castile, had expelled the Jews and had survived. Portugal, reasoned the sovereign, could do the same. So before the end of 1496 Manuel had signed a decree ordering all unbaptized Jews to depart within ten months. For good measure, he included the Moslems, of whom there were still a few in Portugal, but rather less attention was focused on carrying out this part of the decree.[3]

A few months later, and before the ten months expired, Manuel ordered the seizure of all Jewish children under fourteen, so that they might be prepared for baptism. Of all his obnoxious decrees, this was the worst. The multitude of seizures and forced baptisms that next occurred in Portugal has been compared by the historian Herculano to a "cannibalistic orgy." [4] The meaningless farce added thousands of nominal converts to the Christian faith, at the price of untold suffering and breaking-up of families.

As time approached for the adult exodus, the scenes that had

[2] Fortunato de Almeida, *História de Portugal* (Coimbra, 1922-1929), II, 203.
[3] Alexandre Herculano de Carvalho, *História da origem e estabelecimento da inquisição em Portugal* (Imprensa Nacional, Lisbon, 1854-1859), I, 116.
[4] *Ibid.*, p. 127.

Portrait of Vasco da Gama, believed to be authentic. From *Grande enciclopédia portuguesa e brasileira.*

A Portuguese vessel of the nau type. Similar to Vasco da Gama's flagship
São Gabriel. From *História da expansão portuguesa no mundo*.

formerly occurred in Castile were largely duplicated. The original plan was to have the Jews embark at three seaports. Transportation failed to materialize, and they were all ordered to Lisbon, where for awhile they were quartered in and around one large building, to the number of about twenty thousand. Very few actually left the country, because here they were set upon and in most cases baptized by force, although many kicked and struggled to the very last. A handful continued to shout that they accepted the banishment decree but demanded that the government keep its word and transport them. These were at last granted a hearing and received a passage to Africa.[5]

The Moslems suffered less and left Portugal in comparative peace. They naturally went mostly to the countries of their own faith, where they stirred up what reprisals they could against the Portuguese residing there.

This ended one phase of the national crusade against the Jews. Manuel now had thousands of bitter, resentful *Christãos Novos* on his hands. Apparently rather conscience stricken about the whole thing, the king ordered that they be unmolested for twenty years and in the meantime be given further instruction and a chance to prove loyalty toward their new faith.[6]

Isabel professed herself satisfied with the orthodoxy of Portugal. She crossed the frontier and was married to Manuel in October, 1497.

Shortly before this the greatest episode in Portuguese history had begun with Vasco da Gama's departure for the East. João II, before his death in 1495, had gone so far with the plan for discovering India as to choose Estevão da Gama as his commander. This older Gama died before the fleet was ready to sail, and Manuel selected his son Vasco, then a man in the thirties, to head the expedition. The ships, prepared under the supervision of the veteran Bartolomeu Dias, were in seaworthy condition by July, 1497. *São Gabriel,* the flagship, was commanded by Vasco da Gama in person and had the renowned Pero de Alenquer as chief pilot. *São Rafael,* of about the same tonnage and build, sailed under the orders of the admiral's brother, Paulo da Gama. *Berrio* had

[5] Alexandre Herculano de Carvalho, *História de origem e estabelecimento da inquisição em Portugal* (Impresna Nacional, Lisbon, 1854-1859), I, 128.
[6] *Ibid.,* p. 129.

Nicolau Coelho for commander, and an unnamed bark carrying provisions was handled by Gonçalo Nunes, a retainer of the Gama family. About 170 men sailed aboard these four vessels. Bartolomeu Dias in a caravel was to accompany them on the first leg of their journey to the Cape Verde Islands, after which he would turn eastward to carry supplies to the fort at São Jorge da Mina.

With the ships anchored at Restelo, a little below Lisbon on the Tagus, Vasco da Gama and his officers had their final audience with Manuel. They prayed at the church of Nossa Senhora de Belem, founded by Prince Henry the Navigator, and on July 8 went aboard. A great crowd gathered to watch the departure, as though the Portuguese people instinctively knew that a mighty chapter in world history was opening before their eyes.

Once outside the Tagus, a week passed before the ships came within sight of the Canaries. A little farther on, off Terra Alta on the African coast, they stopped a few hours to catch fish for their provision stocks. Poor visibility then separated the ships, but they reunited according to plan at the Cape Verde Islands. Stopping a few days at Santiago to take aboard firewood and some extra provisions, they then parted from Dias who went his way to Mina.

Vasco da Gama, piloted by Pero de Alenquer and surely acting on the advice of Dias, now performed one of the great feats in the history of navigation.[7] Hitherto Portuguese ships sailing south along Africa had hugged the coast. But below the Congo they had found their speed cut down materially by the northward flowing currents. Therefore, Gama's fleet abandoned all contact with the continent and boldly thrust far out into the south Atlantic. From the third of August to the eighth of November, the voyagers saw no land. Describing a great semicircle in the ocean, they sailed far enough south to encounter the westerlies which blew them east toward the Cape of Good Hope. They evidently narrowly missed discovering the Tristão da Cunha group, for they beheld migratory sea birds flying in the direction of those islands. Finally, on November 8, they struck land at St. Helena Bay, a few miles

[7] The best account of Gama's voyage to India and return is the anonymous *Roteiro*, written by a member of the expedition, probably Alvaro Velho. For an English version see *The First Voyage of Vasco da Gama*, transl. and ed. E. G. Ravenstein (Hakluyt Society, London, 1898).

north of the cape. De Alenquer, who had been near there before with Dias, was able to report that the great promontory lay just ahead.

After a brief stop at St. Helena, they put to sea again and rounded Good Hope on November 22. Rather slowly Gama conducted the fleet past Dias's last marker and up the east African coast. By this time, with food running low, water spoiling, and many of the men suffering from scurvy, it was necessary to make contact with civilization soon.

Scarcely knowing what they were looking for, but guided in some degree no doubt by Pero da Covilhã's old letter to João II, the Portuguese passed without sighting the first Moslem settlements on the east African coast. But at the mouth of the Quelimane River they first saw signs of civilized life, and a little later they came to Mozambique, where Arab ships lay loading in the harbor. The Moslem sheik of the place first gave the Portuguese a good reception, but on learning that they were Christians he changed his attitude and Gama had to leave the port in haste. At the next Moslem city, Mombasa, the whole expedition was nearly destroyed by a native stratagem, but managed to escape and reach Malindi, a city in the present Kenya territory. Here the local sultan, although also a Moslem, had political reasons for treating the Portuguese well. He visited their ships in person, and they spent eleven days in his port before venturing across the Indian Ocean to Hindustan.

When Vasco da Gama started the last stage of his voyage, the fleet was piloted by an Indian from Gujarat named Malemo Cana, who had been engaged at Malindi to guide the Portuguese to Calicut on the Malabar coast.[8] This part of the voyage was uneventful, and on May 20, 1498, they cast the first European anchors in an Indian port.

Now a new problem arose—that of making a favorable impression on the *Samuri,* who was the Hindu ruler of Calicut. Since the Portuguese came to trade for spice, their situation was made worse by the presence in Calicut of many Arab merchants, who dominated Indian Ocean trade and had no intention of sharing their monopoly with any Christian newcomers. From almost the

[8] Gabriel Ferrand, "Le pilote arabe de Vasco da Gama et les instructions nautiques des arabes au xvᵉ siècle," *Annales de Géographie,* XXX (1922), 289-307.

moment Gama landed, a contest began between Europeans and Arabs for influence over the *Samuri*.

Weeks of uncertain dealings followed. The Moslems accused the Portuguese of being piratical marauders who had come to spy out the land. Gama, who could only negotiate unsatisfactorily through interpreters, seemed on the verge of being lost more than once. But he proved himself a match for the Arabs, both as a diplomat and an intriguer, and he finally left Calicut late in August with a cargo of spice in his holds.

On the way home the men succumbed steadily to fever and scurvy. *São Rafael* had to be abandoned and burned off Mozambique for lack of hands to work her. The little provision carrier had been emptied and broken up much earlier, so only *São Gabriel* and *Berrio* were left to turn the cape on March 20, 1499. The smaller vessel reached Lisbon in July, but Vasco da Gama did not arrive until September, after he had first rushed his dying brother Paulo to the Azores, in the vain hope that the salubrious climate there would cause his recovery.

The great voyage had lasted over two years, and less than a third of the 170 men who set out had returned. But Portugal had made contact with the East, the real East, and now Spain's barren discoveries across the Atlantic looked poor by comparison. Although the cargo brought by Gama was small, the future appeared extremely bright. In patronizing vein, Manuel now wrote Fernando and Isabel, saying that his men had brought back cinnamon, clove, ginger, nutmeg, and other spices, besides securing rubies and other precious stones and finding gold mines.[9] All this commerce, said the king, was for the moment in Moslem hands, but it could be diverted to the Christians.

Meanwhile, Manuel joyfully greeted his returning voyager and loaded him with rewards and honors. No charge of royal ingratitude can be leveled here, for Vasco da Gama died Admiral of India and Count of Vidigueira, with a large fortune to sustain such exalted rank.

The voyage had to be followed up at once, so in 1500 Manuel sent a large fleet of thirteen ships to India, his new commander

[9] *Alguns documentos do Archivo Nacional da Tôrre do Tombo*, ed. by J. Ramos Coelho and others (Imprensa Nacional, Lisbon, 1892), pp. 95-96.

being Pedro Álvares Cabral.[10] Supposedly Cabral meant to follow the Gama route but, for some reason not clearly understood, the ships, after leaving the Cape Verdes, veered farther to westward than their predecessors. On April 22, 1500, they sighted the Brazilian coast near Porto Seguro. The Portuguese named this new land Santa Cruz, not certain for the moment whether it was an island or mainland. But concerning one thing they were positive. The country lay east of the line established six years earlier by the Treaty of Tordesillas and therefore belonged to Portugal. Cabral sent one ship back to Lisbon to report the discovery, and with the rest he rounded the Cape of Good Hope according to orders. Near the cape, a great storm destroyed several ships, and by a sad chance one of the casualties was the real pioneer of the southern latitudes, Bartolomeu Dias, whose unlucky star again forbade him to see India.

The main fleet proceeded, however, discovering the island of Madagascar on the way. Arriving at Calicut, the Portuguese found the *Samuri* now completely dominated by the Arabs, who had furthered their own cause since Gama's departure. After several unhappy experiences Cabral transferred headquarters down the coast to Cochin, whose ruler hated the *Samuri*. There envoys from Cannanore and Quilom waited on the Portuguese commander, inviting him to use their ports and promising to provide spice in large quantities. By the time Cabral left for home, he had made a beginning toward establishing his country's hegemony over parts of the southern Indian coast.

For the next few years, Portugal sent annual expeditions to India. João da Nova commanded the fleet for 1501, and the next year Vasco da Gama sailed again, in command of twenty ships. Fighting had meanwhile broken out with both Moslems and Hindus, and the fleets took on a thoroughly military character. Each Portuguese expedition suffered heavily from war, shipwreck, and disease, but each brought back a heavy spice cargo.

During the first years of contact with the Orient, the Portuguese learned the science of India voyaging. They learned, for example, how to time their departures from Lisbon so as to

[10] All the sources for Cabral's voyage are included in *The Voyage of Pedro Álvares Cabral to Brazil and India,* transl. and ed. by William Brooks Greenlee (Hakluyt Society, London, 1938).

make the seasonal monsoons, which blew them quickly from east
Africa to Hindustan. Their first thought regarding Brazil was that
it might serve as a way-station to break their voyages around the
cape, but they soon gave up this idea as it involved too long a delay and could often mean missing the monsoon.[11] Only an occasional Portuguese ship bothered with Brazil, to pick up a cargo
of interesting plants or animals or to take on a load of the market-
able dye wood, or *pau brasil,* which eventually gave the new country its permanent name.

Regarding India itself, the Portuguese soon changed many of
their original erroneous notions. They found that the Hindu
religion was not a Christian faith, as Vasco da Gama had first
taken it to be. They also soon learned that their arrival on the
Malabar coast had not brought them to the real home of the
spices. Malabar produced ginger, but this had no great value. Cinnamon bark grew in Ceylon, and the costlier spices came from still
farther east. Calicut, which the Portuguese had first aimed for on
the advice of Pero da Covilhã, was indeed the great distributing
point of the India coast, but it was only one of the important sta-
tions on the long spice trail. Another great emporium, Malacca,
lay many weeks' voyage beyond, near the modern Singapore. And
even on reaching Malacca the voyager would still be far from the
Spice Islands.

During the first years, therefore, these facts became organized
in the Portuguese mind. No real territorial conquests were as yet
attempted, as the European newcomers concentrated on gaining
command of the sea. They were content to buy spices in the Indian markets, although they already aimed at monopoly. Within
a few years they appeared to have accomplished their aim. The
Italian republic of Venice had long bought spice from Arab middlemen at the eastern end of the Mediterranean. But when the
Venetian galleys went to Beirut and Alexandria for the annual
trade in 1504, they found no spice for sale.[12] The Portuguese had
bought out the whole supply in India. An important commercial
revolution was under way, even though the Red Sea trade route,

[11] Alexander Marchant, "Colonial Brazil as a Way Station of the Portuguese India
Fleet." *Geographical Review,* XXXI (1941), 454-465.
[12] Albert Howe Lybyer, "The Ottoman Turks and the Routes of Oriental Trade,"
English Historical Review, XXX (1915), 584.

which supplied Venice, ultimately regained much of its old importance.[13]

When Portugal entered the Indian Ocean, the two most important facts in the picture were the supremacy of the Arab traders and the rising Ottoman Turkish power. A third factor later appeared; the Mogul empire in India, created by the conquests of the eastern Turkish chieftain, Baber, and his successors. The Portuguese were lucky in having established their commercial supremacy before the Moguls invaded India.

The word "Arab" is admittedly used loosely here to describe the trade rivals of the Portuguese. They were of assorted blood and stock, but they used the Arabic language and all followed the Prophet. They had dominated the commerce and shipping of the Indian Ocean for centuries, and sensed a dangerous competition the moment Vasco da Gama appeared. But they could not match the Portuguese as seamen and warriors, and in the contest that followed they lost steadily. Part of their weakness lay in lack of unity and cohesion, for only occasionally did they form a substantial coalition against the Europeans. As long as the Portuguese attempted no land conquests, the Arabs, with their shore bases, seemed to have some chance of regaining the upper hand. But once King Manuel's people grasped the strategic elements of the situation the Arab competition faded fast.

The Ottoman Turks were in full flood of conquest themselves when the Portuguese invaded the Indian Ocean. They needed the revenue from trade, and it was to their advantage to have the new Portuguese monopoly broken and the old routes restored. This was especially true after their sultan, Selim I, defeated the Mamelukes in 1516-1517 and conquered Egypt. Several times the Ottomans cooperated with Portugal's enemies in attempts to oust these western interlopers from the Indian Ocean. It was the good fortune of the Portuguese to have virtually won their fight before the Ottomans gained direct access to the ocean. If they had actually come to grips with the great Turkish power, their small numbers and resources might not have been equal to the test.

Up to 1505 the Portuguese had captured trade and had made satellites of minor Indian states. Their empire building began

[13] Frederic Chapin Lane, "Venetian Shipping during the Commercial Revolution," *American Historical Review*, XXXVIII (1933), 219-237.

when Manuel made Francisco de Almeida his viceroy in 1505, and sent him out with orders to build forts at Kilwa in Africa and at Anjediva,. Cannanore, and Cochin in India. These strongholds would protect friendly peoples from attack by the enemy the moment Portuguese fleets had gone home. They would also provide places where spice could be safely collected and stored while awaiting shipment.

Almeida built the forts as directed, and Portuguese power spread. Both Mozambique and Sofala on the African coast were captured and fortified, and a factory was established at friendly Malindi. When Afonso de Albuquerque was on his way to India to succeed Almeida, he occupied the Socotra Islands commanding the Red Sea entrance. Then he visited the Persian Gulf, where he sacked Muscat in the Kingdom of Oman and compelled the ruler of Ormuz to acknowledge the sovereignty of Manuel.

The obvious inability of the Moslems to stop the Portuguese with divided tactics forced them to make a grand alliance. The mainstays were Egypt, whose resources were dwindling due to the Portuguese deflection of trade from the Red Sea, and the Moslem Sultanate of Gujarat, whose port on the island of Diu was suffering for similar reasons. Several small states were involved, including Calicut, which lay close enough to Portuguese headquarters at Cochin to be useful as a spy.

The allies prepared fleets in the hope of taking Viceroy Almeida by surprise, and in fact the Portuguese were nearly caught napping. They learned of the Calicut danger from a Bolognese Italian, Ludovico di Vartema, who for years had wandered about the East, disguised as a Moslem.[14] On the strength of his warning, the *Samuri*'s fleet was quickly disposed of by the viceroy's son, Lourenço de Almeida, who was next ordered north by his father to keep an eye on Gujarat. But in the meantime the Egyptian fleet had reached Diu and the combined force sailed down the coast and caught young Dom Lourenço in the anchorage at Chaul. The outnumbered Portuguese fought with their usual bravery, but their youthful commander fell and his own ship was taken by the Gujaratis.

This was the first Christian defeat in India, and Viceroy

[14] For Vartema's career, see *The Travels of Ludovico de Varthema*, transl. and ed. George P. Badger (Hakluyt Society, London, 1863).

Almeida knew it must be wiped out at once. He prepared to take command in person, although before he could sail Afonso de Albuquerque arrived from Portugal bearing orders as his successor. Almeida, with his son's death to avenge, would not be superseded just then and flatly refused to make way for Albuquerque until he had settled scores with Egypt and Gujarat. In 1509 he put north and found the allied fleet under the protecting guns of the walls of Diu. Without hesitation Almeida closed, and after the longest battle in the history of Portuguese India won a complete victory, destroying most of the Egyptian ships and putting the rest to flight. Gujarat quickly came to terms and gave the Portuguese every guarantee they asked.

Almeida had now avenged his personal loss and for the time had ended all threat to the Portuguese in India and from the west. He now had to relinquish power to Albuquerque, but before doing so he sent a fleet eastward to discover the distant Malacca. Diogo Lopes de Sequeira commanded this expedition, in which Ferdinand Magellan sailed as a subordinate officer. Sequeira reached the eastern strait late in 1509, but largely through his own carelessness he allowed himself to be surprised and severely handled by the natives. He drew off and sailed away to the west and Malacca went unmolested for two years more.

Albuquerque had now taken over the power, and he was to be the real founder of the Portuguese empire. He first looked for a city to serve as capital, bulwark, and anchor of his country's eastern conquests. He selected Goa, midway up the west coast of India, as the ideal stronghold. Scorning the fears of his doubtful and timorous colleagues, who demurred at the costliness of the undertaking, he decided to capture the place. It proved difficult, and the city changed hands three times before the Portuguese could rest in secure possession in 1510. But Goa fulfilled all Albuquerque's hopes, and rapidly replaced the declining Calicut as the trade emporium of the Indian coast. Some years elapsed before it proved feasible to move the capital there from Cochin, but when the change was made in 1530 it proved permanent, and Goa to this day remains the center of Portuguese India.

The next step in Albuquerque's program called for sealing the Indian Ocean entrances and exits to all comers except the Portuguese. This involved a three-point strategy: first the capture of Malacca, dominating the eastern approach; next the taking of Aden at the Red Sea entrance; and finally the seizure of Ormuz on the Persian Gulf. Although Ormuz had made a halfway submission to Portugal a few years back, Albuquerque knew that nothing short of outright Portuguese possession would serve the purpose.

First came Malacca, and in 1511 he set out for there, to settle with the city for its presumption in attacking Lopes de Sequeira and to make it a permanent Portuguese stronghold. Resistance proved fierce, and Albuquerque had to assault Malacca several times before capturing it. The local sultan escaped and sent envoys all the way to the Ming emperor of China to complain of the aggression of the "Franks." The Son of Heaven, Wu Tsung, contented himself with publishing a decree scolding the western intruders and with ordering the king of Siam, whom he considered his vassal, to throw the Portuguese out of Malacca. But the Siamese ruler, Phra Borom Raxa, had formerly had his own private quarrel with Malacca and felt that Albuquerque had done him a good turn in punishing the place.[15]

Seeing in this gratitude an excellent chance to open trade with Siam. Albuquerque sent a Malay-speaking Portuguese to Phra Borom Raxa bearing gifts. In return a Siamese embassy visited Malacca, and a distinctly friendly atmosphere prevailed.

The importance of Albuquerque's new conquest was realized at once in Europe. King Manuel wrote Pope Leo X a proud letter describing the capture of Malacca. Leo, after congratulating the king on his new possession, issued the bull *Precelse devotionis* on November 3, 1514, by which he forbade any other Christians to interfere with Portugal or trespass on the territories Manuel had won.[16]

Albuquerque's next logical step was to send agents beyond Malacca strait to get in touch with Java, the Moluccas, and China. While still in Malacca, he sent an envoy to Java and ordered Antonio de Abreu to take a small fleet to the Moluccas. Abreu

[15] Henri Cordier, "L'arrivée des portugais en Chine," *T'oung Pao*, XII (1911), 503-508.
[16] *Corpo diplomatico portuguez, contendo os actos e relações de Portugal com as diversas potencias do mundo*, 15(?) vols. (Academia das Sciencias de Lisboa, Lisbon, 1862-1936), I, 275-289.

entered the Pacific in 1511, early enough to be ahead of Balboa, on his "peak in Darien," by nearly two years. He went in person only as far as the Bandas, but one of his captains, Francisco Serrão, proceeded on to Ternate in the Moluccas. There Serrão elected to spend the rest of his days, but he did write letters that got back to civilization, one letter of especial importance being to his friend, Ferdinand Magellan. Serrão thought the Moluccas lay over halfway around the world from the demarcation line agreed on by the Treaty of Tordesillas. This opinion, if correct, meant that the islands rightly belonged to Spain. Magellan took up the theory and later acted on it when he transferred to Spanish service. His famous voyage, which led to the circumnavigation of the globe, started as an attempt to reach the Moluccas by sailing westward and claiming them for Charles V of Spain.

Albuquerque did not live to send a mission to China, but soon after his death Tomé Pires started for Canton. Pires had a sad time dealing with the Chinese, and got the first European taste of that Celestial loftiness which regarded all foreigners, and especially western ones, as being scarcely good enough to walk the sacred soil of China.[17] Nevertheless, his effort marked the first of a series that ultimately established the Portuguese in Macau, a port in Chinese territory.

For the moment, Albuquerque had other important business in hand. He returned to India in 1512 and learned that his former conquest of Goa was endangered by a large native army which was besieging the place. Albuquerque routed the army and raised the siege. He then dealt mercilessly with a number of Portuguese renegades who had joined the enemy, mutilating them by the removal of their noses, ears, right hands, and left thumbs.[18] He resorted to such punishments in order to give an object lesson to any other Portuguese who might be considering treason a profitable course.

The energetic commander, already aged sixty, next sailed westward to complete the mastering of the Indian Ocean. He appeared off Aden in 1513, meaning to take the city and so gain

[17] *The Summa Oriental of Tomé Pires,* transl. and ed. Armando Cortesão, 2 vols. (Hakluyt Society, London, 1944).
[18] *Commentaries of the Great Afonso Dalboquerque, Second Viceroy of India,* transl. and ed. by Walter Gray Birch, 4 vols. (Hakluyt Society, London, 1875-1884), III, 238.

control of the strait of Bab el Mandeb. But at Aden, Albuquerque had the one conspicuous failure of his brilliant career. For once, the Arabs were prepared, and a furious but rather mismanaged Portuguese attack was beaten off. The fleet nevertheless sailed up the Red Sea to study the situation, and Albuquerque at this time had the wild thought of deflecting the Nile from its course and destroying Egypt, which he hated. Nothing came of this, and the old lion retired sullen and beaten to Goa to lick his wounds and prepare for revenge. India claimed his attention for a year and a half, and it was not until February, 1515, that Albuquerque sailed west again, headed this time for the Persian Gulf and Ormuz.

This city was one of the richest in Asia. Since the days of Mongol rule in Persia, two centuries earlier, it had grown and prospered as a trade emporium. Although once nominally subject to the Persian dynasty, it was now for all practical purposes independent under a line of native rulers. At the moment of Albuquerque's approach, the members of this family were quarreling over the succession. He arrived, and the contestants appealed the question to him since, as Ormuz had already submitted to Portugal, they had a right to suppose he came in peace. But King Manuel's viceroy now meant to finish the conquest he had once begun. In a powerful minister, Rais Ahmad, he recognized the most able and dangerous person in Ormuz. He had Rais Ahmad ruthlessly struck down, after which the Portuguese took complete possession of the city. Albuquerque rushed the building of a fort to safeguard the new conquest, but now he fell sick of dysentery and was forced to leave Ormuz and sail for Goa. On the way his ship met a native craft bearing the news from India that he had been superseded and that Lopo Soares de Albergaria, who was his personal enemy, was to be his successor. The shock of learning that Manuel no longer trusted him killed the already ailing Albuquerque, and he died on shipboard in December, 1515, just as the vessel anchored before Goa.

The king, who had listened to Albuquerque's enemies at court and had been talked into replacing him, now realized what a man he had lost. He refused to have the remains of his great conquistador sent home and ordered them buried at Goa, on the theory that as long as the natives could see Albuquerque's tomb Portuguese India would be safe.

Compared with Albuquerque, Lopo Soares proved second-rate. He managed to hold what his abler predecessors had won, but made no further important conquests and was foiled in a second attempt on Aden. That left the Red Sea trade route open, and since the Portuguese never cut this artery of commerce they never gained full mastery of the situation.

"Prester John," the Christian ruler of Ethiopia, had not been forgotten by the Portuguese. In 1512 an Armenian merchant named Matthew, who claimed to have been sent by the Negus, Lebna Dengel, reached Albuquerque at Goa. There he received a gracious welcome and was sent to Lisbon for an interview with King Manuel. The Portuguese officers escorting Matthew considered him a Turkish spy and mistreated him during the journey. But all this changed when they reached Portugal, for Manuel punished his officers and loaded the Armenian with honors. When Lopo Soares went to India to relieve Albuquerque, he took Matthew along, with orders to repatriate him as soon as possible and to send a Portuguese mission with him to the Negus. The opportunity came in 1520, and Matthew entered Ethiopia, escorted by Rodrigo de Lima, a priest named Francisco Álvares, and several other Portuguese. The Armenian died on the way, which may have been just as well because when the Europeans reached Lebna Dengel that ruler denied ever having heard of Matthew. However, he gave Rodrigo de Lima and party a good reception, and they remained several years in Ethiopia. Needless to say, they found Prester John's land rather disappointing, and the narrative later written by Father Álvares gave the first detailed account of the country ever published in Europe. While there, the envoys met an aged Portuguese who had resided in Ethiopia for nearly thirty years. He turned out to be Pero da Covilhã, whom João II had sent on his oriental mission back in 1487! Covilhã gave Álvares a good account of himself and his stay in Africa, explaining that the Ethiopian sovereigns had taken him for a spy and although treating him well, had refused him permission to leave their country. Covilhã also took the opportunity to confess his sins to Álvares and to receive absolution. He explained that, although Ethiopia was Christian, the priests there had a reputation for laxity in keeping the secrets of the confessional, for which reason

he had never availed himself of their services. The Portuguese
envoys offered to take the old man with them, but he declined,
pleading his age and the fact that he had meanwhile remarried
and raised a second family in Ethiopia.[19]

While these important events went on in the East, the Portuguese had been very busy in other places. They paid considerable
attention to Atlantic voyaging and made early contact with parts
of North America. The claim, often heard in Portuguese historical
circles, that Vasco da Gama's countrymen discovered parts of the
New World before Columbus, seems to lack any adequate proof.
But Gaspar Côrte-Real, a native of the Azores, certainly discovered
Newfoundland in 1500 and lost his life making a second voyage
there a year later. His brother, Miguel Côrte-Real, attempting to
repeat the voyage in 1502, was also lost at sea.[20] Soon, however,
Portuguese fishing fleets were making annual trips to Newfoundland waters to catch the *bacalau,* or codfish, that soon became a
staple part of the national diet.

For a time during Manuel's reign Portugal seemed on the
verge of building an empire in Morocco. In the fifteenth century,
Ceuta, Alcácer, Ceguer, Arzila, and Tangier had been won for
Portugal, and other cities had agreed to pay tribute. Peace never
existed for long between Christians and Moslems in Morocco.
Raids and counter-raids took place, and as fast as the Portuguese
captured one town another straightway became a menace to them.
In past years there had been powerful rulers of Morocco, but this
was no longer true and the country now consisted of independent
city states on the coast and tribal tracts in the interior. Manuel
took advantage of the Moroccan divisions to build new forts and
to capture additional cities. His principal agent at first was the
elderly Diogo de Azambuja, who early in the reign of João II
had built São Jorge da Mina on the Gold Coast. Azambuja added
Safi to the list of Portuguese holdings in Morocco. This city,
earlier subject to Afonso V, had gone on enjoying internal autonomy, even though severely handicapped by factional quarrels
among its citizens. One of these factions invited Azambuja to

[19] Francisco Álvares, *Verdadeira informação das terras do Preste João das Indias,*
(Agencia Geral das Colonias, Lisbon, 1943), Ch. civ.
[20] Samuel Eliot Morison, *Portuguese Voyages to America in the Fifteenth Century,*
(Harvard University Press, Cambridge, Mass., 1940), pp. 68-72.

intervene in the dispute, which he did in 1508, building a fort inside the town and installing a Portuguese garrison.

When age compelled Azambuja to retire, Nuno de Ataíde became his successor. King Manuel meant to fringe the whole Moroccan Atlantic coast with a line of Portuguese strongholds to serve as bases for the penetration of the interior. His next act was to seize Azemmour, another city that had been under nominal Portuguese control for years but which had grown lax and defiant about tribute payment. When Manuel sent an expedition to conquer Azemmour in 1513, he tried to make the enterprise a crusade. Pope Leo X was appealed to for moral support, and the Portuguese poet, Gil Vicente, wrote an *Exhortation to War* to drum up enthusiasm at home.[21] Since Manuel's sole purpose was to strengthen his military position in Morocco, the whole thing seemed somewhat absurd to his contemporaries. Moreover, the artificial enthusiasm proved unnecessary, since the Moors tamely abandoned their city and fled without a fight.

The boldest stroke tried by the Portuguese in Morocco was their surprise assault on Marrakech, the ancient capital of the country located a hundred miles from the coast. Nuno de Ataíde made the daring attempt in 1514. With a small force he ascended the Tensift River, which flows near Marrakech, and nearly battled his way into the city. But Moors in overwhelming numbers blocked the way, and Ataíde finally drew off his small army in safety and with slight loss. This glorious failure raised Portuguese prestige rather than lowered it. For the next few years, Morocco, almost to the walls of Marrakech, was subject to the Christians or at least was on a tribute-paying basis. What finally wrecked the fragile structure of Portuguese power was the assassination in 1518 of the Moorish agent, Bentufafa, who had faithfully collaborated in the work of Portuguese empire-building. The brave Ataíde had already died, and with the loss of these two Manuel's hope of a great African domain to match his eastern conquests went glimmering. Before long Portugal began to find the Moroccan holdings a profitless investment and to abandon them one by one.

Manuel lived to learn of the start of the famous voyage by his erstwhile subject, Magellan, but not long enough to learn his fate.

[21] Fidelino de Figueiredo, *Literatura portuguesa,* (Editora a Noite, Rio de Janeiro, 1940), p. 84.

Magellan had come home from India to find that there was little further chance for him to use his talents in Portuguese service, because his old chief, Albuquerque, had handed in what today would be called an unsatisfactory fitness report concerning him. So, after a short enlistment for service in Morocco, where he received a crippling wound, Magellan made a final gesture of loyalty to Manuel by offering to make the westward voyage to the Moluccas for Portugal. Of all possible plans, this was the one least likely to tempt the king, who knew that Portugal's only hope of a spice monopoly depended on keeping all routes closed except the one around the Cape of Good Hope. Moreover, Manuel had taken a dislike to Magellan and he gave the man an unnecessarily curt dismissal, telling him that he might enter any foreign service he chose.

Magellan next busied himself with studies in Lisbon, to reinforce his own conviction that the Moluccas rightly belonged to Castile and that they could be reached by sailing westward. He then went to Spain and was joined there by several other Portuguese who likewise felt disgruntled with conditions at home. He quickly gained an audience with high Castilian officials and presently with the new king, soon to be Charles V of the Holy Roman Empire. Charles responded to Magellan's proposal with downright enthusiasm and ordered immediate preparations for the voyage. At this point Manuel became alarmed and tried by means of saboteurs and diplomatic agents either to keep Magellan from sailing or else to lure him back to Portugal. The king failed to prevent the voyage, but he did create a feeling of suspicion in Castilian official circles that ultimately handicapped the great discoverer. Several Spanish officers who sailed with Magellan went largely to spy upon him.

Preparations went forward, and in 1519 Magellan sailed from Sanlúcar de Barrameda in command of five ships. Despite opposition and mutiny, he discovered Magellan's Strait and conducted three of the vessels across the Pacific. On Mactan, one of the southern Philippine Islands, the commander lost his life in a native skirmish. His companions elected new leaders; and, after wandering for months about the East Indies, they finally visited the Moluccas, where they found that Magellan's old friend, Serrão, had recently died. Since the Portuguese had not yet moved east of Malacca to occupy the Moluccas, the Spaniards were able to obtain a cargo of the highly prized clove. One of the ships, the *Victoria,* commanded by Sebastián de Elcano, then completed the circumnavigation of the globe by running the Portuguese gauntlet and returning to Spain around the Cape of Good Hope. That had not been the original plan of Magellan, who had expected to return the same way that he had come.[22]

Spanish competition galvanized the Portuguese into action in the Far East, and a force of theirs straightway moved into the Moluccas and occupied the island of Ternate. When a second party of Spaniards crossed the Pacific in the track of Magellan and reached the Moluccas, they found the Portuguese there ahead of them. Following a lengthy conflict in the islands, the Spaniards all surrendered and were sent as prisoners to India.

The original question, however, remained unanswered. According to the Treaty of Tordesillas, which country owned the Moluccas? Spain and Portugal both claimed them, and neither party would abate its claims in the least. The Portuguese held the real whip hand, since they could reach the islands much more easily and quickly than the Spaniards could by their remote Strait of Magellan route. Charles V finally realized this and, by the Treaty of Saragossa, in 1529 he sold out for cash to João III, son and successor to Manuel.[23] Although the terms provided that Charles could always revive his claim by refunding the Portuguese money, there was little chance that he would exercise the option, and in fact he never again brought up the matter. In a sense Charles was the gainer, since he had sold something that already belonged to Portugal. Under the original Tordesillas terms, that country was clearly entitled to the Moluccas.

Some years before this, in 1521, Manuel the Fortunate had died. His twenty-six year reign had seen Portugal grow from a small European state with a few island possessions into the first of the great modern world empires. The mighty Spanish conquests in the New World had not taken shape by 1521; the Portuguese

---

[22] The best survey of Magellan's career is Jean Denucé, *Magellan, la question des Moluques et la première circumnavigation du globe* (Brussels, 1908).

[23] Frances Gardiner Davenport, *European Treaties bearing on the History of the United States* (Carnegie Institution of Washington, Washington, D.C., 1917-1937), I, 169-198.

Empire was largely formed. The fame of Almeida and Albuquerque filled Europe; that of Cortés and Pizarro lay still in the future.
Manuel had lived in luxury and pomp unknown since the Roman
emperors. His palaces were the most splendid, his entertainments
the most sumptuous, and his ambassadors the most ostentatious
of any in Europe. His name was synonymous with opulence; and,
if the popular notion of Manuel as a Midas or Croesus was not
entirely correct, the reverse side of the picture did not show up
sharply in his lifetime.

Manuel's hope of gaining the throne of Fernando and Isabel
had come to nothing when his wife, the anti-Semitic Isabel, died,
leaving one infant son who soon followed her to the grave. Manuel
then married Maria, another of Fernando and Isabel's daughters,
but she, being a younger child, was not in line to inherit her
parents' kingdoms. Of Manuel's many children by Maria, João,
the eldest, became the next king of Portugal. Late in life, when
again a widower, Manuel married a third time. This bride was
another Spanish princess, Leonor, a granddaughter of Fernando
and Isabel. Leonor survived Manuel and, after nine years of
widowhood, married Francis I of France. She outlived her second
husband as well and, attempting no more matrimonial ventures,
retired to Spain to spend her last years.

Chapter VI

IMPERIAL PROBLEMS

PORTUGAL, as the first founder of a modern world empire, had no experience to serve as a guide in the government and administration of a vast colonial domain. Furthermore, no one else in Europe had any such experience, so there were no ideas that could possibly be borrowed or imitated. Most nations when confronted by the situation that faced Portugal have attempted to solve the problem by stretching their familiar home institutions to meet the new demands. The Portuguese naturally tried this solution first.

Their earliest colonial problems came with the populating of the Atlantic island groups—the Madeiras, Azores, and Cape Verdes. Here they found it fairly easy to apply European feudal practices. Individual proprietors, called donataries, received islands or parts of islands on certain terms from the crown and undertook to bring settlers from Portugal and to manage them after their arrival.[1] Later on, the Portuguese did the same in Brazil, a land of continental size presenting problems very different from those of the small islands. In Brazil the scheme worked in some places and fell flat in others, often depending on how hostile and dangerous the local natives were.

This solution, of course, could never apply to the Portuguese oriental conquests, where the problem was, first, to manage a great and growing trade, and, second, to arrange for the govern-

---

[1] *Alguns documentos do Archivo Nacional da Tôrre do Tombo,* ed. by J. Ramos Coelho (Imprensa Nacional, Lisbon, 1892), pp. 2, 6-7.

ment of millions of Asiatic subjects. Portugal did not solve this problem all at once but advanced toward a solution a step at a time.

The solution began with a warehouse, constructed at Lagos in Prince Henry's day. There the first products from Guinea were unloaded into the crude building, which became known as the *Casa da Guiné* or House of Guinea. After the prince's death, the government moved the warehouse to Lisbon. Presently, in the reign of João II, the Portuguese built their famous fortification on the Gold Coast at São Jorge da Mina, and so the Lisbon establishment began to be known as the *Casa da Guiné e Mina*. The staff in charge of the lone structure by the Tagus remained for years the nearest approach to a colonial ministry that Portugal had. Naturally the directors of the *Casa* found it necessary to widen their jurisdiction above and beyond the mere handling of trade, because countless other problems had arisen demanding their attention. Then came the year 1499, with Vasco da Gama's return from Calicut bearing oriental spices. The *Casa* thereafter had to concentrate chiefly on the East, and soon it became known as the *Casa da India*. It now maintained a huge establishment for the unloading and distribution of oriental goods. It collected the duties required by the government and rigorously inspected the imports. The *Casa* now also arranged for the supplying and equipping of Portuguese fleets outward bound for India. This called for the handling of numerous contracts and for paying the wages of thousands of employees, both at home and in the Orient. The *Casa* therefore became subdivided into several *Mesas,* or boards, to deal respectively with spices, money accounts, the equipment of fleets, the training of seamen, and the secretarial or paper work that its numerous functions involved. Naturally too, legal and judicial representatives had to be added as the whole administration became complicated.[2]

As the Portuguese empire grew, the problem was created of supplying competent officials to manage it. Manuel bestowed the office of viceroy on Francisco de Almeida as early as 1505, and, although the title then lapsed for a few years it was quickly re-

[2] For the evolution of the *Casa*, see José Gonçalo de Santa Rita, "O govêrno central e o govêrno local," *História da expansão portuguesa no mundo,* ed. by António Baião, Hernani Cidade, and Manuel Múrias, 3 vols. (Editorial Atica, Lisbon, 1937-1940), II, 73-77.

stored. The Portuguese viceroy, who soon came to reside at Goa, was supposedly the king's representative in the East. His distance from home plus the faulty communications gave him great liberty of action. The same applied to the numerous governors, below the viceroy, who ruled the many parts of the far-flung Portuguese Empire. Whenever complaints came in regarding despotic and unjust rule by the governors, the crown might intervene but always did so tardily, after the damage had already been done. The king and his representatives were absolute masters of the overseas empire. Whatever powers the waning cortes might still have at home in Portugal had no application whatever to the colonies, where Manuel and his royal successors governed as despotically as distance and unfamiliarity with local conditions would permit.

In the last analysis, Portuguese supremacy in the Orient had to rest on military and naval strength. The white soldiers who served their king in the East were ordinarily raised by voluntary recruitment at home. In the early days of the empire, when the whole idea was new and interesting, men came forward in the required numbers for service. Later, when the seamy side of Indian life became better known, recruits proved harder to get, and there had to be forced conscription at times. Ultimately the government undertook the transportation of small boys to India, where they served for some years as pages to wealthy officers and *fidalgos,* and where they learned the art of war. When they grew up, these boys naturally passed into the army and had few interests other than soldiering.[3]

Except in time of war, Portuguese soldiers in the East ordinarily did not have to live a barracks life. So long as they stayed in the town or city to which they were assigned, they had liberty to engage the best quarters they could afford. European Portuguese were not supposed to marry while on colonial duty. Many did so in spite of the regulations, but a far larger number took native mistresses and inevitably sired half-caste children.

Some use was made of Indian soldiers. Mercenaries of the first-line variety generally came from states outside Portuguese jurisdiction. Local natives were often given a minimum of military training to make them useful in case their own districts had to be defended. Sometimes, too, they accompanied the Portu-

[3] A. Botelho da Costa Veiga, "Organização militar do Oriente," *História da expansão portuguesa no mundo,* p. 86.

guese on distant campaigns, in the capacity of baggage-carriers or arms-bearers.

Ultimately the Portuguese Orient became divided into twelve military districts, bounded on the west by the Arabian coast and on the east by the territory of Macau in China. The number of soldiers to a district varied greatly; often it was quite small. In the district of Chaul, for instance, only fifty firstline Portuguese troops were stationed, but they were eked out considerably by reserves and mercenaries.[4]

In an empire resting on sea power, the fleet had to be all-important. Three major naval bases at Goa, Malacca, and Ormuz, existed to keep open the Portuguese lines of communication and to dominate the seas to prevent competition from arising. Every year an armada left Lisbon in March or April, timed to catch the monsoon that would blow the ships from east Africa to India by September. Two types of ship made up the fleet—the cargo carriers that were scheduled to return to Portugal the next year and the war vessels intended as replacements for the Indian Ocean squadron. Most of the warships were based on Goa and from there went out on patrol duty to outlying parts of the empire. Malacca had its own permanent fleet, for the purpose of keeping clear the seas east of the straits so that Javanese and Chinese junks laden with valuable produce could voyage in safety.[5]

Portuguese supremacy in the East rested partly on conquest and partly on diplomacy. The usual custom was not to overthrow native rulers but to keep them on their thrones, allow them substantial jurisdiction over their own subjects, and in this way save the expense of installing an all-Portuguese administration. Even in Goa the Indians lived largely under their own laws, administered by a native known as the *tanador,* who appointed sub-officials and collected taxes. A system of alliances held in line the neighboring states that were not under Portuguese jurisdiction and that could be dangerous in case they united against the Europeans. Long before the English achieved the conquest of India, the Portuguese had evolved several principles of government that the Anglo-Saxons later adopted. The most important of these

[4] A. Botelho da Costa Veiga, "Organização militar do Oriente," *História da expansão portugesa no mundo,* pp. 90-92.
[5] Alfredo Botelho de Sousa, "A armada e o império da India," *ibid.,* II, 93-99.

was the policy of concluding alliances with Indian potentates which made them virtually satellites of the European power. Furthermore, the sepoys who played such a part in conquering and holding India for the British were clearly foreshadowed in the limited number of mercenary soldiers employed by the Portuguese.

The great empire of Portugal at its height produced everything but revenue or, to put it another way, cost more to maintain than it yielded in returns. Although King Manuel had a reputation for fabulous riches, his successors could well believe that the great king had taken his wealth with him into the grave. Certainly the treasury at the time of his death contained little or nothing.[6]

Strange as this may seem for a man who during twenty years had been lord of the most opulent trade on earth, the reasons for the poverty are not hard to find. From the beginning, India voyages had been costly. Vasco da Gama's had brought small financial profit and the more elaborate expedition of Cabral showed a loss of 80,000 ducats.[7] Each ship going east had to be manned and equipped at heavy expense. Ships wore out early, and each one was good for only a few round trips to India. The casualty rate, moreover, was high, for shipwreck occurred frequently, each wreck meaning that a heavy investment went to the bottom of the Atlantic or the Indian oceans. As the Portuguese eastern military and civil services grew, hosts of officials had to be paid, and some of them, such as the viceroy and governors, drew heavy salaries. Add to this the inevitable practice that soon developed of private profiteering by many officers to the detriment of the king's treasury, and it will be seen that far more was involved than merely raking profits into the royal exchequer.

Then, too, the extent to which Portugal really monopolized the eastern trade has been exaggerated. From Vasco da Gama's voyage to the end of Manuel's reign, an average of a dozen ships a year sailed to the Indian Ocean, and many did not return. This was a pitifully small number to dominate such an extensive commerce. Venice, the European state most threatened by Portugal's

[6] C. Malheiro Dias, "A metrópole e suas conquistas nos reinados de D. João III, D. Sebastião e Cardeal D. Henrique," *História da colonização portuguesa do Brasil*, ed. by Carlos Malheiro Dias, 3 vols. (Litografia Nacional, Oporto, 1921-1924), III, 10.
[7] Roberto Levillier, *América la bien llamada* (Buenos Aires, 1948), I, 236.

new trade route, was experienced and resourceful. Venetian agents studied the situation in Lisbon and often accompanied the Portuguese fleets as private traders. Since Albuquerque and his successors never closed the Red Sea route, Venice still made some use of it, in collaboration first with Egypt and later with the Ottoman Turks. The Portuguese themselves sold large amounts of spice in Ormuz, some of which was taken by caravan to the Syrian coast and picked up there by Venetian ships for sale in Europe. So, after a momentary setback, the old Italian republic continued to do a substantial amount of business.[8]

The Portuguese do not seem ever to have added materially to the spice available for the European market. If anything, they diminished the total amount in circulation, originally by disorganizing the old trade routes and later by failing to take up all the slack themselves. Statistics show that Portuguese imports failed to lower the pepper cost in Europe, which indicates that the supply did not increase. Profits diminished also from the fact that cargoes suffered greater deterioration on the long voyage around the cape than on the easier journey by way of the Red Sea and Suez. In the meantime, the cost of obtaining spice and bearing it to Europe in Portuguese ships steadily rose, for carrying expenses became greater as the sixteenth century progressed.

The truth was that Portugal was one of the least fitted European countries to engage in imperial ventures. A combination of luck, geographical position, maritime skill, and native daring had given the Portuguese an initial lead they could not hold for long. The nation lacked a large and solid middle class to bear the commercial brunt of the enterprise, and it also lacked large-scale, experienced bankers, such as Italy, Germany, and the Low Countries could provide. And these foreign bankers, taking advantage of the poverty and commercial ineptitude of the Portuguese, soon crowded into the picture. They bought their way into the India fleets, and by advancing money to the crown to pay the expenses of expeditions they often took a first mortgage on returning cargoes, thus guaranteeing the profits to themselves. After a time Antwerp and not Lisbon became the central distributing point for spice in Western Europe. The Portuguese metropolis, despite all the docks and warehouses maintained by the *Casa da India*,

[8] Frederic Chapin Lane, *American Historical Review*, XXXVIII, 219-237.

threatened to become merely another way station, like Malacca or Goa, on the long spice route.

Portugal suffered in ways above and beyond the simple financial deficit. It all represented a mighty strain for a nation that had barely 1,500,000 people at the start of the sixteenth century and possibly less at the end of it. The numbers taken eastward by the Indian fleets were possibly not a high percentage of the total population, but they came out of the nation's best young manpower. Many never returned, whether they ended at the bottom of the ocean, died in war, succumbed to disease, or went native. Men who did come back, like the poet Camões, returned broken in health and, despite the still prevalent belief in eastern riches, fit only to become public charges.

To summarize the situation briefly, the crown of Portugal provided means by which private fortunes could be built, some by its own subjects and some by foreigners. The Portuguese soldiers and seamen did all the dangerous work and shed all the blood. Others, who stayed comfortably in Europe and took no chances, pocketed the bulk of the profits. Portugal ran a vast colonial empire mainly for the benefit of others.

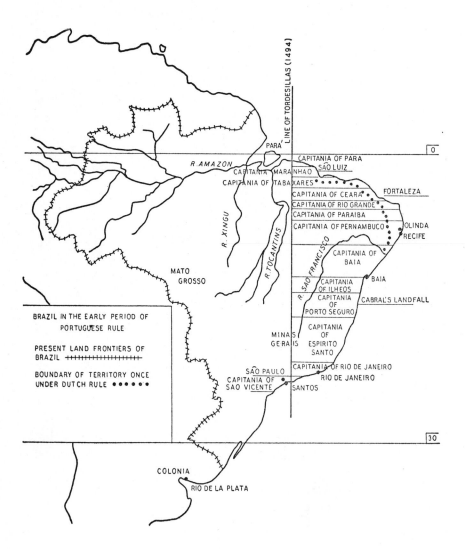

LINE OF TORDESILLAS (1494)

PARÁ

R. AMAZON

CAPITANIA OF PARA

SÃO LUIZ

CAPITANIA MARANHÃO

CAPITANIA OF TABAXARES

CAPITANIA OF CEARÁ

CAPITANIA OF RIO GRANDE

CAPITANIA OF PARAIBA

CAPITANIA OF PERNAMBUCO

FORTALEZA

OLINDA

RECIFE

R. XINGU

R. TOCANTINS

R. SÃO FRANCISCO

CAPITANIA OF
BAIA

CAPITANIA
OF ILHEOS

BAIA

MATO
GROSSO

CAPITANIA
OF
PORTO SEGURO

CABRAL'S LANDFALL

CAPITANIA
OF
ESPIRITO
SANTO

MINAS
GERAIS

CAPITANIA OF RIO DE JANEIRO

SÃO PAULO

CAPITANIA OF
SAO VICENTE

RIO DE JANEIRO

SANTOS

BRAZIL IN THE EARLY PERIOD OF
PORTUGUESE RULE

PRESENT LAND FRONTIERS OF
BRAZIL ++++++++++++++++

BOUNDARY OF TERRITORY ONCE
UNDER DUTCH RULE ● ● ● ● ● ●

COLONIA

RIO DE LA PLATA

Chapter VII

THE PORTUGUESE DECLINE

*W*ITH Manuel gone, the heavy burden of power and responsibility rested on the shoulders of João III, who in 1521 was aged not quite twenty, and who was to reign for almost thirty-six years. Historians have often called João stupid and bigoted, mainly because Portugal established the Inquisition during his reign. Bigoted he surely was, but perhaps not altogether stupid. Any man who could hold the shaky Portuguese Empire together for four decades, and even enlarge it in places, cannot be written off as incompetent. No one, to be sure, has ever called him brilliant, and Camões, when João died, took note of the king's death in a sonnet, which, although respectful, clearly showed that the poet never thought his departed sovereign would shine in the pages of history. Yet whoever studies the career of João gets the impression of a man who had a policy and thoroughly understood his nation's situation in the world. Portugal had now passed largely from the expansive stage to the holding, conserving stage. This meant that some things could be attempted and others could not; it was up to João to weigh every policy and action in the light of these facts.

He had a horror of leaving the empire smaller than when it had come to him. His unwillingness to retreat on any front was perhaps his major weakness, yet he had remarkable success in maintaining this policy of holding fast. Like a greater statesman four centuries later, he had not come to power "to preside over the liquidation" of his country's empire.

95

But a few retreats had to be made. In 1539, João's sage minister, the Count of Castanheira, gave him a most disheartening report on the condition of the kingdom and empire. Every source of revenue, said the count, had been tapped, and every possible cut in expenses had been made. And yet it was still necessary to lessen the burden. Castanheira therefore proposed that the cities of Safi and Azemmour in Morocco be abandoned.[1] They had never been anything but a drain to Portugal, and just then it happened that a new vigorous government had come to power in Fez which would certainly try to push the Portuguese out of these coastal places. João could not bear to accept his minister's undoubtedly sound arguments. He listened to more hot-blooded Portuguese, who advised him never to yield the cities. He appealed to his brother-in-law, Charles V of Spain, for help, only to learn that the Spanish treasury was in much the same shape as his own. João resolved to fight, but before he was ready, the Moors had taken the offensive and were threatening all the Portuguese establishments on the coast. And the places could not be held. Safi and Azemmour were given up first, then Alcácer Ceguer, and finally Arzila, after each had been as nearly destroyed as possible. João felt this loss keenly and regarded himself as a traitor to both Portugal and Christendom in abandoning the cities. His conscience even made him appeal to the pope for forgiveness.[2]

These losses cut the Portuguese holdings in Morocco down to Tangier and the original Ceuta. Once there had been a thought of a great North African empire, but that dream would never be realized now.

In view of the weakness of his country and the vulnerability of his empire, João could scarcely afford the luxury of any European policy other than one of complete or near-isolation. He would submit to almost any insult rather than go to war. He remained aloof from the alliances and alignments of the European powers and thus fought in no continental wars. Relations with Spain were now amicable, due in part to the fact that João had married Catarina of Castile, sister of Charles V. Most of the trouble came from France, then ruled by the pushing and aggres-

---

[1] Malheiro Dias, "A metropole e suas conquistas," *História da colonização*, III, 15-16.
[2] *Ibid.*, p. 16.

sive Francis I. Fortunately for Portugal, Francis always saw his major enemy in Charles V, and so that powerful ruler absorbed most of the shock from France. But on the high seas French privateers made things difficult for the Portuguese, even though they still lacked sufficient knowledge of seafaring to venture many times beyond the Cape of Good Hope.

Francis I of course did not feel bound in any way by the demarcation line Spain and Portugal had drawn at Tordesillas. Once, when a Spanish minister complained of encroachments by French ships in the Atlantic, Francis made one of his most famous remarks, a remark which is usually slightly misquoted. The French king said, "And does it mean declaring war and contravening my friendship with his majesty to send my ships down there? The sun shines for me the same as for the others: I would much like to see that clause in Adam's will that excluded me from the partition of the world." [3]

João patiently bore the depredations of French corsairs for several years, until it became evident that they meant to set themselves up on shore in Brazil. True, Portugal had never colonized this long stretch of coast and had attempted no administration of it, but Brazilian ports in French hands were a thing João could not risk. Any foreigner with a base in Brazil would be in a splendid location to dart out and seize Portugal's spice-laden ships as they returned from the East, usually in poor condition and with depleted manpower.

Therefore, in 1530, João's government took the first step toward the occupation of Brazil, which it still did not particularly want but which had to be held for strategic reasons. An energetic officer, Martim Afonso de Sousa, was given a fleet and told to make a survey of the Brazilian coast, to drive off foreign intruders, and to select a good site and plant a permanent settlement. As Sousa advanced down the Brazilian shore by easy stages, he met and ousted some French interlopers and also discovered white settlers, both Castilian and Portuguese, who had made their homes at various points, either alone or with the Indians. After exploring all the way to the Río de la Plata, he selected the site of São Vicente, near the modern Santos, for his colony. There, in 1532,

[3] António Baião, "A expedição de Cristóvão Jacques," *História da colonização*, III, 63-64.

he established the settlers who had come with him, and soon afterward returned to Portugal with most of the fleet. The rest of Martim Afonso de Sousa's career was connected with India, where he ultimately became viceroy.[4]

It did not take João long to learn that this provided no real solution to the Brazilian problem. One settlement could contribute little to holding a coastline stretching from the equator to the south temperate zone. More colonization was imperatively required, but how and at whose expense? The empty Portuguese treasury made government enterprise impossible, and so resort was had once more to the old feudal idea. João's government, on paper at least, chopped the Brazilian coastline into fifteen grants, or *capitanias,* and bestowed them as holdings on various trusted Portuguese who were called donataries. Each holder of a *capitania* took responsibility for bringing colonists from Portugal and for developing the economic resources of his grant. The donatary could tax and govern his tenants, but assumed certain financial and legal obligations to the Portuguese crown.[5]

The first awards were made in 1534, and within a short time all the fifteen *capitanias* had been assigned. The system succeeded well in a few places, particularly at São Vicente and Pernambuco. In several other regions the colonies that were established managed to endure, though in a down-at-heels, poverty-stricken manner. In still other places the settlements dwindled away and vanished, usually because of Indian hostility. A few grants existed mainly on paper, and apparently their owners thought of them more as real estate investments than as potential colonies. Strangely enough, in their first Brazilian colonizing, the Portuguese overlooked Guanabara Bay, where the city of Rio de Janeiro later grew.

By 1549, the government realized that, while the *capitania* system had accomplished something toward strengthening the hold on Brazil, a further step was necessary. Continued danger from the French and the lawlessness prevalent in some of the *capitanias* called for the appointment of a governor general, to take care of defense and to bring uniformity out of confusion. Tomé de Sousa received the assignment and was appointed donatary of

[4] Jordão de Freitas, "A expedição de Martim Afonso de Sousa," *História da colonização,* pp. 97-164.

[5] Malheiro Dias, "O regimen feudal das donatarias," *ibid.,* pp. 219-283.

Baia, with authority over the rest of the *capitanias,* which were not, however, abolished. With the arrival of Sousa, Baia became the capital of Brazil and remained so until the eighteenth century. Accompanying the governor general were officials, soldiers, additional settlers, and several friars of the newly founded Jesuit order, who had been sent to evangelize the Indians.

Tomé de Sousa proved to be an able official and did his work well.[6] Portugal had reorganized Brazil not a moment too soon, because in 1555 a party of Frenchmen led by Nicolas de Villegaignon made a settlement on Guanabara Bay. It could now be seen what a costly mistake had been made in leaving this splendid harbor unoccupied. The French had high hopes of building for themselves an empire in South America, which they grandiloquently termed "Antarctic France."

Fortunately for the Portuguese, their adversaries were considerate enough to wreck their own enterprise. Several Huguenot clergymen from John Calvin's headquarters at Geneva came to join Villegaignon, bringing with them a number of Protestant laymen. Soon the Frenchmen began quarreling over theology, which led to civil war within the colony. Some of the French returned to Europe; others left Villegaignon's settlement and went to live among the Indians. The leader himself abandoned the enterprise and went back to France. Finally, in 1560, Mem de Sá, one of Sousa's successors as governor general of Brazil, was able to destroy the slender remnants of the French colony. Individual Frenchmen lived among the surrounding Tamoyo Indians for several years more and even made some headway in spreading Calvinism among them. Ultimately, of course, as Portuguese control spread, all traces of Protestant doctrine disappeared.[7] Meanwhile the Portuguese settlement of Rio de Janeiro was founded, and, although the French later menaced other parts of Brazil, they never tried to resume their original enterprise.

This Brazilian interlude never led to open and declared war between Portugal and France. Although João frequently complained of French conduct through his ambassadors in Paris, he never worded his protests so strongly as to close the door to the

[6] Pedro de Azevedo, "A instituição do governo geral," *História da colonização,* pp. 327-383.
[7] Charles E. Nowell, "The French in Sixteenth Century Brazil," *The Americas,* V (1949), 381-393.

possibility of reconciliation. And the French always had their hands sufficiently full in Europe to make them regard Portugal as a secondary issue.

In the Orient, while the Portuguese were being economically vanquished by the dead weight of empire, they could still conquer with the sword. At the outset of his reign João found his eastern possessions badly disorganized, thanks to Albuquerque's incompetent successors, and urgently needing a strong hand. The aged Vasco da Gama was then sent to Goa with viceregal powers; but, having barely reached India, he died on Christmas day, 1524. His successor, Henrique de Menezes, governed with a vigor and suppressed Portugal's eastern enemies with a ruthlessness that recalled the times of Afonso de Albuquerque. The *Samuri* of Calicut had taken what he considered a favorable opportunity to go on the warpath again. With a huge army, he besieged 300 Portuguese in a fort they had constructed in his city. After the small garrison had stood a terrific siege, Menezes arrived with a fleet bearing reinforcements. Although outnumbered approximately twenty-five to one by the *Samuri,* he landed his men and won a sweeping victory.

One triumph, however, seldom solved more than a local problem in the East. The Portuguese empire could not remain static; it had to grow or else wither away. In 1531, Nuno da Cunha, then governor of India, made an attempt to capture the powerful city of Diu, north of Goa, which Francisco de Almeida, years earlier, had intimidated but had not conquered. Cunha assembled possibly the largest fleet ever gathered in Indian waters to attack Diu, but the frenzied resistance of the hard fighting Gujaratis forced him to retire with heavy loss. In 1535, however, the Portuguese largely accomplished their aim by other means. The Gujarat ruler, Bahadur Shah, was being terrorized by the Mogul emperor, Humayan, and was on the verge of fleeing to Mecca, when his advisers persuaded him to make friends with the Portuguese who would then act as his protectors. The advice pleased Bahadur, who permitted the construction of a fortress by Europeans on the island of Diu.

The Moguls soon retired and Bahadur Shah, repenting of his bargain, decided to throw out the Portuguese. He first worked up a grand alliance among the rulers of western India, and even included the Ottoman Turks, who sent ships to his assistance all

Monastery of Batalha—A Fourteenth Century Architectural Masterpiece. *Courtesy of Casa de Portugal, New York.*

Portrait of King Manuel the Fortunate. From *História da colonizacão
portuguesa do Brasil.*

the way from Suez. This first siege of Diu, as it is called to distinguish it from a later one, lasted through most of 1538 and well
into the following year. António da Silveira commanded the Portuguese, who fought with a valor they had never surpassed in
Albuquerque's day. The heavy cannon brought by the Turks far
outclassed their own small artillery, and the defenders held on
only by grim determination. Luckily for them, the Ottomans
quarreled with the Gujaratis and sailed home.[8] Early in 1539,
Garcia de Noronha, the viceroy of India, arrived with an adequate
fleet and compelled Bahadur to make peace.

Noronha's successor was Estevão da Gama, son of Vasco. He
saw a danger in the presence of Turkish warships in the Red Sea
and reverted to Albuquerque's old plan of establishing Portuguese domination there. In 1541, he swept past Aden in the direction of Tór and Suez, pausing to sack the city of Suakim on the
way. He reached Tór and spared it from destruction on the pleading of two friars from Mount Sinai who happened to be there. Bad
weather then prevented Gama from bringing his main fleet to
Suez, and the Turks succeeded in repelling the few ships he
brought. He retired, like Albuquerque before him, having terrorized the Red Sea but leaving it still in Moslem hands.

The second siege of Diu, which came a few years later, was an
even more impressive episode than the first. João III now had as
his governor in India João de Castro, the last of the great Portuguese empire builders, a man in every respect worthy to wear the
shoes of Almeida and Albuquerque. Castro arrived in Goa just
before the new Gujarati ruler, Muhammed, repeated his predecessor's attempt to destroy the Portuguese in Diu. João Mascarenhas, who now commanded that citadel, realized that an attack was
impending when he caught two traitors who had been bribed by
the enemy to explode his powder magazine. But though he was
not surprised, his situation seemed desperate, as with 200 men he
found himself besieged by thousands of Gujaratis, Turks, and
Egyptians, not to mention an Italian renegade who furnished the
brains of the attacking force. The siege began early in 1546, and
João de Castro quickly rushed what reinforcements he could from
Goa. Their arrival increased the manpower available but also
increased the likelihood of starvation. After Castro had labored

[8] Fortunato de Almeida, *História de Portugal* (Coimbra, 1922-1929), II, 317.

eight months, collecting soldiers from every Portuguese post in western India, he arrived with a fleet in November, 1546. So cleverly did he cover his movements, usually working by night, that he slipped his entire fighting strength into the fortress, with the enemy still unaware that the disembarkation had begun. Castro's next problem was whether to remain behind walls or to sally out and fight, for he had most of the Portuguese mobile eastern strength under his command, and a battle, as his counselors warned, meant "risking all of India." The commander took the chance and, after planning his attack well, won so sweeping a victory as to render him total master of the island. Diu was saved, and, more than that, India was saved for the Portuguese.[9] Years went by before another such danger had to be faced.

Elsewhere in the East, the influence of Portugal was extended, largely by peaceful means, in the reign of João III. Trade relations with Siam were increased, and in 1557 the tiny peninsula known as Macau, in southern China, was leased, to become for several centuries the only European foothold in the Celestial Empire. Pushing out from the Moluccas, where they were now firmly established, the Portuguese explored the East Indian Archipelago —the Philippines, the Celebes, and Papua. In 1542, the first party of Portuguese visited Japan and opened the way for a missionary effort by the Jesuits which soon followed.

At home, the most important event of João's reign was the establishment of the Portuguese Inquisition. Events had been working in that direction for years. Manuel's order for the expulsion of the Jews in 1496 had resulted in their forced conversion rather than their departure. Meanwhile, the Castilian Inquisition was hard at work, and many Spanish New Christians, fleeing from persecution, crossed the frontier into Portugal. As early as 1515, Manuel had complained of this to Rome and had asked Leo X to set up a Portuguese Inquisition. The Pope at that time had refused, and the Jews, now ostensibly all Christians, at least breathed freer air in Portugal than they did in Spain. But only for a limited time, because ill winds were blowing. It had become a Portuguese habit to blame the Jews for every local or national catastrophe, from a crop failure to a plague. Rumors ran to the effect that

[9] *História quinhentista do segundo cêrco de Dio,* ed. by António Baião (Coimbra, 1925), especially pp. 86-93.

Jewish doctors and pharmacists were in league to poison Portuguese Christians. Every town and district had its local horror story, ranging from the mutilation of Christian images by the Jews to slaughter of Christian babes for Israelite religious purposes.

Another factor existed by the time of João III, for Protestantism had meanwhile arisen. It never made much headway in Portugal, but a few men there absorbed heretical ideas, and according to Roman Catholic notions these must be nipped in the bud.

João III repeated Manuel's plea for an Inquisition in 1531, when he asked Pope Clement VII for a bull establishing the institution perpetually in Portugal, the Inquisitor General and other personnel to be selected by the crown. The Roman curia again objected, saying very frankly that it considered the whole idea merely a pretext for despoiling the Hebrews of their property.[10] But with the next pope, Paul III, João had better success and in May 23, 1536, obtained the bull establishing his Inquisition. The persons against whom the tribunal would specifically operate were Christianized Jews who had relapsed to their old faith and all persons who accepted the heresies of Luther. The papacy, still distrustful of national Inquisitions, at first imposed limitations on the Portuguese tribunal, but João continued to protest and to maintain that every vestige of tolerance must be removed. Paul III at last succumbed, and by the bull *Meditatio cordis* in 1547 gave the Portuguese Inquisition a free hand.[11]

The first Inquisitor General, the Bishop of Ceuta, was an old, easy-going man, who soon resigned his office to make way for João's brother, Archbishop Henrique, who is described as stupid, vindictive, and a very paragon of intolerance. The most famous case that came up in the early days of the Portuguese Inquisition was the trial for heresy of George Buchannan. This Scottish man of learning had imbibed Protestant views early in life and had made a fine scholarly reputation for himself at a college in Bordeaux. João remodeled the Portuguese university in 1537 and moved it from Lisbon to Coimbra. Buchannan was one of the men to whom he offered a professorship, and the Scot eagerly accepted.

[10] Fortunato de Almeida, *História de Portugal* (Coimbra, 1922-1929), II, 324.
[11] *Corpo diplomatico portuguez*, VI, 166-170.

With a group of Bordeaux scholars, including several Portuguese, he went to Coimbra and commenced his teaching. Suddenly the Inquisition seized him and two fellow instructors, João da Costa and Diogo de Teive. The charges concerned their previous careers and heresies outside Portugal rather than the specific things they had taught at Coimbra.

Evidently King João felt some desire to save the lives of the men he had personally invited to teach in his university, and possibly he pulled some wires to keep matters from going to the limit. At any rate, Buchannan, Costa, and Teive were let off after they had confessed their iniquities and promised to behave in the future. But Inquisitor General Henrique now had a thorough house cleaning at the University of Coimbra, and placed the school in the safe hands of the Jesuit Order.

Buchannan and his colleagues had been lucky. Without friends in high places they might have died by burning, as did many an unfortunate in their time, although sometimes the victim was mercifully strangled before being committed to the flames. There is ample evidence that the crowds in Lisbon, Oporto, or Braga hugely enjoyed these burning spectacles, far more than they would have appreciated the tame theatrical entertainments provided by Gil Vicente or Sá de Miranda.

The Company of Jesus, more popularly known today as the Jesuit Order, entered Portugal a little after the Inquisition. Like the Inquisition, the Jesuits existed primarily to combat heresy, but they had the additional purpose of spreading the Roman Catholic faith by conversion in parts of the world that had never known Christianity. Ignatius Loyola, the founder, was of Spanish birth and French education. He labored for several years in organizing his original handful of followers, and Pope Paul III formally recognized the Company as an Order in 1540.

João III, on learning that the Jesuits existed to convert the unbelievers, straightway became interested and invited Loyola to send missionaries to India by way of Portugal. A formal church organization had been established in the East years before, but, although some conversion work went on, it existed mainly for the Portuguese. The king believed that Jesuits would labor more energetically among the natives. Loyola complied with João's request, and soon the zealous and energetic Francis Xavier was selected to go to India. His magnificent although brief career as a missionary took him to several parts of India, to the Malay Archipelago, and to both Japan and China. Tradition exaggerates when it puts the number of his baptisms at 700,000, but certainly his converts were numerous. In 1549, when Tomé de Sousa went to reorganize Brazil, he took with him several Jesuits, headed by another famous missionary, Manuel da Nóbrega. They set up headquarters in the São Paulo district, and the evangelization of the Brazilian Indians dates from their arrival.

In Portugal itself, the Jesuits at first humbly nursed the sick and aided the poor, but soon their stock began to rise. They gained virtual control of the University of Coimbra after the Buchannan trial, and they soon had won great intellectual ascendancy in the country. Jesuits largely dominated the court of João III in his last years and had a great deal to do with killing the Portuguese humanism that still flourished in the youth of Camões but had begun to disappear by the poet's middle age.

In June, 1557, João, who still had not reached sixty, died suddenly of a heart attack. Nothing better illustrates the decline of physical stamina in the Portuguese royal line than the fact that the king's eleven children, nine legitimate and two illegitimate, all preceded him to the grave. The heir, therefore, was João's three-year-old grandson, Sebastião, the child of the king's fifth son. A regency had to be provided at once, consisting of the little monarch's grandmother and a number of powerful nobles and officials. Sebastião's great-uncle, Henrique, now a cardinal, insisted on his own unsuitable candidate as royal tutor, and thus began the reign that was to end in disaster and national eclipse.

Times were out of joint in Portugal, as many a wise person could see. Economic inequalities between classes had increased, and the most productive elements of the country were in decay. Though large fortunes had come to a few families, through trade, profiteering, or graft in the East, such families usually squandered their wealth in luxurious living or munificent gifts to the church and seldom put it into productive enterprises. An Italian cardinal, visiting Portugal in 1571, reported that trumpets sounded in the Duke of Bragança's palace every time His Grace lifted his cup to take a drink of water. Such silly ostentation was evidently fairly common among the "great" men of the realm, yet often within a stone's throw of their magnificent residences the bleakest poverty could be found.

Portuguese agriculture was declining, because of the steady drift of the peasantry from the land to the cities and the India fleets and because of the increasing use wealthy magnates now made of slaves to till the soil. Negroes, for employment as slaves, began to enter Portugal in small numbers in Prince Henry's time. Accurate figures for their importation in later years are lacking, but by the middle of João III's reign foreigners were commenting on the number to be seen in Lisbon, and by 1550 Negroes made up approximately ten percent of the city's population. In rural Portugal, slaves performed a large share of the agricultural work by the latter part of the sixteenth century. The country had never had people enough for the great imperial ventures undertaken, and the enterprises stimulated by the discovery of India cut steadily widening gaps in the ranks. Even more important, perhaps, than the physical exhaustion was the decline in morale. An apathy had fallen on large segments of the population, and the people whose ancestors had won their magnificent fight for freedom at Aljubarrota were ready, two centuries later, to submit meekly to the national enemy that had once been defeated.

Yet to the very end, the Portuguese showed some flashes of their old vigor. Luís de Ataíde, Sebastião's viceroy in the East. could still gain victories that fired his young sovereign's heart. Paulo Dias, in 1574, commenced the occupation of African N'gola, presently to be known as Angola. Unimportant though this colony seemed at the time, by the twentieth century it would be Portugal's major possession. To the outside world, Sebastião's realm presented as imposing a face as ever.

The young king grew up weak in body but ardent and romantic in disposition. It became evident that he would never be content with the role of a Manuel or a João III. He had no wish to be a huckster monarch, engaged in buying and sellings drugs and spices. The memory of Nuno Álvares meant more to him than that of Henry the Navigator, and he aspired to be the leader of a rejuvenated Portugal returning to the ideals of its national youth. *O Rei Cavaleiro*, or the knightly king as he has been called, planned a crusade, which he did not mean to trust to subordinates but intended to lead himself.

It is hard to imagine any scheme more sterile and less promising than Sebastião's plan to conquer Morocco. In his grandfather's times, Portugal had abandoned its main interest in that country and was now well out of a profitless enterprise. Sebastião resolved to resume the adventure, despite prudent advisers who urged him to marry instead and raise heirs to his throne. In 1574, the twenty-year-old king visited Morocco, where he still owned Ceuta and Tangier. He engaged in a skirmish with the Moors, and returned more bent on his crusade than ever.

Two rivals then quarreled for the Moroccan throne, and the weaker party appealed to Sebastião for aid. The young king mustered what fighting men were still available in Portugal and hired mercenaries from abroad. His uncle, Philip II of Spain, promised a little help but felt no great interest in the enterprise. In June, 1578, Sebastião sailed from the Tagus at the head of more than 20,000 soldiers, about half of them Portuguese and the rest recruited in Germany, Holland, Flanders, Italy, and Spain. He bore with him the sword and shield of Afonso Henriques, objects that had been guarded in a Coimbra convent for centuries.

Muley abd el-Halik, Sebastião's Moroccan opponent, first showed some fear of the King of Portugal by his refusal to stand and fight. He waited until the unskilled young monarch had marched his army into an arid hill country back of Arzila. Days of marching, plus the effects of heat and thirst, reduced the morale and strength of the European soldiers. Suddenly the Moors gave battle at Alcácer Kebir on August 5, 1578. Their numbers, and the untenable position into which they had maneuvered Sebastião, told the story. Before nightfall the young king was dead and his army annihilated, with scattered driblets of soldiers making their way back toward the coast. None of the survivors could actually recall seeing the king die, and this fact later gave impetus to the Portuguese legend of "Sebastianism," which held that the monarch still lived and would presently return to his people.[12]

Portugal had lost its king and its army at one blow. It next had to lose a heavy percentage of the portable national wealth, for hundreds of men of rank remained prisoners of the Moors. These must be ransomed, and their families made valiant sacrifices to

[12] The story of Sebastião's Moroccan campaign is told by J. M. de Queiroz Veloso, *Don Sebastián, 1554-1578*, transl. by Ramón de Garciasol (Madrid, 1943).

scrape together the money required. They sold off their fine garments, their jewels, and their silver plate to raise funds—all to be poured into Morocco. The ransom price of Portuguese *fidalgos* ranged anywhere from 5,000 to 16,000 *cruzados*. Many a family in comfortable circumstances found its standard of living drastically cut.

Sebastião's only legitimate male relative in Portugal was his great uncle, Cardinal Henrique, who was now a man in the late sixties. He of course took the throne, but most Portuguese knew this to be a temporary makeshift, since the real solution to the succession problem would be provided after the cardinal's death.

Two candidates within the country had claims. The Duchess of Bragança was a granddaughter of Manuel the Fortunate, but no one felt much enthusiasm for her, largely because her husband, the duke, was an impossible character and one of the most hated men in Portugal. António, the Prior of Crato, on the other hand, had a sizable following. He was an illegitimate son of one of the brothers of João III, and he made no secret of his dislike of the religious career that had been earlier thrust upon him. Old King-Cardinal Henrique might have helped António's cause by acknowledging him as his own successor. But Henrique hated his bastard relative and refused to make any such declaration.

Philip II of Spain, on the score of blood and birth, actually had the best claim to Portugal, for his mother had been one of Manuel's daughters. Already his agents were busy in Portugal building a party for him there and working to prepare a favorable state of mind in the country. One of those bought for cash was João de Mascarenhas, the gallant defender of Diu in 1546, who in his sordid old age sacrificed the reputation he had won in his heroic youth. Certainly the bulk of Portuguese people did not want a Spanish king, knowing well that he would mean a disguised form of annexation to Spain. But this was not the Portugal of Aljubarrota. In that older day, the people had thought for themselves and had felt master of the situation. Royal absolutism in the sixteenth century had ground the self-reliant instincts out of the home Portuguese. No counterparts of the Master of Avís, João das Regras, or Nuno Álvares appeared now, and even had they come forward they could have done little with the weary and apathetic people.

At first there was some slight hope that King Henrique might receive a papal dispensation, marry a young wife, and beget heirs. But the pope acted slowly in the matter, and meanwhile the elderly ruler's health failed so fast that the idea was out of the question. Henrique died on January 31, 1580, without having named a successor.

António of Crato prepared to claim the crown, but Philip of Spain gave him little chance to organize his following. Twenty thousand Spanish veterans crossed the frontier in June, commanded by the renowned Duke of Alba. Portugal resisted weakly. A makeshift army, bravely but unskillfully commanded by António, was brushed aside at Alcántara and Alba entered Lisbon. The prior fled the country and, after a visit to England and France, turned up in the Azores, where, with a little aid from Catherine de Medici, queen-mother of France, he managed to set up a shortlived "government in exile." On the mainland Philip had everything his way. A Portuguese cortes, assembled at Tomár, meekly chose him king, although Philip did make some promises that Portuguese national institutions would be respected.

The people of Portugal, however, knew the situation for what it was. Philip might talk about keeping the two crowns separate and the two colonial empires apart. What had really happened was that Portugal had lost independence and might soon lose national identity as well. The "Babylonian Captivity" had begun.

Chapter VIII

PORTUGUESE CULTURE IN THE GOLDEN AGE

*A*N interesting historical phenomenon is the manner in which a nation's cultural flowering closely coincides in point of time with its political greatness. Periclean Athens and Augustan Rome saw the worship of the muses reach their height. Much later the England of Elizabeth and the France of Louis XIV attained poetic levels that have never been surpassed in those countries. The Spaniards had their *Siglo de Oro,* or Golden Century, immediately following the rise of Spain to world power status. And in Portugal the situation was the same. The genius of the Portuguese during the fifteenth and sixteenth centuries unfolded in all lines—not in merely a few.

The most conspicuous contributions were in literature.[1] Earlier, during the middle ages, Portugal had produced a galaxy of songs, lays, ballads, and chronicles comparable to the better known products of Spain. *Cantares de Amigo* and *Cantares de Amor,* of which mention has already been made, flourished at the time of King Dinís and especially at his own royal court. The names of quite a few Portuguese troubadors who lived at this period, or even earlier, have been preserved. There is some evidence that a Portuguese work of epic type once existed, based on the Christian victory over the Moors at Salado in 1340, but this poem, if ever written, is lost beyond hope of recovery.

---

[1] Comparatively little Portuguese literature, old or new, is translated into English. Most of the interpretations presented here follow Fidelino de Figueiredo, *Literatura portuguesa* (Editora a Noite, Rio de Janeiro, 1940).

Portugal may well have been the pioneer in creating romances of chivalry, those blood-and-thunder novels of knight-errantry persisting to the time of Cervantes, who laughed the final degenerate ones out of existence. There is reason to think that *Amadis de Gaula* (Amadis of Gaul), the best and most famous of such romances, was the work of a Portuguese, Vasco de Lobeira, sometime late in the fourteenth century. It appears likely too, that Lobeira based his prose work upon an earlier Portuguese version in verse.

It was the historians, however, rather than romancers, who laid the foundations of Portuguese prose. Passing over early chronicles, dealing with purely local events and lacking all claims to literary merit, we turn to Fernão Lopes as the father of Portuguese historiography. In 1434, King Duarte created the royal post of *cronista-mor,* or chief chronicler, and appointed Lopes to fill it. In writing of the reigns and deeds of Portuguese kings, Lopes had access to the archives and records of the realm, and his abilities as a writer and investigator have won him the title of "The Portuguese Froissart." His works still have high value for the student of medieval Portugal.

The first chronicler to deal with overseas expansion was Afonso de Cerveira, who wrote of the discovery of Guinea, apparently during the time when Prince Pedro was acting as regent for his young nephew, Afonso V. For reasons never fully explained, Cerveira's account was suppressed shortly after Pedro's death. Gomes Eanes de Azurara, the squire and companion of Prince Henry, used it, however, in composing his own *Chronicle of the conquest of Guinea,* describing the great achievements of the renowned prince-navigator. The suspicion exists that Cerveira was Pedro's historian, just as Azurara was Henry's, and that the story as originally told by Cerveira differed in some ways from the version that has come to us. Be that as it may, Azurara furnishes what is now the earliest information regarding the original Portuguese discoveries. Modern impressions of those events have been completely shaped by him.

Through the rest of the fifteenth century, Portuguese historians were still largely chroniclers. Ruy de Pina is particularly outstanding among them for having produced an "inside," gossipy narrative of the reign of João II. The tone is extremely laudatory, and Pina seemed to admire the king quite as much for his feats of chicanery as for his solid virtues. For all that, his account of the great monarch's career is by far the best.

Perhaps the greatest Portuguese historian, prior to Herculano in the nineteenth century, was João de Barros, who lived from 1496 to 1570. With him the chronicle ceased to hold the stage, and history on the grand scale came into its own. Barros, whom the government subsidized by the award of a paying position, conceived his work according to a great plan which would include four continents: Europe, Africa, Asia, and Santa Cruz, by which he meant Brazil and hence the New World. In addition to history, he thought it his duty to write an all-embracing geography and a work on commerce.

Barros evidently accomplished a great deal of his plan, but only the historical work entitled *Decades of Asia* survives. He consciously modeled his *Decades* on the history of Livy the Roman, and this gave it elegance of style as well as providing an honorable precedent for its extremely patriotic tone. Beginning with a brief and fairly fanciful account of ancient history, as he understood it, Barros skimmed lightly over the story of the Iberian peninsula and the creation and development of Portugal. He then plunged into the history of exploration and discovery under Prince Henry and João II. He next brought the Portuguese into the Indian Ocean with Vasco da Gama, and described the building of their oriental empire. If an inordinate amount of national vanity appeared in his narrative, Barros compensated for this by being careful and conscientious concerning his facts, which he had unrivaled means of checking because of his government connection. The style was lofty and, though at times artificial, gave the reader a thrilling as well as an accurate account of events. When Barros died, his still unfinished work was continued by Diogo do Couto, who, though inferior as a scholar, had the advantage of a long residence in India, which made for greater realism.

Other sixteenth-century Portuguese naturally took a hand at writing the story of the eastern conquests. Fernão Lopes de Castanheda, although generally inferior to Barros, surpassed him in accuracy for some periods and events. Gaspar Correa, who was the weakest of the three, nevertheless had the advantage of living for years in India. This gave him a surer touch in writing of events and localities personally known to him.

Damião de Góis (1502-1574) certainly bears the palm as the most cultured Portuguese humanist of the sixteenth century. He had virtually every talent and advantage that a man could have in those days, since he was a scholar, diplomat, businessman, social-light, soldier, musician, art collector, and general bon-vivant. On the historical side, Góis is best represented by his *Chronicle of the most serene lord King Manuel*. Many of the events covered in this work were also dealt with by Barros, whom Góis surpassed in critical spirit and freedom from national bias, but whom he did not equal in style.

Góis spent many years of his life abroad in the diplomatic serv-ice. He lived in Flanders, Holland, Poland, Prussia, the Scandi-navian countries, and Italy. During his northern travels Góis made the acquaintance of such men as Erasmus, Luther, and Melanc-thon. These experiences, although highly interesting, ultimately cost him dearly. After the establishment of the Portuguese Inqui-sition, a Jesuit priest denounced Góis as a heretic. Twice the great humanist escaped unscathed, but the Inquisition refused to forget him, and in his old age he was hailed before it a third time. On this occasion the verdict went against him, and he spent twenty months in prison, after seeing all his property confiscated. Al-though ultimately released, he returned to his home in Alenquer barely in time to die. The fame of Góis rests more upon his diversity of interests, his eventful career, and his fine humanistic spirit than upon any one piece of writing. Except for the poet Camões, he has probably been studied more than any other Portu-guese of his century.

The Portuguese theater got off to a fine start in the sixteenth century, only to be smothered and to languish until its nineteenth century revival. Gil Vicente (1470?-1536?) wrote the first good works for the Portuguese stage. He was evidently of bourgeoise birth, because he once served as inspector of goldsmiths and later was elected a member of the *Casa dos Vinte e Quatro* (see Chapter III), which was an association of guild masters. In early life, Gil Vicente wrote non-dramatic works, mostly poetry. He also served at times as pageant director and master of festivities for the court, but his heart lay always in the theater. All told he wrote forty-four pieces for performance on the stage. His earliest works were pri-marily religious in tone and formed a logical continuation of the church pageants of an older day. Within a few years, however, Vicente began to write farces with entirely secular themes. Some dealt with historical subjects; others had plots invented by the author. One work, which does him more honor in the execution than in the conception, was his *Exhortation to War,* written to aid King Manuel's mock African crusade that resulted in the capture of Azemmour in 1513.[2] This was a magnificent dramatic spectacle with patriotism as its theme.

Gil Vicente's third period, which was also his best, saw him produce his most solid dramatic work, still secular in type. There was now some attempt at real character portrayal with philosophical speeches for the learned auditors and lower comedy touches for those of baser mind. Some of the dialogues of Gil Vicente have, in translation, a near-Shakespearian sound. The dramas of Gil Vicente were rather formless, and the author disregarded fixed standards and rules. He made no attempt to observe the classic unities and brought into his plays all types of characters and action. Since no Portuguese professional stage existed in his time, all performances of these works evidently took place at the court or in the homes of the nobility.

Sá de Miranda (?—1558) was the real successor to Gil Vicente and in a sense his only successor. Early in life Miranda traveled in Spain and Italy, and in the latter country particularly he met men and encountered ideas that helped to shape his future. His first poetic efforts appear to have been mostly sonnets in the Italian style and eclogues (pastoral poetry), which he wrote in Castilian and which were inspired partly by the Spaniard Garcilaso de la Vega. He then turned to theatrical comedy and produced several good pieces, but later succumbed to the spell of the classical drama which was now being felt in the Iberian peninsula. At least one of his classical tragedies, *Cleopatra,* is known in fragmentary form, but scarcely enough survives to permit a judgment.

Portuguese dramatists were now generally adopting the classical rules of composition, with the inevitable result that their work became largely imitative. António Ferreira, in his tragedy *Castro,* told of the sad amours of Prince Pedro and the *formosa donzela,* Dona Inês, which a little later were described so much better by Camões in the *Lusiads.* Ferreira also turned to classical comedy,

[2] See Chapter V.

which the rules stated must be written in prose, even as tragedy must be in verse. His play, *Jealousy,* is based on the theme even then not very new, of the touchy husband who insists on keeping his wife imprisoned in the house while allowing himself the utmost latitude in extra-marital affairs. *Bristo,* another of António Ferreira's comedies, has the common renaissance theme of many suitors competing for the hand of a fair damsel. Each of these exercises all the ingenuity he possesses and avails himself of the aid of third parties. In ideas at least, the Portuguese drama of Ferreira had traveled a long way from the simple, religious themes of Gil Vicente's early career.

The Portuguese theater, born in the sixteenth century, died in the same century. The establishment of the Inquisition in 1536 had something to do with the decline, but it is worth noting that the Inquisition had no such effect in Spain. Works of a dramatic nature continued to be written in the seventeenth and eighteenth centuries, but evidently they had small interest even for contemporaries and are seldom deemed worthy of study today.

Although Portuguese activities in Africa, Southern Asia, and the Far East were generally official and with government backing, the little nation produced more than one "Marco Polo" who went adventuring alone and lived to write of his wanderings. Travel literature had existed as far back as the time of the Egyptian Pharaohs, but never in world history has there been so much to write about as in sixteenth- and seventeenth-century Portugal. Duarte Barbosa, Tomé Pires, Fernão Mendes Pinto, and Bento de Góis, to mention but a few, enriched their country's literature and at the same time added to the world's store of geographical knowledge. Not all these works can be described here, but two of the authors seem worthy of special mention.

Fernão Mendes Pinto until recently enjoyed a reputation as a liar and a braggart, but seems now to have been at least partly vindicated. The Mendes Pinto adventures, if authentic, surpass the probably fictitious ones which Captain John Smith claimed for himself. They began in childhood when he ran away from Lisbon and when the ship on which he sailed was captured by Moorish pirates. For their own reasons, his captors, instead of selling him in Morocco, put him ashore in Portugal. Next, at the age of twenty-six, Mendes Pinto sailed for the East where he wandered

about for the next twenty-one years. Usually making India the
point of departure for his trips, he, by his own statement, visited
the Red Sea, Ethiopia, Ormuz, Malacca, Sumatra, Siam, Burma,
China, and even Tibet and Mongolia. He was possibly a member
of the first European party to set foot in Japan, and even if he
was not it seems likely that he did go there ultimately. In more
than one other Far Eastern place Mendes Pinto claimed to be the
first European visitor. In the course of his travels he entered the
Jesuit Order, which he soon left for want of vocation with the em-
phatic consent of his colleagues. Returning to Portugal, he gave
in his *Peregrination* an account of the places he had visited and
the sights he had seen. It is no wonder that his tale was received
with some reservations, but Philip of Spain was enough impressed
with Mendes Pinto to award him a pension after becoming ruler
of Portugal in 1580.

Some years later there came a Portuguese traveler to rival
Mendes. Bento (Benedict) de Góis was a native of São Miguel in
the Azores. He joined the Jesuit Order and went out to India to
work in a modest capacity. There he learned the Persian language,
and this accomplishment no doubt explains his selection for a
great exploring mission. Asia north of the Himalayas was still
completely unknown to Europeans. Marco Polo had crossed the
continent overland, ultimately arriving in the teeming land of
Cathay to the east. This, as we know, was China, but the sixteenth-
century Portuguese, who had reached China by sea, felt grave
doubts about identifying it with Polo's Cathay, since their own
impressions did not entirely agree with the account of the old
Venetian traveler. Cathay, therefore, was lost, and the Jesuits felt
an urge to find and Christianize it. So Bento de Góis was selected
to make the search, and he prepared with all the care his limited
knowledge permitted. Proceeding first to the Mogul capital, Agra,
he received money, men, and letters from the great emperor
Akbar. He then struck out for vast, unknown central Asia, one of
his companions being an Armenian from Lahore named Isaac.

Modern geographers have succeeded in tracing his route
through Kabul, Badakshan, Yarkand, Aksu, Turfan, Hami, and
all the way to Suchow near the western end of the Great Wall.
Here Góis sadly realized that the old Cathay was none other than
the now-familiar China. Here too he received a letter from Matteo

St. Peter on the papal throne, painted by Grão Vasco Fernandes in the sixteenth century. From *Grande enciclopédia portuguesa e brasileira.*

The tower of Belem, near Lisbon, built on the spot where Vasco da Gama embarked for India. From *História da expansão portuguesa no mundo.*

Ricci, head of the Jesuit establishment in Pekin. The Portuguese traveler was already near death from illness and privation, and, on hearing from Ricci, exclaimed, *"Nunc dimittis servum tuum, Domine."* [3] A few days later he died, having, as a contemporary wrote, "sought the Kingdom of Cathay and found Heaven instead." His Moslem companions, misunderstanding the journal he had kept, tried to destroy it, but the faithful Isaac bore the fragments to Ricci, who with Isaac's help was able to piece the itinerary together. Góis, therefore, was able to add little to literature, but he did explore hidden lands where no European had gone since Marco Polo and where none was to follow him until the nineteenth century. His lonely death in western China occurred in 1607, but three centuries later the Azoreans of São Miguel honored their traveler by erecting a monument in his honor.

In the sciences, Portuguese renaissance contributions invariably had something to do with geography, cosmography, and the overseas empire. As a result of their voyages down Africa and into the Atlantic, the Portuguese by the time of Prince Henry's death had become the foremost European navigators and users of nautical instruments. About 1496, Abraham Zacuto, a Portuguese Jew of Castilian birth, produced a set of declination tables for the accurate determination of latitudes that were superior to any others of their time. Zacuto's work was followed by the invention of improved astrolabes for astronomical aid in navigation.

The Portuguese school of cartography began with the engagement of the Majorcan Jew, Jafuda Cresques, by Prince Henry sometime after 1420. Nevertheless, few Portuguese map specimens have survived from the fifteenth century, although many foreign mapmakers of the period used data furnished by the Portuguese. The government, not wishing to share its overseas knowledge with outsiders, put an embargo on the export of maps from the country. For some years, any foreigners wishing to know the latest limits of geographical discovery had to arrange for smuggling maps out of Portugal. A good example is the case of the Italian duke, Ercole d'Este, Lord of Ferrara. Anxious to gain this desirable information, he had his Lisbon agent, Alberto Cantino,

[3] *Cathay and the Way Thither*, transl. and ed. by Sir Henry Yule, 4 vols., 2d. ed. (Hakluyt Society, London, 1913-1916), IV, 248.

bribe a Portuguese cartographer who made a beautiful planisphere in 1502 which Cantino was able to send home to Italy. This map, one of the finest of its time, later somehow disappeared from Ferrara and, in the nineteenth century, turned up in use as a mural decoration in a Modena sausage shop.[4]

The most famous of the Portuguese cartographers were a father and son, Pedro and Jorge Reinel, who worked together in the first quarter of the sixteenth century. They kept especially abreast of the progress of discovery at the far end of the Indian Ocean, and their maps show the progressive stages of the Portuguese advance.[5] They were among those Portuguese who ultimately deserted with Magellan to go to Spain, where they proved valuable in helping the great voyager to make his final plans.

In the mathematical sciences, sixteenth century Portugal can boast the name of Pero Nunes (1502-1578), a man of European reputation and one of the foremost mathematicians and cosmographers of the time. He translated from Latin into Portuguese the thirteenth century *Tractatus de Sphera* by the Englishman Sacrobosco, which was still considered basic for an understanding of geography. Nunes, however, approached his task with an independent mind, making his own emendations and comments as he wrote. His *Book of Algebra* is another of his achievements, this having been first written in Portuguese and then translated into Castilian, the author hoping thus to gain a wider public and hence a greater sale.[6]

Garcia da Orta (?-1568) was a pioneer in the study of oriental medicines and drugs. He spent thirty years of his life in India, where he was physician to a series of viceroys. He also went on scientific and exploring journeys about the Deccan, being often the welcome guest of the Sultan of Ahmednagar. He exchanged medical knowledge with Hindu, Arab, and Persian physicians, collected specimens and data, and learned the origins and properties of the native drugs. His book *Colloquy of [Indian] simples and*

[4] Duarte Leite, "O mais antigo mapa do Brasil," *História da colonização*, II, 225.
[5] Armando Cortesão, *Cartografia e cartógrafos portugueses dos séculos xv e xvi*, 2 vols. (Seara Nova, Lisbon, 1935), I, 249-305.
[6] Luciano Pereira da Silva, "O ‹Libro de Algebra› de Pedro Nunes," *Obras completas de Luciano Pereira da Silva*, I (Agencia Geral das Colonias, Lisbon, 1943), 187-197.

drugs, published at Goa in 1563, was unique at the time it was written. Although a landmark in scientific history, it is little known today outside Portugal where it was re-issued twice in the nineteenth century.[7]

In the visual arts Renaissance Portugal never equaled Italy or Spain, yet did produce some creative minds worthy of remembrance. The fifteenth century king, Afonso V, although a political failure, was at least a generous patron of the arts which he genuinely appreciated. Approximately thirty painters are known to have flourished at his court, of whom only two, a Fleming and a Florentine, were foreigners. The accounts of Afonso's treasury frequently show large sums being set aside for the salaries and expenses of these artists. Nobles and courtiers followed the king's example and became lesser Maecenases themselves.

Needless to say, most of the art was religious. One of the finest of the Portuguese painters was Nuno Gonsalves, a contemporary of Afonso, who is particularly known for his magnificent work adorning the altar of São Vicente in the cathedral at Lisbon. The scene represents a youthful Saint Vincent who stands receiving the adoration of various groups from Portuguese society—princes, priests, and plebians. Henry the Navigator, wearing the habit of the Order of Christ, appears in one of these groups, and this is believed to be the only authentic portrait of the great prince.[8]

Nuno Gonsalves showed the influence of the Flemish school of painting; in the next century Italian ideas became predominant. Manuel the Fortunate sent several Portuguese artists to study in Rome, and Italian painters settled in Lisbon. Perhaps the greatest of all Portuguese painters was Vasco Fernandes, who worked in Viseu in the first half of the sixteenth century. Details of his life are scarce, and legend has stepped into the breach to the extent of attributing to him many works that could not possibly have been his. Many other artists certainly painted at Viseu in his time and modern criticism finds it hard to decide which of the numerous works pouring from there were executed by "Great Vasco" himself. The major ones attributed to the master are scenes from the life of Christ, beginning with the *Marriage of the Virgin*

---

[7] See Conde de Ficalho, *Garcia da Orta e seu tempo* (Lisbon, 1886).
[8] José de Figueiredo, *O pintor Nuno Gonçalves* (Typ. do Annuario Commercial, Lisbon, 1910).

and following in some chronological order to the death of John the Baptist.[9]

Gothic architecture flourished for a time in Portugal, reaching its peak in the superb Batalha monastery, built by João I on the field of Aljubarrota as a thank-offering for his victory over the Castilians in 1385. The king ordered the work begun immediately following the battle and it went on through his entire reign, several architects being in charge at various times. It was added to in later years by other Portuguese sovereigns.

Toward the end of the fifteenth century, the type of architecture known as Manueline began to develop in Portugal. Some have called the Manueline style chaotic, for it was neither medieval nor classical but eclectic. The great discoveries of the Portuguese furnished many new ideas for decoration and adornment, and often the constructors threw together all manner of material without much rhyme or reason. One of the really fine Manueline specimens is the celebrated tower of Belem, built on the spot where Vasco da Gama boarded his ship to depart for India. The tower was designed to be a military fortification and thus suggests strength and solidity. The harmony of its proportions at once strikes the beholder's eye. It has a somewhat oriental look, and the explanation seems to be that its builder, Francisco de Arruda, had lived in Moroccan Safi and Azemmour.

But the real glory of Manueline architecture is the church and monastery of the Jeronimos in Belem, which in later times has become Portugal's Westminster Abbey, the burial place of the country's illustrious dead. King Manuel ordered this built in thanksgiving for Vasco da Gama's successful voyage, to preserve the memory of the mighty accomplishment. The king did not live to see its completion, which came in the time of his successor, João III.

That there was a Portuguese renaissance sculpture is evidenced by the fact that literally thousands of figures and images, some very fine, survive in the churches. But, as in many other forms of art, the names of the makers are lost to us forever. The Portuguese sculptor evidently did not seek the eternal fame that his Italian contemporary did, and so, while the works of the local Verrocchios and Donatellos live on, their names do not. All Portuguese

[9] Fortunato de Almeida, *História de Portugal* (Coimbra, 1922-1929), III, 743-750.

renaissance art was in fact more anonymous than that of Italy. Painters, goldsmiths, glass workers, miniaturists, illuminators, and designers all undertook contracts with kings, nobles, cathedrals, and monasteries. Their surviving handiwork shows that usually they performed well, but in general they left no traces of their own identities.

Until the sixteenth century Portugal had only one university, located in Lisbon. Although this had once been a respectable institution, it had since declined to the point where able Portuguese students often preferred to go abroad for their training. King Manuel reorganized the university about 1503 and gave it new statutes, but what it needed more was wide-awake professors who could instill a proper spirit into their students. João III understood this better than did his father, and in 1537 he transferred the university to Coimbra, giving it new teachers and a new curriculum modeled on Salamanca in Spain. A turn for the better came at once, and Coimbra, despite some weaknesses, became the intellectual center of Portugal. It held that place through the following centuries, and in time to come it educated not only the élite of Portugal but many Brazilian students as well. During the second half of the sixteenth century an additional Portuguese university was founded at Évora, which, however, never equaled Coimbra in fame

Chapter IX

CAMÕES

In the first half of the sixteenth century Portugal had astonished the world with great deeds of discovery and conquest. The tiny nation, still only four hundred years old, seemed to "bestride the earth like a colossus." Therefore it was only fitting and proper that the century in which this first of modern empires arose should also furnish the epic poet who would sing his countrymen's achievements for all generations to come. The moment produced the man, and Camões appeared. In writing the *Lusiads* he provided both the glorification and the epitaph of imperial Portugal. Living as he did in the twilight of Portuguese historical greatness, he furnished his countrymen with consolation for the long centuries of national obscurity that were to follow the few generations of glory that had so quickly passed.

It is impossible to overestimate the importance of the man and his work. Dante means a great deal to Italy, as does Shakespeare to England and Cervantes to Spain. But not one of this great trio fills quite the place in his country's history that Camões does in that of Portugal. Part of the reason, perhaps, is that Italy, England, and Spain have produced other literary geniuses, approaching if not quite equaling the stature of these giants. Portugal, on the other hand, has only this one contribution to make to the small section of the literary pantheon reserved for supreme geniuses. Camões, unlike the others, is completely a national poet, and his masterpiece from beginning to end is devoted to the story of his country. Alone and unaided he gave Portugal an epic literature and a modern language. This explains why he continues as a living force wherever the tongue is spoken.

There are various signs that in the generations before Camões the Portuguese, who felt that their mighty accomplishments deserved fitting recognition, had begun to bemoan the absence of a great national poet. João de Barros, the historian, had tried in his learned way to create a monument to the national past in his *Decades*. But he instinctively knew that something more was needed, and that a book of history, even a great book, would not quite serve the purpose. Garcia de Resende, himself an historian and a collector of Portuguese verse, had complained that his countrymen were careless about recording the national deeds of which they had so many to their credit. A few men had even attempted epics, but until Camões came to the rescue the attempt had fallen very flat indeed. It is kinder to let these efforts rest in peace than to give them publicity here after their centuries of well-earned oblivion.

Concerning Luiz Vaz de Camões, as is often true with great men, there are controversies as to place and date of birth.[1] These learned debates have no important place here, although a good deal of literature in Portugal and elsewhere has been devoted to the subject. Both Lisbon and Coimbra claim to be the poet's birthplace, with the evidence apparently inclining a little in favor of Lisbon. The year usually accepted is 1524. The Camões family, originally called Caamaños or something similar, had originated in Spanish Galicia but had moved to Portugal before the end of the fourteenth century. The poet's father was Simão Vaz de Camões and his mother was Anna de Macedo. Very little is known about the parents, although Anna lived a very long life and survived by several years her famous son who died at the age of about fifty-six. Two years after his death, a government document showed that the modest pension conceded him late in life had been continued for the aged Anna.

The Camões family was of "gentle" blood, though never a part of the nobility. There was no particular stigma in this, however, because many of the most blue-blooded Portuguese, descended from the ancient *fidalgos,* had never received specific titles from

[1] A good account of the poet's life in English is Richard F. Burton, *Camoëns, His Life and His Lusiads,* 2 vols. (Bernard Quaritch. London, 1881).

the crown and, from what evidence we have, did not particularly care to receive them.*

The great poet, then, inherited a fairly good name and a family tradition, but also inherited a genteel poverty which he did little to amend. Financial troubles beset him all his life, since he was never a very provident soul and what money he did acquire, at least in his younger and more daring years, slipped easily through his fingers.

Camões in his later 'teens was educated at the University of Coimbra, which had been moved from Lisbon to the provincial city as recently as 1537. His university years made a deep impression upon him. Not only did he like the studies but he liked Coimbra as well. More than once in his later poetry he recalled the pleasant days of youth, spent by the waters of the "sweet Mondego." The picture we get of Camões as a student is that of an adolescent who denied himself none of the pleasures or even dissipations of "bright college years," but who at the same time dearly loved books and learning. These happened to be the richest years of the Portuguese renaissance, before the blighting hand of the Inquisition and the growth of religious intolerance had combined to stifle humanism. Camões was by interest and instinct a classicist. He became fluent in Latin and certainly learned to read Greek. He did not neglect modern languages, and mastered Castilian and Italian as well as their literatures. Although his fundamental piety and religious orthodoxy were never seriously questioned, it is clear that his taste ran more to pagan than to Christian learning. He particularly loved Greek mythology, and his phenomenal memory for its details in later life shows how thoroughly he mastered the subject. The great *Lusiads* were written mostly in the East, when Camões had left Coimbra far behind him and when he had few opportunities to refresh his memory with books. The *Lusiads* are filled with mythological allusions, often of the obscure type that would make even a professional classicist consult the texts in order to be sure of himself. Yet

* An interesting reflection of this attitude is found in the modern novel *A illustre casa de Ramires* by Eça de Queiroz. The hero, Gonçalo Ramires, a young nineteenth century gentleman descended from the most illustrious *fidalgos*, is offered a title by the king because of his growing influence in politics. He refuses disdainfully, saying that the House of Bragança, far junior to his own, has no power whatever to bestow additional distinction on the House of Ramires.

Camões almost never makes a mistake, whether writing in Indian Goa, Chinese Macau, or African Mozambique. His knowledge of history is also surprising. It might be expected that he would know the past of Portugal in detail, but his knowledge of world history, subject of course to the inevitable limitations of the sixteenth century, shows what could be accomplished even then in a few years of concentrated study.

To be a humanist four hundred years ago by no means meant neglecting nature and science. Camões certainly neglected neither. In his poetry he showed himself a nature lover who could describe a scene, a landscape, or an oceanic disturbance as well as he could call to mind some adventure of a Grecian god or hero. Astronomy had made some strides as a science in Camões's time, and Portugal, as the main seafaring nation of that century, was fully abreast of the latest advances. The movements of the heavenly bodies appealed to Camões both as a scholar and as a man of poetic imagination. The twentieth-century Portuguese mathematician, Luciano Pereira da Silva, has made a searching and interesting study of the astronomy of the *Lusiads*. He finds that the poet's genius was as unerring here as in other subjects and that his astronomical knowledge stands up well when put to a critical test.

Camões was still less than twenty years old when he left the university to go to Lisbon. During the next few years in the capital he seemed undecided about what to do next and what use to make of his life. Although poor, he moved in high social circles, even if not exactly a member of the Portuguese court, then presided over by the dour João III. The young man's budding genius had been recognized, and already he wrote abundantly. But now he demonstrated another of his boundless capacities, which was for falling in love. He did so over and over again in the course of his life, each occasion furnishing a theme for some of his best poetry. In spite of being repeatedly enamored, it is worth noticing that he never married, even though his financial troubles were not so great as to put marriage out of the question. One might almost suspect that he preferred a hopeless love, of the Dante-Beatrice, Petrarch-Laura, kind, which, due to economic barriers or other adverse circumstances, could either not be requited or else had no chance of resulting in anything but distant, though scarcely silent, worship by the poet.

During this first residence in Lisbon, Camões loved a lady whom he called Natercia, which turns out to be a thin disguise for the name Caterina. The identity of this Natercia is not certain, but the most accepted theory is that she was Dona Caterina de Ataíde, a young lady of the court a few years senior to Camões. The same version says that Caterina in her heart by no means rejected the poet but was kept from him by family considerations. She died, not many years later, when Camões had already gone to India, and according to this version the news of her death caused him to write one of the most beautiful of sonnets, beginning with the words

> Alma minha gentil que te partiste
> (My gentle soul that is gone away)

But Camões did not spend all his time in Lisbon sighing over unattainable *donzelas*. His poetic muse being constantly at his elbow, he wrote many things on many subjects. Remembered now mainly as an epic poet, his talents in youth turned mostly toward the lyric. He tossed sonnets about in reckless profusion, many of them of extremely high caliber. Since Gil Vicente had created a Portuguese theater a generation before, society taste leaned toward the drama, and Camões showed an interest in composing for the stage. One such effort proved both the cradle and the grave of his ambitions as a playwright. He wrote a one act skit called *El-Rei Seleuco,* which was performed privately in the home of a nobleman. The plot, taken from an episode in Hellenistic history, bore just enough resemblance to a recent eyebrow-raising occurrence in the Portuguese royal family to make certain people think it in questionable taste. King João III did not attend the performance, but soon learned of it from various well-wishers, and to say that the king was "not amused" would be an understatement. Having now no chance, at least for the moment, of finding favor in royal eyes, Camões determined to go into temporary, but not too distant, exile by enlisting for service in Morocco. Although not fitted either by training or temperament for military life, he became a private soldier and spent two years in North Africa. Here, in an obscure engagement, either from the faulty priming of a flintlock or from enemy fire, Camões lost his right eye. The accident caused him more mental than physical suffering, for although it did not hamper his activity in the least it injured his pride. Thereafter, he declared, ladies poked fun at him behind his back and even hurled insults concerning his *cara sem olhos* (face without eyes). Since Camões had his full share of physical vanity, it seems reasonable to guess that the insults existed mostly in his own imagination.

He returned to Lisbon in 1549, sans eye, still poor, and aged about twenty-five. His prospects there being as meager as ever, he decided to do the conventional thing for a poverty-ridden *fidalgo* by enlisting for India, for which his previous African service had been the normal and usual training. For various reasons his departure was delayed several years, and Camões spent the time largely in the company of a wild and reckless set of companions. His crowning escapade was the assault and wounding of a royal official in the streets of Lisbon by night. For this he was arrested and jailed, but the imprisonment did not last long. The wounded royal officer was generous enough not to bear a grudge, and the fact that Camões had already enlisted for India told in his favor. In 1553, then aged about twenty-nine, he was allowed by the government to embark for Goa, which, since its capture by Albuquerque over forty years earlier, had been the seat of Portuguese power in the East.

Camões had enlisted for a term of three years, again as a private soldier. On arrival at Goa, he found that his regular duties were not very arduous. He took part in a few campaigns, and from all evidence gave a good account of himself as a fighter. He also had plenty of leisure and used most of it for writing. The rumor is that he found plenty to criticize in the administration at Goa and did so in his verse, so that the heads of the government came to look upon him with fear and suspicion. At any rate, when his original enlistment had expired, Camões was allowed or ordered to go still farther eastward to the comparatively new Portuguese establishment in China. He was given the one substantial and lucrative post he held in his entire life, evidently with the idea of "kicking him upstairs" and getting rid of him as an unwelcome critic and commentator around Goa.

It may be that a certain amount of legend has accrued to the poet's life in China. He lived most of the time in Macau, the city near Canton which the Portuguese had acquired by lease from the Ming emperor a short time before. It is certain that Camões had started work on the *Lusiads* before leaving India and that he continued writing while in China. Visitors to Macau are still shown the Camões grotto, where tradition says the poet used to work, although there is more than a little doubt concerning the truth of this story.

The nature of Camões's appointment in Macau had been such as to permit his making some profit, as was considered only right and fair for a colonial official exiled to such outlandish parts in those times. But a reform wave had recently swept through the Portuguese government, and the king had instructed his higher officials to make a vigorous turnover among the appointees. Camões was one of those whose official scalp was forfeit, doubtless as a scapegoat for higher and more guilty officers, and he was ordered back to Goa in 1558. Taking with him his main treasure, the almost finished manuscript of the *Lusiads,* he sailed for India, only to be shipwrecked off the Mekong River. One of the most famous Camões stories, doubtless fairly authentic, tells how the poet swam to safety, clutching and holding above water the manuscript of his immortal poem. At least the *Lusiads* were somehow preserved, and Camões was rescued, to be taken first to Malacca and then to Goa.

He lived several years more in India before returning to Portugal. His fortunes varied in Goa this time. Several times arrested and jailed for either corruption in office or for debt, he also had the good fortune once or twice to encounter high officials who had known and liked him in Lisbon and who helped to make his life easier. During the second stay in Goa occurred the famous incident of his invitation to several friends to dine. Each guest, on being seated at the table, found an original verse of poetry at his plate instead of the more substantial fare he had expected. However, an excellent dinner was soon forthcoming, for Camões, who was in fairly comfortable circumstances at this time, had merely taken the opportunity of playing a literary joke.

After various financial ups and downs in India Camões started home to Portugal and made the first leg of his journey, to Mozambique, on borrowed money. Here, without a *rei* to his name, the poet lived until 1569, when a ship bearing several of his friends, including the historian Diogo do Couto, arrived on its way to

Lisbon. The friends managed to collect among them enough passage money for Camões, who finally reached home after seventeen years in the Orient, now almost fifty years of age and bringing as the sole fruit of his adventures and travels the completed manuscript of his *Lusiads*.

Just how he lived during the next few years and just who bore the expense of getting the first edition through the press is not exactly known, but presumably friends came to the rescue once more. Press censorship in Portugal had become very strict, and the priest commissioned to look over the work evidently balked somewhat at the prominent part played in it by pagan gods and goddesses. But this did not prove serious enough to hold up publication, and the censor may have been mollified by a passage which Camões slipped in, obviously as an afterthought and for his benefit. In this verse, toward the end of the poem, the goddess Venus, in describing the true cosmography to Vasco da Gama and his companions, is made to say that she and the other divinities were always merely fables.

The first edition of *Os Lusiadas* appeared in 1572 and the second before the end of the year. The poem created no great excitement, but from the beginning there were some who appreciated its true greatness. In Italy, Torquato Tasso knew and admired the epic and referred in his own writings to the author as "Il colto e buon Luigi." The reigning king of Portugal, young Dom Sebastião, having no personal interest in poetry, was prevailed on to award Camões an annual pension of 15,000 *reis*, which was a modest sum but enough to keep a small family in comparative comfort in those days. The direct descendants of Vasco da Gama, who now rejoiced in titles of nobility and landed patrimonies as the result of their ancestor's discovery of India, showed no apparent interest in the work which has as its main purpose the lauding of Vasco's great achievement. This was entirely to be expected, for the Gamas did not cultivate the muses, and had Vasco been living at the time there is every reason to suppose that he would have been as indifferent as the rest. But people of taste and culture in Portugal soon took notice of the *Lusiads* and realized that their country had at last produced something remarkable.

The active part of Camões's life was over. Although still not an old man in years he was worn out. He was merely another India veteran, and the nature of his life had been such as to break a man early. His remaining years were spent in Lisbon in a kind of genteel poverty, although not actually in want, as later imaginations, prone to magnify the misfortunes of poets, insisted on believing. He had brought home from his wanderings a Malay servant named António, who remained faithful to the end of Camões's days. But the story that António went begging in the streets to provide bread for his master seems to have no foundation. Although the pension from the king was sometimes a bit in arrears, matters did not get to the starvation point. Until almost the end of his days the bard hoped and rather expected that further favors would be forthcoming from the crown. These hopes ended in 1578, when Sebastião went off to Morocco to lose his life in the last hopeless crusade.

Camões died in June, 1580, just before the events that ended Portuguese independence and caused the country to pass under the Spanish yoke. No one can regret that he did not live longer, for his life was so indelibly associated with the life of his country that it seems impossible that he could have survived the blow. In 1880, three centuries after his death, the Portuguese government decided that the remains of Camões should be deposited in the Jeronimos in Lisbon, which is the Westminster Abbey of Portugal. By that time all memory of the poet's grave had been lost, and so a body was disenterred from the place where he was supposed to lie and placed with due ceremony in the Jeronimos. No one seriously supposed that these were the right remains, but the nation nevertheless paid tribute in effigy to its great man. At the same time, what was supposed to be the body of Vasco da Gama was brought from the family estate at Vidigueira and also laid in the Jeronimos.[2] Even here, it was later found, an error had been made and a rather insignificant member of the Gama family had been substituted. The mistake appears to have been rectified later in an unostentatious manner.

Having said so much about the poet, it is now time to speak of the poem. Camões, not in the least an imitator, made no secret of the fact that the *Aenead* of Virgil had served somewhat as his

[2] Details regarding the Camões-Gama festival of 1880 will be found in A. C. Teixeira de Aragão, *Vasco da Gama e a Vidigueira* (Lisbon, 1898).

model. The themes have something in common, for just as the Roman poet wrote of the legendary wanderings of Aeneas from Troy to Italy, the Portuguese genius described the voyage of Vasco da Gama from Portugal to India and home again. As Virgil begins with "Arms and the man I sing," so Camões, in his opening line, refers to "As armas e os barões assinalados." But he aspires to do more than tell the story of one voyage, however noteworthy. His greater theme is the noble history of Portugal and the people whose heroic deeds reached their climax with the discovery of India. Camões is too much of an artist to try his readers' patience with a straight chronological narrative. He adopts the bold expedient of beginning in the middle of his theme and finding opportunities and occasions to revert to what had gone before.

In the first canto of the poem the ships of Vasco da Gama have already rounded the Cape of Good Hope and are moving up the east coast of Africa, approaching Mozambique. The gods from Olympus take notice of what the Portuguese are doing and, with Jupiter presiding, hold a conference to consider the matter. Bacchus turns out to be the enemy of the Lusitanians, as he fears that his own exploits in the Orient will be overshadowed if the Portuguese are allowed to go there. But Venus, the mother of Aeneas and hence the patroness of the Romans, is very fond of the Portuguese, who resemble the ancient race. Even their speech reminds her of the beloved Latin. Therefore, she speaks out strongly for Vasco da Gama and his countrymen and is stoutly seconded by Mars, to whom the warlike qualities of the Portuguese have a strong appeal.

During the rest of their journey up the East African coast the Portuguese are persecuted by Bacchus, who comes to earth in disguise to incite the Moslems against them, but Vasco and his men are saved by Venus. Camões cleverly works the Olympian deities into the actual experiences of Gama with the hostile Africans and provides an explanation of his varying fortunes based upon their supernatural interventions. Finally Jupiter sends Mercury to guide the Portuguese to the friendly African city of Malindi, where, in actual history, Vasco da Gama procured the pilot who conducted the ships across the Indian Ocean to Calicut.

During the pause at Malindi, Camões has the opportunity to bring in the earlier parts of his story. The friendly local sultan asks

Vasco da Gama about Europe and Portugal, and the commander gratifies his curiosity in a narrative that lasts through several cantos. He begins with a description of Europe, its nations and its people. Next he more particularly describes the Spanish peninsula, calling it the "Head of Europe," and from there on he concentrates on Portugal. From the time of Afonso Henriques he proceeds reign by reign, naturally emphasizing the themes of greatest poetic interest.* One of the highlights of the *Lusiads* and one of Camões's supreme poetic flights is the handling of the Inês de Castro incident, in which the doomed lady begs for life kneeling at the feet of King Afonso IV. Following his description of her murder, Camões tells how Inês was long remembered by the maidens of Portugal, who made almost a cult of the story of her love for Prince Pedro, and of how their tears formed a fountain of love at Coimbra.[3]

Gama proceeds with his narrative through the battle of Aljubarrota and the enthronement of the Avís dynasty. The discoveries sponsored by Prince Henry are passed over rather lightly, because Camões is glorifying the Portuguese nation rather than its princes. He quickly proceeds through the reigns of Afonso V and João II, saying something of the preparations made by the latter sovereign for the discovery of India. Next Gama tells of the accession of King Manuel and of his own selection to command the great expedition. There is a moving description of the departure from the Tagus. Most effective of all is the speech of the "velho" (old man), who from the crowd on shore addresses the departing voyagers. This old man, who represents the conservative spirit of Portugal, prophesies endless suffering and loss for his people as a result of the momentous step that is now being undertaken.[4] But the adventurers proceed and round the Cape of Good Hope. There they are met and accosted by the giant Adamastor, the spirit of the cape, who for untold ages has guarded this mighty promontory whose secret the Portuguese, first among men, are about to penetrate.[5] They pass Adamastor and reach Eastern Africa, at which point Camões had begun his story.

* It may be added parenthetically that the real Gama would probably not have known this history, since he was a rather unlettered man.
[3] *Os Lusiadas*, III, 118-135.
[4] *Ibid.*, IV, 94-104.
[5] *Ibid.*, V. 39-59.

Guided by a reliable pilot, the ships cross the Indian Ocean, though even here the villainous Bacchus makes trouble by persuading the sea gods to send a terrible storm, from which, however, the Portuguese safely emerge. The seventh and eighth cantos tell the story of their stay at Calicut and their rather unsatisfactory dealings with the *Samuri* and his factotum the *Catual*. At last, in canto nine, Vasco and his crews push off for home with what spice they have been able to secure. Venus helps and protects them as usual, and finally conducts the mariners to an idyllic resting place, which seems to be historically suggested by Vasco's brief stay at the Azores on his way home. There the nymph Thetis, who is the mother of Achilles and hence knows heroes when she sees them, foretells the future deeds and glories of the Lusitanians, mentioning by name such valiants as Francisco de Almeida and Afonso de Albuquerque. Venus then displays to the Portuguese the true nature of the globe, accompanied by her explanation that she and all the gods are nothing but imaginary creatures, and the voyagers return to Lisbon. The narrative part ends here, although Camões dedicates a few concluding stanzas to King Sebastião, apparently by way of apology for not including the events of his own reign.

Here then was Camões's legacy to Portuguese nationalism; a legacy that was sorely needed and proved extremely useful in the dark days of Spanish rule that lay just ahead. The Portuguese public did not truly appreciate the gifts of Camões until the glory of which he sang had departed forever.

Some mention has already been made of the lesser works of Camões. The poet did not shine greatly as a playwright, but had he persevered with drama he might have rescued the Portuguese stage from its abrupt decline after the death of Sá de Miranda. Next to the *Lusiads,* his best remembered products are his sonnets, some of which are among the most beautiful in any language. Attempts to translate them into English usually leave something to be desired because of the matter of rhyming—easy in Portuguese but very difficult in some other languages including our own.

From the seventeenth century to the twentieth, attempt after attempt has been made to do justice to the *Lusiads* in English. Perhaps the best effort is that published in 1881 by Sir Richard Burton, who is better known as the translator of the *Thousand*

Nights and a Night.[6] Burton had the "feel" of the Portuguese language as few others have had, and even coined English words where he felt the existing vocabulary inadequate to translate the spirit of Camões. In this he was largely following in the footsteps of the great poet, who, as he wrote, was molding and partly creating the Portuguese language of our time. Any fluent reader of the modern tongue will have no great difficulty with the work of Camões. He will not find it so easy with the writings of any earlier Portuguese. This is merely another testimony to the genius of the greatest man Portugal has ever produced.

[6] *The Lusiads,* 2 vols. (London, 1880). A recent English translation by Leonard Bacon could not be consulted for the present study.

Chapter X

THE BABYLONIAN CAPTIVITY

PORTUGAL began the sixty-year era of Spanish Hapsburg rule enjoying the nominal status of a junior partner kingdom. In the course of time it sank to the stature of a conquered province. Things looked fairly well at the opening of the period, but even then there was no doubt that the Spaniards had the whip hand and meant to be masters.

Philip II of Spain, the first of his name to rule Portugal, made a number of solemn promises following the cortes of Tomár that elected him king in 1581. He guaranteed that the Portuguese cortes should assemble only in Portuguese territory and that all the old *forais,* liberties, and laws would remain inviolate. Except for possible nominees from the royal family, all viceroys, governors, and other officers of important rank should be Portuguese. The same would hold true of high appointees in the church. The Spanish and Portuguese colonial empires were to be kept separate; each to be governed by its own officials. The two coinages should remain distinct, and above all those legal cases involving Portuguese subjects and interests should not be transferred outside the country for trial. Philip promised, wherever he might be, to have always available a council of six Portuguese to advise him on Portuguese affairs. In all, he agreed to twenty-five articles, which, if faith was kept, would assure Portugal of an independent future and of no more than a personal link with Castile.[1]

Whoever scans Philip's list of guarantees in the light of what

[1] Fortunato de Almeida, *História de Portugal* (Coimbra, 1922-1929), IV, 32-36.

came later, however, will notice the omission of two very important items. There was no promise to refrain from using Portuguese tax money for purely Spanish expenses. Likewise, Philip forgot to guarantee that Portugal would not be stripped of military and naval strength to serve his other empire. Perhaps it would have made no difference had these points been included, for the Spaniards ultimately broke both the spirit and the letter of the whole agreement. From first to last, the three Hapsburg Philips who governed Portugal thought of themselves as Spaniards with a vassal kingdom to exploit in the national and imperial interests of Spain.

António, the Prior of Crato, continued to be troublesome to Philip II for a few years. A band of his partisans gathered on Terceira in the Azores, and the rest of the islands also declared for him. The prior himself first rushed off to England, where he asked Queen Elizabeth for help. Since the queen did not feel ready for open war with Philip, she declined to be involved, and António went to France, where he had better luck with Catherine de Medici, mother of the young Henry III. Catherine recognized him as king of Portugal, and as a trifling return for French support the prior agreed to cede Brazil to France! [2] Much as the Portuguese wanted a home-born ruler at that time, it is doubtful whether António was worth quite such a price.

The prior shipped a few hundred French and English volunteers off to Terceira and in 1582 followed them himself with a French fleet commanded by an Italian named Filippo Strozzi. Philip of Spain had not taken the Terceira resistance seriously up to this point, but now he decided to crush the movement. He prepared fleets in Lisbon and Seville, but without waiting for the Seville contingent the Spanish Marquis of Santa Cruz, Philip's best admiral, sailed for the Azores with the Lisbon squadron. He trapped Strozzi's ships off the island of São Miguel, capturing some and scattering the rest. The badly wounded Strozzi was dragged before Santa Cruz, who brutally ordered him knocked over the head and thrown into the sea. António had been at Terceira during the battle, and on learning the bad news he quickly slipped off to France. Catherine de Medici stuck to her bargain and tried again to aid him, but Santa Cruz in the mean-

[2] Marques Guedes, *A aliança inglêsa* (Editorial Enciclopédica, Lisbon, 1943), p. 206.

time had ended all resistance in the Azores. With this beachhead gone, anyone could see the hopelessness of António's cause. The prior wandered between England and France for the rest of his days, still seeking aid. He accompanied Sir Francis Drake and John Norris in their raid on Coruña and their attempt on Lisbon in 1589. His hopes of a Portuguese rising in his favor at that time came to nothing, and he retired with the English. He died in France six years later, still full of plans to gain the throne of Portugal.

But when all prospects for António vanished, the Portuguese popular mind turned in another direction and concocted the fantastic belief known as "Sebastianism." [3] All the national disasters and humiliations stemmed from that fatal day of Alcácer Kebir when King Sebastião had died. But, on second thought, was the king really dead? None of the survivors had seen him die, and although it was perfectly possible to learn from Moroccan sources where he had been buried, a great many Portuguese preferred bright hopes to a discouraging realism. So presently a widespread belief developed that Sebastião still lived and would presently return to liberate his people. The king, according to one of the theories, was undergoing penances in some holy place in expiation for his headstrong arrogance in leading the nation to disaster.

With so many expecting Sebastião's return, a standing invitation was thus furnished to pretenders of every ilk to come forward and claim to be the rightful ruler of Portugal. The late king had been only twenty-four in the year of Alcácer Kebir. Most of the people had never seen him, and those who had were willing to make generous allowances for the inevitable changes wrought by time.

During the first seven years after the fatal battle two "Dom Sebastiãos" appeared. The first was a young fraud from Alcobaça, who in 1584 set up as a hermit near the village of Albuquerque and impressed the neighboring peasants with his imitation holiness. He told wild stories of the battle of Alcácer Kebir, giving himself the air of a participant. His impressive silences and mysterious words, when they asked him about Sebastião, soon caused some of the local rustics to believe him the king. Although he was

[3] For the history of Sebastianism, see Miguel Martins d'Antas, *Les faux Dom Sébastien* (A. Durand, Paris, 1866).

but twenty years of age and completely unlike the departed monarch in appearance, his fame spread like wildfire until the Lisbon authorities had to take action. They arrested him, exposed him as an impostor, and sent him to the galleys as an oarsman. The last known of him is that in the year 1588 he departed with Philip's "Invincible Armada" against England and never returned.

Almost at once, another Dom Sebastião appeared in the person of a young monk named Mateus Álvares. He passed from the monastic to the hermit life, and also collected devotees near the village of Ericeira. He made a point of praying aloud, within earshot of listeners, and of addressing himself as "Infeliz Sebastião!" (Unhappy Sebastian!) People of wealth and rank flocked to see and hear this pretender. When the government sent an official to examine the doings of Mateus, an irate crowd put the agent to flight. Next, young Álvares began distributing titles and royal favors. He selected a queen and crowned her with a diadem removed from an image of the Virgin in a nearby church. News of this caused the authorities to send a substantial force to arrest Mateus, some of whose partisans gave their lives in his defense. The pretender was captured at last, taken to Lisbon, and executed there in 1585.

Almost ten years went by before another Dom Sebastião appeared. This time it was an ex-Spanish soldier, Gabriel de Espinosa, who on his retirement from the army had set up as a pastry cook in the Castilian town of Madrigal. Nearby, in a convent, lived Doña Anna, the illegitimate daughter of the late Don Juan of Austria, Philip II's half-brother. A patriotic Portuguese friar, Miguel dos Santos, acted as Anna's confessor, and, although he knew perfectly well that Espinosa was humbly born, he persuaded the lady that the pastry cook was the king of Portugal. Anna, who had been forced to take religious vows against her will, actually expected to marry Sebastião (Espinosa), go to Portugal with him, and raise a revolution which would make them king and queen. This wild scheme came to grief when Espinosa's mediocre brain proved unequal to carrying out the part as the friar had planned it. The impostor took to boasting of his coming marriage with a great lady and his prospects of a throne. The Spanish government seized all three, sentencing Anna to four years' solitary confinement and the friar and pastry cook to execution. The sentences were carried out in 1595.

The last of the Sebastiãos was Marco Tullio Cattizzone, an adventurer from Calabria. He appeared in Venice in 1598, when various Portuguese of the exiled António faction had settled in the city. Perhaps Marco scarcely expected his adventure to land him on the Portuguese throne, but he hoped to make profit from it at least. In conjunction with a few of the pro-António gentlemen, he made up a fantastic story of his wanderings since Alcácer Kebir and began to impress various gullible Portuguese whom he met. Marco somehow learned a great many details that any plausible Dom Sebastião would have to know about himself. His greatest handicap was an absolute ignorance of the Portuguese language, which he covered by saying that he had made a vow not to speak it for a certain period of time. The Spanish ambassador in Venice considered him dangerous enough to obtain his imprisonment by the authorities, but he was released through the intervention of João de Castro, grandson of the great viceroy of India. When Marco emerged from prison, Castro and most of the honest Portuguese who met him, knew at once that this could not be their king, to whom he bore no resemblance. A few still clung to the pretender, largely because they would not admit they had been duped. They accompanied him to Florence, where the Medici grand duke seized and delivered him to the Spaniards. Cattizzone was taken to Spain, to be executed at San Lúcar in 1603 after first being mutilated.

That ended the pretenders. Twenty-five years had now gone by since Alcácer Kebir, and Sebastião had become only a memory and a tradition to most Portuguese. A few more years and the odds began to mount against his continued existence, even granting that he had survived the battle. But in a hazy way Sebastianism lingered for another generation. When the Duke of Bragança restored Portuguese independence and became king in 1640, he declared that if Sebastião should reappear the throne would be turned over to him. The departed monarch would then have been eighty-six years old.

Meanwhile the Portuguese learned year by year what a price they had paid for their Spanish king. Their first sharp lessons came in the form of attacks by foreigners. Since beginning her conquests overseas, Portugal had remained as aloof as possible from the politics and wars of Europe. Spain had followed a different course. Although Philip had not inherited the Holy Roman Empire of his father, Charles V, he still owned territory in several parts of Europe and participated in every major war. At the time he seized Portugal he was trying to crush the political and religious revolt of the Netherlands and was on the brink of open war with England. He had also taken sides in the civil wars in France over religion, and the new Bourbon dynasty which presently came to power there under Henry IV looked on Spain as the natural enemy. The Portuguese had no serious quarrel with any of these three countries, for, while their commerce had been bothered by French and English freebooters, matters had always stopped short of war. Now all this changed. With Philip in control of Portugal, his numerous enemies became Portugal's enemies. And, as he tried to use his smaller kingdom in carrying out his plans, the hostile countries found it easier to retaliate against Portugal than Spain.

In 1588, the Spaniards used Lisbon to assemble their great armada for the attack on England. Philip's governor in Portugal, young Cardinal Albert of Hapsburg, worked zealously to add a large Portuguese contingent to the fleet, which went along and was lost in the general destruction. The next year, the Englishmen Drake and Norris retaliated by attacking Lisbon. In 1594 Philip tried economic pressure against the Dutch, with the Portuguese being the principal sufferers as usual. Up to this time the Netherlanders had been allowed to trade through Lisbon in spite of their war with Spain. But now the king ordered fifty of their ships confiscated as they lay in the Tagus and clamped a tight embargo on any more trade with the Dutch. As a result Portugal lost a valuable commerce and a useful means of distributing the products of the colonial empire through Europe. But even worse was in store when the Netherlanders reasoned that they could just as well go east for the spices themselves. In 1597 their first ships returned loaded with cargo from Java, and Lisbon found itself bypassed. The Dutch were better merchants than the Portuguese and their cities had better locations for marketing the goods in Europe. Due partly to geographical remoteness, Lisbon had never been an ideal distributing point, which explains in the main why

the supremacy had long ago passed to Antwerp. Now because of
Dutch enterprise, the center was about to shift to Amsterdam. The
handwriting was on the wall for Portugal, and the letters became
large and bold indeed when the Dutch founded their East India
Company in 1602.

In 1598 Philip died, having reigned forty-two years over Spain
and seventeen over Portugal. The double world empire he ruled
in his later years has been likened to a mastodon, staggering under
its own enormous weight and ripe to be attacked by smaller, more
vigorous enemies. The Iberian Peninsula, with its seapower vanishing and all manner of weakness setting in, could not hold the
entire unwieldy structure together in the face of the foreign
attacks now impending. Portugal scanned the future with an
empty treasury and a vanishing navy and merchant marine. The
India fleets still made their annual voyages from Lisbon to Goa,
but scarcely half as many ships went now as in the palmy days of
the empire. The perils of the voyage had become greater than
ever. Poor ship construction, overloading, and bad distribution of
the cargoes aboard, counted for some of the loss. The foreign
corsairs took a steadily mounting toll. Even in the East, as Portuguese prestige dropped, native enemies began to raise their heads.

But Portugal had still lost no important territory by 1598. An
able sovereign, interested in the problem, could have done something to better the situation. Instead, there came to the throne
Philip III of Spain and the second of Portugal. The late king,
with all his faults, had possessed some of the elements of greatness and above all a tireless industry. The new one was an indolent monarch, caring mostly for pleasure and willing to leave the
business of government in the hands of favorites, particularly the
Duke of Lerma, who quickly learned that the best way to stay in
favor was to keep the king amused. As a result, Portugal and
Spain received a lax, extravagant administration at a time when
neither country could afford it.

Philip visited Portugal only once during the twenty-three years
he ruled. The *camara* (municipal council) of Lisbon first broached
the subject of a royal visit in writing to the king in 1609. Philip
declined for the moment, saying that he lacked funds to make the
trip and pointing out that the royal palace in Lisbon needed re-
pairs. Therefore he commissioned the *camara* to undertake the

rehabilitation and to collect a *serviço* (cash donation) from other Portuguese *camaras* for the purpose. The Lisbon council sent out the call for money and the replies soon began to come in. Some allowance can be made for the natural reluctance of all subjects or citizens to part with cash for government support, but if half the excuses were valid Portugal must have been in bad shape indeed. One city stated that its only residents with money were Jews, all of whom were in the hands of the Inquisition. Another place declared that a recent plague had cut it down in size from a city to a village, with a total stoppage of farming, cessation of trade, and heavy debt for everybody. Still another city said that hard times had caused many of its people to emigrate from Portugal.[4]

Somehow, in spite of all this, the money was raised. Philip then showed his lack of regard for Portugal by delaying his visit for another ten years. When he arrived, in 1619, he remained three months, doing nothing in particular except enjoy the expensive hospitality the Portuguese had provided in hope of getting better government in the future. They received no satisfaction beyond empty promises.

Philip had violated the original Hapsburg agreement with Portugal many times. He introduced Spanish officials into the Portuguese administration in spite of his father's solemn promise. As viceroy of Portugal in 1617 he named the Count of Salinas, a Spaniard, even though the count had no connection with the royal family. Philip once sent a Spaniard to take command of the Portuguese army, but this general had to retire when the officers refused to obey him. On another occasion a Spanish fleet tried to take possession of the Portuguese India squadron before it reached Lisbon, but had to give up the attempt on meeting a determined resistance. By the death of Philip, in 1621, forty years after his father had taken over Portugal, relations between the two countries had deteriorated badly and the Portuguese felt more determined than ever to cast off Spanish government at the first good opportunity.

Their colonial empire had suffered all through the reign of Philip III. The Dutch interest in Brazil had steadily grown, and the Hollanders kept raiding Portuguese coastal settlements there,

[4] Fortunato de Almeida, *História de Portugal* (Coimbra, 1922-1929), IV, 87-89.

in preparation for their later effort to conquer the whole enormous colony. Foreigners also plagued the Portuguese in West
Africa. Already, in 1582, the French had captured and held for a
short time the old fortress of São Jorge da Mina on the Gold
Coast. They were soon driven out, but Mina before long lost its
former importance because the Dutch began to trade freely along
the coast and finally planted their own settlement a few leagues
from the Portuguese fort. They also made their own trade agreements with African chiefs, and the growing Dutch wealth, con-
trasted with the poverty of Portugal, gave them much better
bargaining power.

On the east coast of Africa, the forces of the Dutch East India
company assaulted Mozambique in 1608. Their commander,
Pieter Willemz Verhoeven, captured and razed the city, but the
Portuguese troops held out in a convent which they had made into
a citadel. Finally Verhoeven had to retire and the defending commander, Estevão de Ataíde, found himself still master of ruined
Mozambique.

In India and farther east the Dutch showed that they had come
to stay and to dominate. They seized the island of Amboina and
also took possession of the Moluccas, although a spurt of vigor
on the part of the Portuguese soon drove them out. The energetic
Hollanders quickly grasped the importance of the Malacca Straits
and tried to capture the town of Malacca. A makeshift force of
Portuguese and Japanese, commanded by André Furtado de Mendonça, defended the town and not only held it but inflicted heavy
loss on the Dutch before they retired.

So, by 1621, Portugal had met competition all along the line
and, though yielding at a few points, had resisted sturdily at
others. The future belonged to the enemy, for reasons perfectly
clear. The Portuguese had grasped the trade and lordship of the
East at a time when most of Europe was not ready to offer competition. Spain, the only potential rival in the day of Manuel the
Fortunate, had been shunted off on another line, partly through
the voyages of Columbus and partly through clever Portuguese
diplomacy in arranging the Treaty of Tordesillas. But now the
main powers of western Europe were ready to take a hand, and
from the moment they started the bulk of the Portuguese empire
was doomed. There is no real point in saying that the Spanish

Hapsburgs caused the collapse. They may have hastened it a little by their incompetent rule, but the major fact is that Portugal stood in the way of stronger powers—the Netherlands, England, and France. Regardless of who now ruled Portugal and of how it was ruled, those countries were sure to reach out for the spoils of empire and were equally sure to seize them.

Even in the seventeenth century, the century of their decline, a few fragments of sunset glory could be snatched by the Portuguese. They pushed the conquest of their new Angola colony with some vigor. Their travelers, including the renowned Bento de Góis, who was mentioned earlier, explored places in wild Central Asia that not even the Polos had visited. Their empire, though it shrank in a few places, still expanded in others. They won the mastery of Ceylon in a curious way. Several native kingdoms existed on that large island, and the overlord of all was João Paria Pondar, a baptized Christian. Paria Pondar died in 1597, leaving a will in which he named Philip of Portugal and Spain as his heir. On the strength of this the Portuguese moved into Ceylon, but soon several of the local rulers tried to expel them and to resume full independence. A war broke out, which with changing shape and altering personnel lasted for several years. It ended with the Portuguese in control everywhere, and they held the island until the Dutch finally took it from them.

Philip IV of Spain, and the third of Portugal, inherited his troubled empires in 1621, at the age of sixteen. He had two possible models to follow; his grandfather, who represented unflagging industry, or his father, who represented laziness and the pursuit of pleasure. He chose to follow his father's example, and became an indolent monarch. Again there was an all-powerful minister, the Spanish Count-Duke of Olivares, a man of some ability, who, if the cards had not been stacked against him, might have accomplished something to better the world position of Spain. In Portugal, Olivares became bitterly hated, because he adopted a policy of Castilianizing all parts of the peninsula which would have meant blotting out whatever were left of the independent Portuguese institutions. In Catalonia he followed a similar policy, and it was largely this combination of Portuguese-Catalan resentment that ultimately gave Portugal a chance to strike for independence and to gain it.

Meanwhile, in the Orient, the Dutch, now aided by the English, struck the Portuguese a series of ruinous blows. The two Protestant nations attacked the whole eastern empire—Mozambique, Ceylon, Malacca, China, and the Moluccas. The English fortified the Sunda group commanding the Malacca straits and nullified Portuguese control of this strategic waterway. In India they acquired Surat, not far from Diu, and pushed their way to commercial supremacy in that part of Hindustan. One of the saddest blows to Portuguese prestige was the loss of Ormuz, the magnificent trading city on the Persian Gulf conquered in 1515 by Albuquerque. Shah Abbas, the ruler of Persia, who had been fairly friendly with Portugal up to 1622, suddenly turned to an alliance with the English and besieged Ormuz with a large army. The Portuguese did not let the Persian Gulf go easily, and Rui de Andrade, their last great admiral in the East, fought a magnificent fight until the Anglo-Persian combination overwhelmed him.[5]

The Netherlanders, as the history of their imperialism plainly shows, made a systematic attempt to duplicate the Portuguese empire in both hemispheres. Already they had spread into Sumatra, and they presently seized the Moluccas, avenging their first defeat there by the Portuguese. In 1619 they had built Batavia in Java, which became the new eastern center of the spice trade and soon outstripped Goa. No Treaty of Tordesillas limited the Dutch to a one-way approach to the Indies. The Netherlanders, Schouten and LeMaire, rounded Cape Horn in 1616, and after that their countrymen could use the Pacific Ocean route whenever convenient.

Next the enterprising Dutch tried Brazil, in which they had been interested for years. In 1621 they founded their West India Company as a counterpart to the great East India corporation. The Netherlands government gave this new organization full trading and colonization rights in Africa from the Tropic of Cancer southward, and duplicate privileges in all parts of the Western Hemisphere. To North Americans, the most important result of the Dutch West India Company's work is surely the colonization of Manhattan Island and the lower Hudson River. But in the sixteenth century the Hollanders regarded Brazil as

[5] Fortunato de Almeida, *História de Portugal* (Coimbra, 1922-1929), IV, 107-108.

their important goal, and it was into that great Portuguese possession that they poured most of their money and manpower. In
1624, one of their fleets, commanded by the renowned sea rover
Pieter Pieterszoon Heyn, captured Baia, which was weakly defended by the Portuguese. This threw a scare into the ordinarily
indifferent King Philip and he sent a strong combined Portuguese-
Spanish armada, which retook Baia a year later when Heyn had
moved on with most of the Dutch fleet.[6]

More effort than this was required to save Brazil for Portugal,
however. Within a year, Heyn was back, terrorizing the coastal
shipping and raiding settlements. In 1630 the Dutch captured
Olinda, the richest town in Brazil, today a suburb of the city of
Recife (Pernambuco). For several years Hollanders and Portuguese battled for the possession of nearby Recife, but Dutch reinforcements poured in faster, and in 1635 the city surrendered to
them. Since Recife had the most strategic location of any Brazilian settlement, the Dutch planned to use this as a base for
conquering the rest. Their West India Company showed that it
meant business by appointing Johan Maurits of Nassau, one of
the most distinguished men in the Netherlands, to be governor in
Brazil, in the hope that he would soon win mastery of the South
Atlantic. For several years Johan Maurits won repeated successes
and stretched the area of Dutch control approximately to the
Amazon. By 1640, when Portugal broke loose from Spain, Brazil
seemed as good as lost.[7]

Humiliating though all this was, the Portuguese thought more
of their home situation than of colonial losses. In 1624, the
camara of Lisbon informed Philip that the city could not possibly
defend itself in case of a determined foreign attack, since it had
neither arms nor up-to-date fortifications. The Dutch were not the
only ones driving Portuguese commerce from the seas, for even
the Moslem pirates of Algiers took a hand. Their ships assaulted
Portuguese vessels with impunity in the Mediterranean and even
in the Atlantic, where for a time they were in danger of cutting
off the codfish supply from the Newfoundland Banks. In 1635 and
1636 Portugal had a wheat shortage and, in spite of many past

[6] C. R. Boxer, "Salvador Correa de Sá e Benevides and the Reconquest of Angola
in 1648," *Hispanic American Historical Review*, XXVIII (1948), 485-486.
[7] *Ibid.*, pp. 487-488.

humiliations at Dutch hands, had to admit a fleet of Netherlanders to the Tagus bearing grain to sell at enormous prices. For years Portuguese in great numbers had been abandoning their unhappy country. Some went to Brazil, but many chose to live in nearby Spain. By 1640 it was estimated that a quarter of Seville's population was Portuguese, and in more distant cities, such as Madrid, the language of Camões could be heard frequently in the streets.

Olivares had chosen to plunge Spain into the Thirty Years' War on the Catholic side, and for this he needed men and above all money. Although the Portuguese had not the slightest wish to be belligerents, their Spanish masters expected them to pay a full share of the war expenses and to contribute soldiers. With Portugal's sources of revenue drying up, it is no wonder that the country fell behind in its regular taxes besides failing to raise the levies that Spain demanded from time to time. The government then passed to extraordinary means of extorting revenue, such as the imposition of half-annates. The ruling was that all important officials receiving public appointments should turn over to the king's treasury half of the profits that their first year's employment brought.[8] The result might easily have been foreseen, for thereafter appointments went regularly to the men who would promise to make the largest payments. In other words, the government made bargains with would-be grafters, who naturally expected to recoup their losses, plus a handsome interest, from the suffering public.

Olivares needed his own creatures to carry out his policy, and abandoned all pretense of any longer living up to the old guarantees of a Portuguese administration for Portugal. The last Spanish governor was a woman, Margaret, Duchess of Mantua, who at least qualified for the post by belonging to the Hapsburg family. But she gave all evidence of despising Portugal, and filled the administration with Spaniards and Italians. Margaret and Olivares together meant to sweep the remaining Portuguese institutions to the winds. This would open the way for the final step the count-duke had in mind—the outright annexation of Portugal to Spain. Although it was not a new idea in high Spanish circles, there had been fear of attempting it until now.

[8] Fortunato de Almeida, *História de Portugal* (Coimbra, 1922-1929), IV, 124-125.

Preparations for the step must be made by luring as many high-ranking Portuguese nobles and clergymen from the country as possible, by withdrawing the native armed forces from the kingdom, and by continuing to grind down the country by taxes. The most dangerous Portuguese individual in Spanish eyes was João, Duke of Bragança, who, because of his royal descent, now had the best claim to the Portuguese throne. For several years Portuguese national hopes had centered in the duke, but as Bragança was not a man of great courage or decision he felt more embarrassed than elated at being so prominent. Olivares by no means overlooked him and prepared to get him out of the way by making him master of arms for Portugal. This meant placing Bragança in command of the soldiery. The next move would be to order him and his troops away on a foreign assignment, and during their absence the final annexation step would be taken.

The Olivares program of unifying Spain through the suppression of local rights had also been applied to Catalonia. The proud Catalans had a list of grievances similar to Portugal's, and in the year 1640 they revolted. A royal letter reached Bragança, ordering him to prepare to lead his troops to help suppress Catalonia. Several other Portuguese nobles also received orders to go. These men held quick conferences and decided that they could scarcely hope for a better moment to strike for independence. Spain now had two wars on hand, and every Spanish soldier was needed to wage them. The difficulty from the Portuguese angle lay in converting the timid Bragança to a plan of action. As he continued to hesitate, some of the rasher ones talked of offering the throne to his brother, Duarte, or even of proclaiming a republic. Gradually the duke was won over, largely by his wife, Luisa de Guzman, who, although Spanish herself, desired to be a queen and worked to stimulate her faltering husband.

A group of nobles planned the revolution well. On December 1, 1640, they assembled in Lisbon. They traveled by different carriages to the royal palace, swarmed inside, and overcame the weak guard. One of them, the venerable Miguel de Almeida, threw open a window and shouted to the populace outside, in words reported as follows: "Liberty! Liberty! Long live King João IV! The Duke of Bragança is our rightful king! Heaven awards him the crown to revive the realm. The promise of Christ to Afonso Henriques will be fulfilled!" [9]

Margaret of Mantua, taken completely by surprise, tried to appeal to the conspirators' "loyalty" to Philip of Spain. Carlos de Noronha, one of the rebels, informed the lady that she had her choice between leaving the room by the door or by the window.[10] Margaret had no aspirations to martyrdom, and since defenestrations were fairly common in those times she left the room under guard.

Next the noblemen rode through Lisbon, shouting their news to the crowd. People excitedly thronged the streets and took up the cry, all acclaiming the new king, João IV. The *camara* of Lisbon joyfully embraced the revolution. A Spanish fleet anchored in the Tagus surrendered without a struggle. A commission was hastily set up in Lisbon to govern until the arrival of Bragança, who had not accompanied the conspirators. As fast as the news reached the rest of Portugal the country passed over to the revolution. No one offered more than a token resistance in the name of Philip of Spain.

On December 15, 1640, Bragança was crowned king of Portugal as João IV. The sad sixty years had ended.

[9] Luiz Augusto Rebello da Silva, *História de Portugal nos séculos xvii e xviii*, 5 vols. (Lisbon, 1860-1871), IV, 157.
[10] *Ibid.*, p. 162.

Chapter XI

PORTUGAL RESTORED

$\mathcal{N}$ATIONAL independence had been regained, but it would have taken a brave prophet in 1640 to say with any confidence that the new freedom would last. After all, the palace revolution that enthroned João IV had succeeded more through Spanish weakness than through Portuguese strength. As far as anyone then living knew, Spain's debility might be only temporary and Portugal might soon be assaulted by overwhelming force. For years, therefore, the new Bragança dynasty lived under the shadow of a possible reconquest. This danger was real, and only with the passing of much time did the Spaniards abandon the hope of regaining Portugal, if indeed they have ever quite abandoned it.

Even within the country all was not secure. Philip of Spain still had Portuguese partisans, in spite of the unanimous way the nation seemed to accept the new national dynasty. The Archbishop of Braga, Sebastião de Matos de Noronha, had been a Spanish supporter and had lost power and prestige through the revolution. Now he quietly worked up a conspiracy, based on the theory that Spain would soon reconquer Portugal and that the friends of Philip IV could win his undying gratitude by removing João IV through assassination. The plan failed for the same reason that the old plot to kill João II had miscarried back in 1484. One of the conspirators turned king's evidence and revealed the whole scheme to the new ruler. Arrests and trials followed, with executions for some and imprisonments for others. One of those arrested was the Portuguese Inquisitor General, who was soon released, either because of his high position or because the evidence against him was deemed insufficient.[1]

In January, 1641, soon after his coronation, João IV called a cortes in Lisbon to which all three estates sent representatives in the time-honored Portuguese manner. There was much to do, and the times would permit no delay. The national fortifications had been neglected for years and must be repaired at once. The Portuguese navy must be restored and coastal defenses strengthened. Above all the weak army needed to be increased and placed on a war footing. Fortunately, the cortes understood the needs perfectly and assembled in a generous mood. It voted the subsidies required and also unanimously passed a law forbidding the inheritance of the throne in the future by any foreign prince, whatever his relationship to the Portuguese king.

Another problem demanding immediate attention involved gaining foreign recognition. As quickly as possible, João IV sent envoys to the pope and to the governments of France, the Netherlands, England, Denmark, and Sweden.[2]

The agents bound for Rome had to avoid Spain and the Spanish holdings in South Italy, and so were routed through France and from Marseilles to Cività-Vécchia by sea. Their arrival placed Pope Urban VIII in an embarrassing position, because the Spanish ambassador had been urging him to publish a brief denouncing the Portuguese rebellion and also to discipline the numerous Portuguese clergymen involved in it. Urban had declined to do this, being unwilling to appear as a mere agent of Spanish imperialism, and he had been upheld in this stand by the French ambassador, whose government, then dominated by Cardinal Richelieu, was anxious to have Portugal remain independent. But this did not keep the Spaniards from troubling the Portuguese envoys who were headed by the Bishop of Lamego. Spies shadowed them wherever they went in Rome, and once or twice armed bravos assaulted them. Urban in the meantime proved personally friendly enough but delayed recognizing Portugal. The bishop finally left

[1] L. A. Rebello da Silva, *História de Portugal* (Imprensa Nacional, Lisbon), IV, 389-407.

[2] These diplomatic efforts are described by Fortunato de Almeida, *História de Portugal* (Coimbra, 1922-1929), IV, 161-178, and by Edgar Prestage, *Diplomatic Relations of Portugal with France, England and Holland from 1640 to 1668* (Voss and Michael, Watford, England, 1925).

for home without accomplishing his mission. This meant, among other things, that new bishops appointed both in Portugal and in the colonies could not receive the papal sanction. Urban meanwhile proposed a halfway solution that did not satisfy the Portuguese at all. The next envoy to Rome, Nicolau Monteiro, barely escaped assassination by the Spaniards in broad daylight. Although the Portuguese plea for recognition now had the powerful backing of Cardinal Mazarin, Richelieu's successor in France, the new pope, Innocent X, could not bring himself to affront Spain.

Matters dragged on for years, until the patience of King João became exhausted. Pope Alexander XII, who began to reign in 1655, was willing to arrange for the affairs of the church in Portugal in a left-handed way but still refrained from addressing João as king. João died and his successor, Afonso VI, carried on the negotiation, but it was obvious that Spain still enjoyed the greater favor in Rome. Not until the Spaniards at last signed a peace treaty with Portugal in 1668 did the papacy receive a Portuguese mission and award it full standing.

João's envoys went to Paris in 1641, proposing a league against Spain to consist of Portugal, France, and the Netherlands. They suggested invading the enemy's country from several sides and giving aid to the Catalan rebels. But they found their proposed arrangement complicated by agreements France already had with the Dutch, who had been fighting Portugal for years and even then held much of Brazil. While Richelieu valued Portuguese help, he considered the Netherlands a more valuable ally and would do nothing that might alienate the Dutch. The Portuguese mission gained French recognition for João IV's government but fell short of accomplishing its full program.

Simultaneously the Portuguese commenced negotiations at The Hague. The Dutch, at this time, had a double game to play. On the one hand, they desired to weaken Spain, and so they recognized Portugal as an independent state. On the other hand, they had every wish to continue conquering the Portuguese Empire. They compromised by consenting to a ten-year truce with João, but took their time about ratifying it. At the same time they rushed instructions to their overseas officials to seize as much Portuguese territory as possible before the truce went into effect. What they particularly wanted was to gain a foothold in Angola and thus to insure their new Brazilian possessions of a slave supply.

In London, João's emissaries signed a treaty with Charles I in 1642 by which they gained English recognition. But no real help could be counted on for years from Portugal's ancient ally, because Charles had already reached almost the breaking point with his parliament and the English civil war was about to begin. Another twenty years and England would again be ready for a real Portuguese alliance.

In Copenhagen the Portuguese got evasive replies from King Christian IV of Denmark, who for the moment had his own reasons for not antagonizing Philip IV of Spain. Sweden, then dominated by Chancellor Axel Ochsenstierna in the name of young Queen Christina, was definitely hostile to Spain and made no trouble over signing a rather conventional treaty of peace, friendship, and freedom of trade.

So, despite the delays created by the papacy, Portugal had diplomatic standing in Europe within two years of regaining independence. The situation on the Spanish frontier showed that the conspirators of 1640 had chosen their moment well. No huge armies poured from Castile into Portugal. The only real danger zone was the Alentejo district, which would have offered an easy route to Spanish forces had they been available. But Olivares at first could send only weak contingents across the frontier, and for a time there was merely border fighting, with the Spaniards laying siege to a few towns which resisted successfully. Early in 1644 a somewhat stronger Spanish force invaded across the Guadiana, but Matias de Albuquerque, one of the few experienced Portuguese commanders, defeated the enemy at Montijo and drove them home.

The truth was that at this very time Spain was losing what was left of her military power. The great defeat at Rocroi in northern France in 1643 by the French Prince Condé dealt the Spanish army a blow from which it never recovered in that century. The Spanish name lost all its terror, and the military reputation enjoyed since the time of Fernando and Isabel now vanished. Ultimately Spain recovered Catalonia but continued the losing war with France, which ended finally with the Peace of the Pyrenees in 1659. Needless to say, Portugal gained greatly from its large neighbor's troubles.

As soon as news of the restored national independence had time to reach the overseas possessions still held by Portugal, they gave their allegiance to the new Bragança government. The Madeiras and the Azores, being closest, declared first. Next came the adherence of the Portuguese part of Brazil, beginning with Baia, where João was approved by acclamation. The southern *capitanias* followed Baia's example. A short time later Mozambique acknowledged João. Goa and Portuguese India came next, and no place celebrated the restoration more vociferously than did Macau in distant China.[3]

So Portugal came out of the "Babylonian Captivity" still in possession of a colonial empire—a shrunken one to be sure, but nevertheless an empire. The really crucial points now were Brazil, where nothing permanent had been settled by the ten-year truce, and Angola, to which the Dutch were beginning to extend their operations. Brazil, as Johan Maurits of Nassau and his countrymen now realized, had small value without a steady supply of Negro slaves. Most of the slaves came directly across the South Atlantic from Portuguese Angola. The economically minded Dutchmen therefore felt that they needed the African colony. The situation put Portugal and the Netherlands in the queer position of being allies in Europe against Spain and enemies everywhere else in the world.[4]

Obeying his instructions, which were to seize all possible Portuguese territory before the truce went into effect, Johan Maurits sent ships from Recife to Africa in 1641. The Dutch took São Paulo de Luanda, the main settlement of Angola, and for good measure seized the island of São Tomé. It seemed that the Hollanders had triumphed in the southern Atlantic and that in a few more years they would own both Angola and Brazil.

But the tide now turned. The Portuguese in northern Brazil had taken heart from the mother country's revolt for independence. Uprisings against the Dutch broke out, secretly encouraged by the Portuguese governor at Baia. Johan Maurits, having served his term of office, went home in 1644, and his loss was a telling one for the Dutch. The struggle of the Portuguese to recover

[3] Rebello da Silva, *História de Portugal* (Imprensa Nacional, Lisbon), IV, 202, 344, 351-353.
[4] C. R. Boxer, *Hispanic American Historical Review*, XXVIII, 489.

Brazil was long and, though the recapture of Recife in 1654 broke the back of Dutch resistance, the Netherlanders continued to threaten for several years more. Before completing their reconquest of Brazil, the Portuguese had struck back at Angola in 1648, recovering São Paulo de Luanda and following this soon with the capture of São Tomé.[5]

The western part of the empire had been saved, but in the Orient Portugal was not so fortunate and her holdings there shrank year by year. The Dutch had completely taken over Ceylon by 1655, and still earlier had captured Malacca. The Portuguese spice trade became largely a thing of the past, and the Portuguese eastern empire, save for a few dots on the map, was mostly a memory by the end of the seventeenth century. Portugal went down fighting in the East, and not all the single engagements were won by the enemy. But within a generation after their national restoration, the Portuguese had ceased to be an important factor in the Orient. The nation's colonial future lay in Brazil and Africa.

João IV lived until 1656. Although not a brilliant monarch, he gave the country reason to think well of him. He had brought Portugal through a trying period, and while he could not save the whole colonial empire he saved more than anyone had a right to expect. For almost sixteen years he had occupied a throne that many expected to topple at any minute. With the European powers, João had been forced to assume a poor-relation status and to go, hat in hand, begging favors. His own life had been no more secure than his throne, for Spain waged a personal vendetta against him. Another Spanish-inspired plot to assassinate João in 1647 failed only because the hired killer's nerve vanished at the last moment. João's brother, Prince Duarte, was arrested in Austria by the king of Spain's Hapsburg relatives, turned over to the Spaniards, and taken by them to Milan where he died.

The loss of Duarte proved particularly unfortunate after the king's death, because the successor, Afonso VI, was an abnormal boy of thirteen. Sickness that attacked him in early childhood affected mind as well as body, and even at the time of his father's death many felt that he would never grow to be a sound man. Yet

[5] C. R. Boxer, *Hispanic American Review*, XXVIII, 510.

for twenty-seven years this poor creature bore the title King of Portugal.

At first his Spanish mother, Luisa de Guzman, managed affairs as regent. The boy king grew better physically, but refused to study or train himself for royal duties. Instead he cared only for vulgar pleasures with companions of a low type. Neither his mother nor the better courtiers could influence him; and, when in 1662 he took complete possession of the government, there seemed little hope either for the dynasty or for the country. Fortunately for all concerned, the king finally handed effective power over to the Count of Castelo Melhor, one of the most energetic and intelligent noblemen of the country.

Just before this time, Portugal, at a heavy price, had renewed and strengthened the old alliance with England. The English civil war had ended in the victory of Parliament and the beheading of King Charles I in 1649. There followed nine years of government by Oliver Cromwell, who took the title of Lord Protector. Soon after Cromwell's death, in 1658, a movement began which ended in the restoration of monarchy under Charles II in 1660. The new king, still unmarried, was induced to accept as his wife Catarina of Bragança, the sister of Afonso VI of Portugal. Afonso's government gave England a magnificent dowry with the princess.[6] It ceded Tangier, which had been captured from the Moors almost two centuries earlier and added the island and territory of Bombay in western India. The English received trading concessions in Brazil and India, with the right to keep any former Portuguese possessions they might recover from the Dutch. England, for her part, agreed to defend Portugal in case of invasion and to protect the overseas colonies as well. It was a heavy price to pay for such protection, but the Portuguese, whose European and world position was still shaky, felt that they had made a reasonably good bargain.

The Portuguese princess went to England and was married in the spring of 1662. Plain and insignificant in appearance, she had small chance of capturing the heart of that magnificent royal roué, Charles II. During the twenty-three years her husband lived, Cata-

[6] *Collecção dos tratados, convenções, contratos e actos publicos desde 1640 até o presente,* ed. by José Ferreira Borges de Castro, 30 vols. (Imprensa Nacional, Lisbon. 1856-1879), I, 234-257.

rina had to resign herself to a life of neglect, with at least the consolation that her sacrifice brought some security to Portugal.

Ever since the year 1640, a dreary frontier war had dragged on with Spain. In 1659, the French and Spaniards had ended their own long conflict by the Peace of the Pyrenees, and the government in Lisbon naturally feared that this would lead to a new Spanish effort against Portugal. There was indeed some attempt to prosecute the war on a larger scale. Once the Spaniards captured Évora, an important place not far from the frontier, but they lost the battle of Ameixial in 1663, and this was followed by decisive defeats at Castelo Rodrigo and Montes Claros. Within a few years Spain gave up. Philip IV died in 1665 and Carlos II took the Spanish throne, a ruler even younger and more incompetent than Afonso VI. The peace treaty, signed in Lisbon early in 1668, conceded Portuguese independence, with only the Moroccan port of Ceuta remaining in Spanish hands.[7]

Public policy dictated that a marriage be arranged for King Afonso VI, but since the rumor ran freely in European courts that he could be no normal husband, prospects were not particularly bright. The Count of Castelo Melhor tried to combat this report by circulating rumors that the king had already sired a bastard daughter. However, the best queen Portugal could acquire was an orphan princess, Maria of Savoy. She married Afonso in 1666 but, although reported beautiful, seems to have attracted no great interest on her husband's part. The Portuguese Court at that time, having no competent supervision, had fallen into free and easy ways. Castelo Melhor, although possessing great abilities as an administrator, took no steps to improve the situation and seemed to feel that his own power depended on letting the scandals continue. King Afonso's brother, Dom Pedro, as heir to the throne and the most responsible member of the House of Bragança, became alarmed by the whole situation and began to hate Castelo Melhor. Presently he accused the count of trying to poison him, and although he never adequately proved his charge he brought enough pressure to bear on his brother to obtain the count's banishment from court. Nevertheless, the king's sympathies lay with Castelo Melhor, whom he meant to call back the moment conditions grew more favorable.

[7] *Ibid.*, I, 357-417.

The House of Bragança next gave Europe plenty of material for gossip. Queen Maria asked for and obtained an annulment of marriage on the grounds of Afonso's incompetence. Almost at once she married his brother Pedro, whom the Portuguese cortes in the meantime had officially proclaimed heir. In view of the obvious unfitness of Afonso for government, the next logical step seemed to be his deposition and Pedro's elevation to the throne. But the cortes members differed over the exact procedure to be followed. The commoners wanted an immediate deposition of Afonso and coronation of Pedro. The clergy and nobles thought this too extreme, and so, after a conference with leading jurists and theologians, the prince took the title of governor, allowing Afonso to be called king until his death.*

Maria's exchange of husbands and the promotion of Pedro took place in 1668. Afonso, to the surprise of everyone, lived another fifteen years, and as long as Castelo Melhor had freedom of action the powerful count could have started a movement to restore him to full royal powers. For that reason, Pedro's government tried to arrest Castelo Melhor, who fled the country and wandered through Spain, France, and Italy. Finally he arrived in England, hoping to receive protection from Afonso's sister, Queen Catarina. She did befriend him, and he managed to live comfortably in England until after Afonso's death, when Pedro allowed him to return to Portugal.

Afonso, meanwhile, had been moved to a fortress on the island of Terceira. Except for his confinement, he was allowed to live and conduct himself as he pleased. The insanity made rapid progress, but some people continued to regard him as the possible head of a party. When a plot to rescue him from Terceira was discovered, Pedro had the king, now violent at times, brought back to Lisbon and placed under guard in the palace at Sintra. There he spent his last nine years, being occasionally calm and tractable and at others times a raging maniac. He died in September, 1683, and a few months later his former wife, Maria, long married to Pedro, also died.

Maria had borne only a daughter to her second husband, who now at long last was crowned Pedro II of Portugal. With no male

* This replacement of Afonso by Pedro was one of the last important acts of the expiring Portuguese cortes, which by the eighteenth century had ceased to exist.

heirs and now approaching forty, Pedro needed a wife immediately, though several years had to be consumed in negotiating for the hand of Maria Sophia, daughter of the Elector Palatine of the Rhine. However, the German queen, once married to Pedro, performed her part of the bargain remarkably well by producing six children, five of them male.

King Pedro II had to steer his nation through a troubled period of European history. Since the Treaty of Westphalia in 1648, the harmony among the great powers had declined, partly because of the growing ambitions of Louis XIV of France and partly because of the rising problem of the Spanish succession. Carlos II of Spain had been physically and mentally weak from birth. He could have no heirs, and almost from his accession in 1665 it became known that he would be the last of his line. Since the Spanish dominions in Europe were still substantially the same as Philip II had left them, the powers began very early to plan the succession. Louis of France became the leading candidate for the Spanish throne, either in his own right or in the name of one of his numerous descendants. On the other hand, England, the Netherlands, and Hapsburg Austria could not allow a disguised annexation of Spain to France and planned counter measures. Portugal had definitely swung into the English orbit by the renewal of the old allegiance several years earlier, and because of this and the nearness of Spain, Pedro II was bound to be interested in the question.

Carlos II finally expired in 1700, after naming Prince Philip, grandson of Louis XIV, as heir to his whole vast empire. Many others had claims, even Pedro of Portugal, though no one, himself included, took him seriously as a candidate. But on one point most European nations could agree: the urgency of preventing French Philip from ruling Spain as a satellite of his grandfather. When the English, Dutch, and Austrians formed a grand alliance against Louis XIV, Portugal remained loyal to England and entered the war.

Soon after the fighting began, the Portuguese strengthened their English ties by ratifying the Methuen agreement in 1703. This treaty reaffirmed the old military and political alliance. But the important part of the agreement, signed by John Methuen for England and the Marquis Alegrete for Portugal, dealt with trade.

"His Sacred Majesty," as the King of Portugal was now called, guaranteed henceforth to let English wool and woolen goods freely enter his country. In return, Queen Anne admitted Portuguese wines to England on a reduced duty basis.[8] Since most of the wine shipped to England was port, the treaty, in the words of a later wag, bequeathed gout to English gentlemen for the rest of the eighteenth century.

There is reason to believe that the Methuen-Alegrete Treaty proved economically profitable to Portugal. It certainly led to a great agricultural expansion in the Douro region, which had previously been in decline and which now became a sea of grape vines. Since Portugal had no chance of becoming an important wool producer, the nation lost nothing by turning mainly to England for its supply. Henceforth there was less Portuguese dependence on Spain for cloth, while England, at the same time, bought less wine from France. The Spaniards and the French, being the main sufferers, denounced the Methuen Treaty in bitter terms and declared that by it Portugal became the economic and political slave of England. These charges seem rather far-fetched, and the later facts, insofar as they can be interpreted, do not bear them out.

Meanwhile, Portugal took part in the peninsular phase of the war of the Spanish Succession. The allies used Portuguese territory as a base for an invasion of Spain, during which Madrid was captured in 1706. But since most of the Spaniards had by now become supporters of the French Bourbon Philip, the city could not be held for long. During the brief allied occupation, the Portuguese soldiers with the invading force gave the Spanish civilians in Madrid some rather rough handling, regarding this as revenge for the many humiliations their country had received from the Spaniards.

In 1706, at the height of the war, King Pedro II died, leaving the throne to his eighteen-year-old son, João V. The new sovereign, though green and untried, regarded his father as a great man and resolutely supported his allies of the anti-Bourbon coalition. The war went on, and in the peninsula steadily turned in favor of the Franco-Spanish forces, although in other regions the

[8] Marques Guedes, *A aliança inglêsa* (Editorial Enciclopédica, Lisbon, 1943), pp. 310-313.

English Duke of Marlborough and the Austrian commander, Prince Eugene, continued to win victories. It became evident finally that Philip V, the French king of Spain, could never be dislodged, but that he could be deprived of all the Spanish Hapsburg territories outside Spain. Negotiations for peace began in 1712, and the following year, at Utrecht, Portugal signed separate treaties with France and Spain.

The European frontier between Portugal and Spain remained the same as ever, although in America the Portuguese gained the small settlement called Colonia do Sacramento on the Río de la Plata, in the present territory of Uruguay. Colonia, which was chiefly useful for smuggling contraband across the river to Buenos Aires, had changed hands before and would do so several times more in the eighteenth and nineteenth centuries. Elsewhere in the world, the series of treaties signed in 1713 at Utrecht made important changes, but these were of no particular interest to Portugal, save for the European clauses, which deprived Spain forever of Sardinia, the Two Sicilies, Gibraltar, and the Spanish Netherlands.

In the early eighteenth century the Portuguese could regard themselves as a rich nation once more, though the bases of national prosperity were as unsubstantial as the old ones which had rested on the vanished spice trade. With most of the eastern empire lost, Brazil had become the brightest star in the Portuguese crown and produced the revenue that allowed the Lisbon court to live in affluence. Portugal now belatedly compensated for the onetime neglect of Brazil by paying chief attention to the great South American colony.

That colony was growing rapidly. Most of the expansion was the result of interior explorations conducted by roving bands of Brazilians in search of gold, silver, emeralds, slaves, and anything else of value. The explorers were mostly Paulistas, meaning that they came from the district of São Paulo, and their expeditions were usually called *Bandeiras* (Banners) because each party customarily went provided with a flag. The government sponsored some of the expeditions; others followed private individuals who bore the costs themselves. Some *Bandeiras* represented respectable enterprises; others were mere armed marauders in search of Indians to rob or enslave. But their activities all added up to one long term result—the enormous expansion of Portuguese Brazil. They completely disregarded the artificial barrier arranged with Spain by the outmoded Treaty of Tordesillas in 1494. From first to last the *Bandeiras* trebled the area of Brazil.

They made a great gold strike in the region of Minas Gerais, and also found gold in Mato Grosso, although not in the same abundance. Emigrants from all parts of Brazil and from Portugal itself poured into the mining settlements at Cataguases, Ouro Preto, Diamantina, and Mariana. A few years later, in 1729, the adventurers made the first important diamond strike, also in the Minas Gerais area. Both the gold and diamond rushes were accompanied by the scenes usually associated with such bonanzas. Wildness and lawlessness prevailed, with drinking and gambling rampant, and with slight respect existing for human life. Boom towns grew and flourished, ultimately becoming ghost towns to serve as the remaining witnesses to bygone glories.

The Portuguese Crown reaped a fine revenue in gold and precious stones. João V became the diamond monarch par excellence, just as Manuel had once been king of drugs and spices. He handed the jewels around liberally as presents; and, though the diamond market became glutted, the wealth of the Portuguese sovereign was again the talk of Europe. And this time it was the once despised and neglected Brazil that had yielded the prize! As a result, Portugal valued the Brazilian trade in the same way that the commerce of India had once been esteemed. Thousands of Portuguese migrated to make their homes in Brazil, until the government felt obliged to place a ban on emigration. The home authorities backed the South American colonists to the limit in any disputes with their Spanish neighbors.

At home, João V proved an intelligent monarch, although rather extravagant and with a taste for too much luxury. His court existed on a splendid basis, even though scandal several times touched the king's name. João for several years had as his mistress a nun, Paula Teresa da Silva, and as a reward for her devotion Paula's convent of Odivelas received magnificent gifts from the public treasury.[9] The king was not the only Portuguese of his time to consort with nuns, and the practice became so widespread and

[9] Fortunato de Almeida, *História de Portugal* (Coimbra, 1922-1929), IV, 279.

serious that the church superiors at last had to take vigorous action.

In general, however, João was a serious ruler. He used some of the fluid wealth from Brazil in an honest attempt to stimulate Portuguese industry, expand and improve agriculture, enlarge commerce, and advance science and learning. He succeeded better as a patron of letters and arts than as an economist. Under his direct protection, the Portuguese Royal Academy of History was founded. When the French naturalist, Merveilleux, visited Lisbon to carry on some work, João invited him to stay and gave him a well-paying government sinecure. Another Frenchman, Le Quien, who visited Lisbon to work on a history of Portugal, received from the king a pension and the right to wear the habit of Prince Henry's old Order of Christ.

João also worked to revive the Portuguese navy and merchant marine. The naval improvement was needed, even in times of general European peace, to fight off the ever-dangerous Barbary pirates and to convoy the growing trading fleets that went annually to Brazil and returned. João's brother, Dom Francisco, had naval training and a knowledge of ship construction, and he helped the king bring about a certain restoration of Portuguese sea power.

Portuguese diplomacy took a turn for the better in this reign, since João insisted on being represented by able men at the courts of his brother monarchs. Although Portugal was now definitely a second-rate European power, the time had gone by when the country needed to assume the humble, subordinate position that had been necessary in the early years of the restoration. The nation commanded general respect, and foreign governments no longer relegated Portugal to a satellite status.

A few more places had been lost in the Orient; not to European enemies this time but to native states. The powerful dynasty of Oman, once subject to Portugal but now independent, captured Mombassa and several other towns on the African coast north of Mozambique. In India, the Maratha Confederacy, which had risen on the ruins of the dying Mogul empire, wrested a number of cities in Western Hindustan away from the Portuguese. But Portugal did not mind these losses greatly, because the fact had long been accepted that the eastern empire was largely a thing of the past. The great gains in Brazil far more than counterbalanced the decline in the Indian Ocean.

The reign of João had been largely one of peace, following the close of the Spanish Succession war. The main interruption had been a small naval expedition eastward in the Mediterranean against the Turks in 1717, with the purpose of saving the now decrepit Republic of Venice from a complete debacle. The revived Portuguese Navy beat a Turkish fleet off Cape Matapan and returned to the Tagus covered with glory, although without having greatly changed the Eastern Mediterranean situation.

After a generally prosperous and successful reign, João V died in 1750 at the age of sixty-two. The year before his death, in return for liberal loans to the papacy, Pope Benedict XIV had bestowed upon him the title of *Rei Fidelissimo,* meaning Most Faithful King. This title had no great value but was highly cherished, since it gave the Portuguese sovereign an appellation to match those of the Spanish and French rulers, who were "Most Catholic" and "Most Christian," respectively. José I, the eldest surviving son of the late king, succeeded to the throne in 1750.

Chapter XII

ENLIGHTENMENT AND REVOLUTION

*E*XCEPT for a few historians, no one today recalls much about Louis XIII of France; the person remembered is Richelieu, his minister. The achievements of George II in England have made small show in history beside those of his ministers, Robert Walpole and William Pitt. And similarly in Portugal, on reaching the time of José I, the student finds the king shunted into an insignificant role and the leading part taken by the Marquis of Pombal, who rejoiced in the magnificent name of Sebastião José de Carvalho e Melo.

The late João V had outlived most of his seasoned ministers and diplomats. The new José I, although thirty-six years old, lacked experience and had to find advisers at once. His father had never liked Carvalho e Melo, but one of the old ministers had left a memorial in which he spoke well of the man. So José hastened to appoint him to the posts of Foreign Affairs and War. The king distrusted a "two party" system and wanted only one point of view in his government. Carvalho e Melo, as chief minister, took care of this by permitting only one opinion—his own. The powerful new minister was already over fifty and had diplomatic experience in European courts, including London and Vienna. He had no conspicuous record of success as a diplomat but had picked up many ideas of government in foreign parts. He was not a member of the nobility by birth, and the title, Marquis of Pombal, did not come to him until 1770, late in his career. But he is best remembered by his title, and so it will be simplest to call him Pombal from the start.

During the first five years of his government he did not let the Portuguese public know how drastic his rule would be, if indeed he had fully planned his course, which may be doubted, because he was no great planner. He showed that he considered the state superior to the church, and took several opportunities to cut down the authority of the Portuguese bishops. Whether or not he was anti-religious is a matter of opinion; but anti-clerical he certainly was. His enemies claimed that while in the Netherlands he had become a convert to Jansenism, although this charge is seldom taken seriously. In 1751, Pombal curbed the Inquisition and ruled that henceforth no *auto da fé* should take place and that no religious executions should be carried out without government consent.[1] This almost put the Inquisition out of business for the rest of his administration; and, although he later made some use of it, he did so more in the interest of royal absolutism than of religious orthodoxy.

On November 1, 1755, Portugal suffered the greatest natural catastrophe in its history. The city of Lisbon suddenly began to tremble, buildings to shake and fall, and cracks to open in the earth. Tidal waves from the ocean rushed up the Tagus and swept the streets, filling houses and bearing people away. Fires broke out in many buildings and hordes of persons, including the sick and infirm, to whom flight was cut off, died horribly in the flames. Criminals broke from the jails and galley slaves from the ships, to add to the general terror by robbing and looting. In addition to the ruined private homes, many churches, convents, palaces, libraries, and military installations were wrecked. Artistic objects, historical documents, and priceless books were lost. At least 5,000 people died on the day of the quake, and as many more died within the month from their injuries.[2]

King José and his family were reduced to living for months in country cabins. The sovereign now leaned more heavily on his ministers for advice than ever, and the Lisbon earthquake definitely promoted Pombal to the dictatorship of Portugal. When

[1] John Smith, *The Life of the Marquis of Pombal*, 2 vols. (Longman, Brown, Green, and Longmans, London, 1840), I, 65.
[2] Fortunato de Almeida, *História de Portugal* (Coimbra, 1922-1929), IV, 309.

José asked those about him what to do in the emergency, the Marquis of Alorna gave the famous reply, "bury the dead and feed the living." But it was Pombal who acted on the advice. For eight days and nights he made a carriage his headquarters, driving about the city and organizing relief work. Gradually, he and others brought some order out of chaos and mobilized the authorities for action. Religious orders and public spirited citizens improvised hospitals; officers with squads of soldiers went through the streets, burying the dead and rescuing the wounded. Bakers and tradesmen, who would have seized the opportunity to profiteer, were strictly forbidden to charge higher than normal prices for their wares. Provisions bought or commandeered in every part of Portugal were sent to Lisbon, and ships lying in the harbor with cargoes useful in the emergency had to disgorge them. Gradually the police and soldiers ran down the escaped criminals, and all rioters received summary punishment.

The rebuilding of Lisbon, planned by the architect Eugénio Santos, required years and went on long after the time of Pombal. But the new Lisbon that rose on the ruins of the old was essentially the brain child of the powerful minister. Wider, straighter streets and better constructed buildings replaced the crowded thoroughfares and alleyways that dated from the middle ages and the reign of Manuel. In spite of the tragic loss of life, Lisbon profited architecturally from its partial destruction.

By now, Pombal had won such ascendancy over the king that all attempts to dislodge him—and there were many—recoiled on the heads of the plotters. He governed the country until the death of José in 1777. Saint or devil, Pombal is the best remembered Portuguese of the eighteenth century. His countrymen have judged him in various ways, depending largely on their stand on the clerical question and on their political views. To hold him up as a paladin of liberalism is certainly wrong, for he never showed instincts other than those of an autocrat. To class him as a great economist is out of the question, for most of his economic measures failed. He did not shine in foreign affairs, and failed to better Portugal's world position in the least during the twenty-odd years of his government.

Pombal is generally placed in that group of eighteenth-century statesmen known as the "enlightened despots," who meant to use their despotic powers for their subjects' welfare. But it is hard to see that he accomplished much along these lines. His suppression of the Inquisition might be counted in his favor, but many believe he took this step more to get rid of a rival than for any sincere love of liberty of conscience.

Nevertheless, Pombal set out to remake the Portuguese state according to ideas he had acquired both at home and abroad. He disliked England but recognized that nation's greatness and thought he understood the basis of British prosperity. Like a true eighteenth century disciple of the French minister, Colbert, Pombal believed in mercantilism and held the theory that wealth consists of the precious metals, gold and silver. He decided that too much gold was leaving Portugal in English pockets. More than a hundred British firms had either headquarters or branches in Lisbon. In Oporto, since the Methuen treaty, Englishmen had set up an economic dictatorship over the Douro wine growers. Steadily they had forced prices downward for the Portuguese vineyardists, partly because the English wine market had become satiated, and partly because, as middlemen, they could make their own terms.

Pombal first ruled that the British must stop taking money out of Portugal and instead must exchange it for native merchandise. The law was economically unsound, and England rushed Lord Tyrawley to Lisbon to make a protest. During Tyrawley's stay, Pombal arrested three British naval officers for trying to carry 45,000 *cruzados* aboard their ship. But at length he had to give way on the main issue, and in place of the total prohibition on gold exports to England he put a 2% tax on exported gold. Even this became a "dead letter" in time.[3]

In an attempt to aid the Douro vineyardists, Pombal formed a great Portuguese company for marketing the wine, not primarily to enrich the company but to create a counterweight to the influence of the British buyers. But this measure, designed to help national agriculture, proved one of Pombal's most unpopular efforts. The company had the right to sell wine at retail as well as wholesale, and this threatened tavern keepers for miles around Oporto. The local Jesuits found their interests opposed to the monopoly, and they encouraged popular resistance. It is even said

[3] Marques Guedes, *A aliança inglêsa* (Editorial Enciclopédica, Lisbon, 1943), p. 330.

that they went so far as to declare company wine unfit for sacramental purposes. A crowd attacked the residence of the company head in Oporto, and other officials received rough handling. Pombal struck back hard, and not only crushed the Oporto riots but sentenced some leaders to death and punished over 400 others in various ways.

The company established with all this violence seems to have made slight difference in Portuguese economy, except perhaps to build a few private fortunes. Wine exports increased a little in the next twenty years, but hardly enough to pay for the damage caused by the Oporto riots.

In 1758, Pombal took advantage of a plot against King José's life to deal with his enemies in the nobility. The king received a bullet in his right arm while riding home in his coach from an evening spent with the young Marchioness of Távora. Pombal ordered many arrests, which included the male members of the Távora family, among them the husband of the lady. It came out that the would-be killer had been the Duke of Aveiro, who under torture extended his confession, truthfully or not, to implicate the Távoras. There followed a number of executions, in which Aveiro, the Távoras, and several others were killed following barbarous tortures. The marchioness herself, who was judged guilty of no greater crime than adultery, went away to easy confinement in a convent. She at length received the intercession of Madame du Pompadour, whose place at the French court of Louis XV was similar to the one the marchioness had lost in Portugal.[4]

Years later, after the fall of Pombal, another tribunal reviewed the case of the Távoras and decided that there had been a miscarriage of justice. But in all fairness it must be said that the later proceedings were inspired by Pombal's deadliest enemies.

During the Távora trial, some implication had been dropped of Jesuit involvement in the plot against José. Farfetched though the charge was, Pombal eagerly seized upon it, since he considered the time now ripe to settle scores with the Company of Jesus. The Company was hostile to him and could be dangerous as well, for the Jesuits still had great influence over the Portuguese people and sometimes over the king himself. Pombal had run afoul of them years earlier when they had preached against a monopoly he

[4] Fortunato de Almeida, *História de Portugal* (Coimbra, 1922-1929), IV, 321.

had founded and in which he had taken a direct financial interest, to sell slaves in the Brazilian provinces of Pará and Maranhão. Perhaps he had been on the verge of expelling the Jesuits from the Portuguese court in 1755; at least the rumor ran to that effect. If it was true, the earthquake postponed the event, but only until Pombal felt ready to make a clean sweep.

He felt ready late in 1758, while the Távora trials still went on. He placed guards around every Jesuit house in Lisbon and had the places rigorously searched for evidence of many kinds. Next, in January, 1759, he arrested ten leading members of the order and as the year passed took further steps against the Jesuits. The charges against the Company were wildly exaggerated; and, while few will deny that the order had some faults, these accusations were out of all reason. The Portuguese government ruled that the Jesuits should be suppressed in every part of the empire, their property confiscated, and their schools closed. Some of the members of the order were deported to Italy, others remained in Portuguese prisons. As rapidly as possible those Jesuits at work in the colonies were rounded up and brought home. Many were not of Portuguese nationality, and these were generally allowed to go to their own countries in peace.

The church in Portugal did not maintain a united front in support of the Jesuits. The Company had always had many ecclesiastical enemies, and in general the hierarchy abided by the government's wishes in this matter. Cardinal Saldanha, the Patriarch of Lisbon, cooperated with Pombal and published a pastoral letter warning all devout Portuguese to shun contact with the fallen Jesuits.[5]

The suppression of the Company in Portugal is the most famous of Pombal's acts. The Jesuits, in over two centuries of association with the country, had both good and bad achievements to their name. They had been invaluable as missionaries in Brazil, Africa, and Asia. Their intellectual influence on the home country had been less good. The motives of Pombal in suppressing them, however, will not stand scrutiny, for he feared them chiefly as an obstacle to his own power.

He had started a fashion in Roman Catholic countries. In 1764, France, largely through the efforts of another minister,

[5] Fortunato de Almeida, *História de Portugal* (Coimbra, 1922-1929), IV, 373-374.

Choiseul, expelled the Jesuits; and in 1767, Spain, then dominated by the Count of Aranda, took the same step. In 1773, Pope Clement, at the request of both the Portuguese and Spanish governments, suppressed the order altogether. It did not resume its existence until 1814.

The rest of Pombal's career and actions must be summarized briefly. The Seven Years' War, in which England and France as usual were arrayed against each other, broke out in 1756. Portugal, having no grounds for intervention, at first remained neutral. But in 1762 Spain entered the war as an ally of France, having a little earlier signed the Family Pact, by which the two Bourbon rulers acknowledged their mutual interests. One of the prizes offered Spain was Portugal, still bound as an ally to England. Franco-Spanish forces mobilized on the frontier in preparation for an invasion. Pombal had made no real preparations for the war which had long been visible on the horizon, and the enemy appeared likely to capture Lisbon. The Bragança family made hurried preparations to leave for Brazil or some other colony. England hastily rushed regiments to Portugal and a few Swiss mercenaries were hired. Fortunately, the invasion, when it came, was half-hearted, which gave the Portuguese some time for preparation. Fortunately too, the major powers were then on the point of signing a peace treaty, which they did in Paris early in 1763. The war, therefore, affected Portugal but slightly, beyond causing a great deal of fright.

Pombal made changes in colonial administration, and it would be straining a point to say that his efforts were not sincere. Although he has not left a very popular memory in Portugal, he is more highly regarded in Brazil. Among the achievements of his administration were the reversion of several of the old Brazilian *capitanias* to the crown; a very desirable change; and the elevation of Brazil, in 1763, to the status of a viceroyalty with its capital at Rio de Janeiro. Pombal stimulated immigration and in his time at least 20,000 newcomers poured into Brazil, mostly from the Azores. He permitted freer trade in several important commodities and had some Portuguese naval construction performed in Brazil. He also improved defenses and military installations. Thus Pombal accomplished much to place Brazil in a united, self-reliant condition, fit to assume independent status forty years after his death. Nothing, to be sure, would have been farther from his wishes, but the Brazilians rightly regard him as a landmark in their history.

Pombal, being fifteen years older than his king, had little reason to expect to survive him. Yet the marquis, at the age of seventy-eight, was still in office when José died early in 1777. The heir this time was a daughter, Maria Francisca, who became Maria I. There was no chance whatever that she would keep Pombal in power. Among her first actions was a release of prisoners jailed by the marquis, some of whom had been in confinement since the Távora case. Pombal resigned his office and was allowed to go away to his country estate.

Examination of the Portuguese exchequer, after he was gone, destroyed any reputation Pombal may have had as an economist. The treasury, while not empty, was in bad condition, and unpaid government bills ran to huge amounts. Servants, officials, and functionaries had not received salaries or wages for a long time. The army scarcely existed, and the navy, revived back in the time of João V, was now down to a dozen ships rotting in the harbor. Pombal may have handled matters better in his younger days, but his final legacy to Portugal was sad.

Maria I was forty-two years old when the failure of her parents to provide male offspring raised her to the throne. She had long been married to her uncle, Pedro of Bragança, her father's brother, a man now nearing sixty. Pedro was given the courtesy title *El-Rei*, but remained in fact prince consort until his death in 1786. The couple had several children, of whom the third, João, ultimately inherited the throne. Maria and Pedro were in no way a distinguished pair, being reasonably pious, reasonably indolent, and reasonably stupid. The group of uninspiring ministers that took over the government posts seemed to promise a quiet and uneventful reign.

The first years were largely occupied with undoing various acts of Pombal. The Távora case was reopened, with a complete vindication for everyone, living or dead, who had been involved, except the Duke of Aveiro and three humble accomplices. The idea of restoring the Jesuits came up but had to be dropped because of the unfavorable international situation. France and Spain, having followed the lead of Pombal in expelling the order, would have taken a Portuguese change of front with ill grace. Even the pope might be offended, since his predecessor had abolished the Jesuits a few years before.

Pombal, on his retirement, was not allowed to spend his last few years in peace. Those who had nursed grievances for years commenced bringing lawsuits against him. One in particular roused his ire: a charge of having sold property under false pretenses. The accuser added several defamatory declarations regarding Pombal's career in office, although these were irrelevant to the case. The old marquis flung himself into the business of defense and wrote a self-vindication which contained statements damaging to the memory of José I. When the queen reviewed the case, she ordered the part reflecting on her father taken out and destroyed. Next she sent officials to interrogate Pombal, but these men found him fast failing in health and strength. Maria's decree, handed down in August, 1781, pronounced the marquis guilty of many crimes deserving punishment, but in view of his age ordered no punishment beyond banishment from the court. The next year Pombal died, and so bitterly did hatred pursue him that the monk who preached his funeral oration was disciplined by his superiors.

Europe was now headed for the era of the French Revolution, and no country, least of all weak Portugal, could avoid being deeply affected. When the first disturbing news came from Paris in 1789, the Lisbon court took the same disapproving attitude as did the other European governments. Two years more and the full seriousness of the French troubles began to be felt. At this point the mind of Queen Maria, never one of the best, gave way. Several things contributed to the breakdown: mourning for her deceased husband Pedro, worry over the dark clouds hanging over Europe, and, as some say, the demands of her confessor, who was not satisfied with the steps taken to undo Pombal's actions. By January, 1792, no one could pretend that the queen was any longer fit to govern. Her eldest living son, João, became ruler in fact from that time, though he waited seven more years before using the title prince regent. The old queen lived until 1816, and had occasional lucid spells, but took no further part in the government.

Portugal shared in the general rush of European monarchies

to declare war on France after the execution of Louis XVI in 1793. First making treaties of alliance with Spain and England,* the government of Prince João sent a small army to Catalonia to cooperate with the Spaniards, who had initiated fighting and maneuvering against the French along the Pyrenees. Following a few preliminary successes, the Iberian allies suffered heavy defeats, and the Portuguese lost most of their fighting equipment in a disaster early in 1794. Soon after this Spain felt ready for peace and signed the treaty of Basle with France the next year. The Spanish government of Carlos IV took this step without consulting or including Portugal, who was left with only such threadbare comfort as the English alliance gave.

Spain next re-entered the war as an ally of France, which made the Portuguese position more uncomfortable than ever. The Madrid government, dominated by Minister Manuel de Godoy, having once decided to change policy made a complete about-face. It now shelved the fear of revolutionary France in favor of the ancient ambition to swallow Portugal. Even before Godoy undertook troop mobilizations on the frontier, the Portuguese sensed their danger. The English naval victory off Cape St. Vincent in 1797 and the arrival of a few British regiments in Lisbon did little to soothe their nerves.

Portugal rushed a negotiator to Paris to try for respectable peace terms. This agent, António de Araujo, believed his country to be in a frame of mind to accept anything, for in 1797 he signed an agreement promising France an indemnity and the cession of part of northern Brazil.[6] Desperate though Prince João's government then was, it would not concede so much, and Portugal refused to ratify the treaty.

Luckily for the Portuguese, Spain hesitated to invade their country without French support, and France during the next three years was mainly occupied with Bonaparte's Egyptian expedition and with the War of the Second Coalition. Not until 1801, when Bonaparte had meanwhile installed himself as First Consul of France, did the Franco-Spanish allies focus their attention on Portugal again. A drastic ultimatum from Madrid then paved the

* The old British alliance treaty did not provide for Portuguese automatic entry into any English war.
[6] Marques Guedes, A aliança inglêsa (Editorial Enciclopédica, Lisbon, 1943), p. 365.

way for war, and Spanish armies poured across the frontier in several places. The octogenarian Duke of Lafões, in charge of Portuguese defenses, offered only weak opposition, and in a few weeks the invaders seized the whole Alentejo district. All through the brief campaign peace negotiations had been under way. The officers knew this, and many of them did not take the war seriously. "Why should we fight?" asked Lafões of the Spanish general, Francisco Solano. "Spain and Portugal are two beasts of burden. England drives us and France rides you. Let us dance around and make plenty .of noise, but for God's sake let us not do each other any real harm. They would certainly laugh at us if we did!" [7]

Godoy did not take the whole thing as a joke, however, because he wanted glory and spoils. Although Portugal was allowed to exist for the moment, it lived under the constant threat of a new occupation and had to cede the city and district of Olivença to Spain. This small area, which is the only territory ever lost by Portugal in Europe, was never regained, since Spain remained in possession after the fall of Napoleon. England, meanwhile, wrote Portugal off for lost and occupied Madeira and Goa, fearing that otherwise they would fall into enemy hands.

For the next few years Prince Regent João and his people lived under a Damoclean sword. France sent as minister to Lisbon the rough soldier, General Jean Lannes, later Marshal of the Empire, who adopted bullying tactics, affronting and insulting whom he pleased. Bonaparte, who crowned himself Napoleon I in 1804, smashed the Third Coalition at Austerlitz the next year, crushed Prussia at Jena in 1806, and forced the Russian Tsar beyond the Niemen before making the Tilsit alliance with him in 1807. Having dealt thus with the major continental powers, Napoleon now felt ready to deal with the small fry, including Portugal.

In June, 1807, the Corsican emperor assembled an army of 30,000 men at Bayonne under the command of General Andoche Junot. The force was known to exist for the invasion of Portugal in case the prince regent failed to accept all Napoleon's terms. The demand which came from Paris to Lisbon in August ordered Prince João to break all relations with England and declare war, to seize British subjects and merchandise in Portugal, and to close

[7] Fortunato de Almeida, *História de Portugal* (Coimbra, 1922-1929), IV, 467.

his ports to any traffic with the English. João vacillated, as he usually did in grave emergencies, and the British minister, Lord Strangford, began to advise evacuating the Portuguese Court to Brazil.

Junot's army moved into Spain from Bayonne in October, and a few days later France and Spain signed a treaty at Fontainebleau arranging for a division of Portugal into three parts. The boy king of Etruria, grandson of Carlos IV of Spain, would receive the northern provinces with the title King of Northern Lusitania. The Alentejo and Algarve in the south would become the hereditary principality of Godoy, who would add to his mouthfilling Spanish title "Prince of Peace" the additional one of King of the Algarve. Central Portugal would remain on deposit until a final peace agreement settled its fate.

Since the Fontainebleau treaty was secret, the Portuguese did not immediately learn the future the allies had in store for their country. But they knew Junot's army to be on the move and realized that the French destination was Lisbon. Prince João had been on the verge of abandoning England, but the drastic Napoleonic ultimatum now drove him back into British arms. A few days before the Treaty of Fontainebleau he signed an agreement with England in which he recognized the possibility that he soon might have to leave for Brazil. He virtually threw himself on the protection of George III and guaranteed to give the English trading rights in Brazil to compensate for whatever they might lose in Portugal.

The French army entered Portugal on November 19, 1807, and two Spanish forces invaded the country in the north and south. By the 24th Junot was at Abrantes, and on the 29th he was a few miles from Lisbon. The Portuguese could have resisted him easily had they but known it, for he brought a weak army made up largely of raw recruits. Discipline deteriorated in the French ranks, and it was a very unimpressive host that Junot finally brought into the capital.

João put off his decision to depart until the last moment and had made no preparations for a voyage to Brazil or anywhere. As a result, the final embarkation took place amid scenes of comical confusion. João, his wife Carlota Joaquina, their children, and old Queen Maria were hastily bundled into coaches and rattled down to the waterfront to board ships that had not been prepared to receive them. The aged and insane Maria had but vague notions of why they were leaving. Report says that as her coachman frantically whipped his horses to make more speed, she called out to him, "Not so fast. People will think we are running away." [8]

By late in the day of November 27, the royal family, with the court and several thousand people, had been loaded on the ships, which were escorted by Portuguese war vessels and a small English squadron. Bad weather prevented them from getting out of the Tagus until the 29th, and that evening Junot entered the city unopposed.

[8] Tobias Monteiro, *História do imperio. A elaboração da independencia* (F. Briguiet & Cia, Rio de Janeiro, 1927), p. 59.

Chapter XIII

THE CONSTITUTIONAL STRUGGLE

*T*HE royal family remained away from Portugal fourteen years, and during that time important changes came both to Brazil and to the mother country. The Brazilians enthusiastically welcomed their sovereigns, feeling that this meant an upward step for them. They were not deceived in their hopes, because Prince Regent João soon passed decrees favoring the colony, whose pride took a new bound and whose national feeling further increased. The relative positions of Lisbon and Rio de Janeiro became suddenly reversed. Rio, which up to then had been a mere colonial capital, emerged as headquarters for the whole large Portuguese empire, whose government was carried on from there. Portugal, small and abandoned, lay for the moment in French possession, with far from brilliant prospects of regaining supremacy.

João, before leaving, had hastily named a council to administer the country, but the French paid little attention to this. Junot behaved as absolute master. He formed most of what remained of the Portuguese army into a single unit and marched it away to France, although a third of the men deserted before reaching the Pyrenees. Napoleon named the remainder the "Portuguese Legion," and these troops served him until the Russian campaign of 1812.

The home Portuguese, as soon as they recovered from the shock caused by the Bragança flight to Brazil, did not tamely submit to the French. Junot, with the full backing of Napoleon, began

178

systematically plundering the country, levying contributions where he pleased and forcing private donations of gold and jewelry. The Portuguese, true descendants of conquerors and heroes, waited their moment to strike back.

The chance came soon. Early in 1808, Napoleon deposed the Bourbon royal family of Spain and gave the throne to his brother Joseph. The result was an immediate Spanish popular revolt, and the French found themselves with a Peninsular War on their hands. Portugal rose at the same time. In Oporto, Braga, the Trás-Os-Montes province, and other places in the north, the population attacked the French. Southern Portugal joined the revolt immediately, and Junot found himself losing control of the country.

England for years had awaited just such an opportunity to strike at France on the continent. The Duke of Portland's ministry sent money to a governing junta formed in Oporto, and followed this with Sir Arthur Wellesley and 8,000 men, who landed there in August, 1808. The British commander quickly defeated the French in two engagements; and a few days later Napoleon's generals agreed to leave Portugal, provided they might keep their equipment. Since the British were not yet in condition for a full offensive, and since the Portuguese needed to gain time, they both consented to this peaceful evacuation. Before the end of the year Portugal was again an independent country, being governed now by a new junta or council.

Needless to say, the war had only begun. Wellesley rushed the training of Portuguese recruits before the French could strike their next blow. In 1809, from far Brazil, the prince regent named General William Carr Beresford marshal of the new Portuguese army. At about the same time, João made an agreement for a loan from England, to be guaranteed out of the revenues of English-held Madeira and various of the Brazilian exports.

During 1809 the French Marshal Nicolas Soult, Duke of Dalmatia, slipped into Portugal from the north and occupied Oporto. Some of the citizens there had grown disgruntled over the cowardly flight of the Braganças and moreover did not like their English allies. Soult made friends with a group of these men, who thought of setting up the marshal on a throne of Northern Portugal and ultimately making him ruler of the whole country. It appears that Soult was tempted by the scheme, so much so in fact that several of his own officers became alarmed and conspired against him. Wellesley and Beresford quickly ended the matter by attacking and driving the French from the country.

Later in the year Wellesley took his Anglo-Portuguese force into Spain and won a victory at Talavera, but soon retired to prepare for the heavy counterattack he knew would come in 1810. Foreseeing where the assault would be delivered, he built a series of three fortifications called the "Lines of Torres Vedras," reaching from the Tagus to the Atlantic. True to his prediction, the French struck from the northeast toward Lisbon, and the English and Portuguese slowly retired before them to the pocket between the Tagus and the sea. Marshal Massena had overall command of the invaders, with Ney and Junot as his chief subordinates. Wellesley, who in the meantime had been created Duke of Wellington, knew the French custom of living off the countries they invaded. As Massena advanced, he had the land abandoned by the population, and ordered all food destroyed that could not be carried away. Before Massena reached the Torres Vedras lines, his troops had begun to suffer severely for want of provisions, and Wellington's army had weakened the French with rearguard engagements. Massena did not dare to assault the lines and began to move back toward the Spanish frontier. Meanwhile Soult had orders from Napoleon to support Massena by means of an attack from the south through the Alentejo. But the French could not coordinate efforts as far apart as these, and Soult delayed so long near the frontier as to be of no help whatever.

After Torres Vedras, the Peninsular War moved entirely into Spain. From 1811 until the beginning of 1814, Wellington with his English-Portuguese troops went from victory to victory. When Napoleon abdicated early in 1814 to go to Elba, the allies had crossed the Pyrenees and were campaigning near Bordeaux.

The return of the emperor from Elba to France the next year, his hundred days of rule, and final defeat at Waterloo did not affect Portugal. But meanwhile, in a preliminary peace conference, it was arranged that French Guiana, which had been conquered by the Brazilian forces of Prince João, should be given up, and that Portugal should get back Olivença. When the European powers met at Vienna for the final settlement, the ablest of the Portuguese diplomats, the Count of Palmela, headed his country's delegation. The great powers soon changed their minds about compelling the return of Olivença and decided that the matter lay entirely between Spain and Portugal. Fernando VII, the restored Spanish Bourbon monarch, did not choose to disgorge, and the Portuguese had to write Olivença off as a loss.[1]

As a concession to England, the question of the slave trade was brought up at the Congress of Vienna. Portugal opposed complete abolition of the traffic because Angola and Brazil depended on it so greatly, but finally consented to declare the trade abolished in all colonies north of the equator.

This seemed the logical time for the Braganças to return to Lisbon. Instead, Prince Regent João showed a decided preference for Brazil, and his next step was to elevate the colony to the status of a kingdom, equal to Portugal in rank.[2] The French diplomat Talleyrand suggested the change to Palmela at Vienna, believing that with this new relationship Portugal and Brazil could preserve their unity and avoid the ill feeling that had recently caused England and Spain to lose their New World possessions.[*] João accepted the proposal, to the joy of the Brazilians and the dismay of most Portuguese, since the latter had the unrealistic and far-fetched notion that Brazil could be made a helpless colony again. Moreover, João refused to abandon his Rio de Janeiro residence, although the great European powers joined in urging him to return to his Portuguese capital.

Only in 1816, nine years after the flight from Lisbon, did the death of the aged Maria allow the prince regent to become João VI. By this time he seemed more a Brazilian than a Portuguese monarch. He had already thrown the South American seaports open to trade, established the Bank of Brazil, permitted the import of printing presses, and given Brazilians important posts in his government. Now Brazil as a kingdom threatened to outshine little Portugal by far.

The Portuguese meanwhile feared that they had only exchanged masters, expelling the French to make way for the Brit-

[1] J. M. de Queiroz Veloso, *Como perdemos Olivença* (Oficina "Ottosgráfica," Ltda., Lisbon, 1933).
[2] Renato de Mendonça, *História da política exterior do Brasil, 1500-1825* (Mexico City, 1945), pp. 82-83.
[*] Though Spain was still fighting in America to retain her colonies, Talleyrand already counted them as lost.

ish. Marshal Beresford governed the country as regent for João and showed none of the liberal tendencies commonly associated with England. Portuguese army officers in particular resented the foreign domination and conspired several times against Beresford, who suppressed the plotters with a heavy hand.

Yet the Portuguese picture had its bright side. The country made a quick recovery from the ravages of the war. Agriculture flourished, and increased building fast repaired the damages left by the military campaigns. The people seemed contented and reasonably prosperous, but the French revolution and the presence of French forces in the country had made changes that did not appear on the surface. Freemasonry, which had made its appearance, sowed a constant propaganda, not only against Beresford but against the absent João VI. Just across the frontier trouble also brewed in Spain, where Fernando VII had followed a systematic policy of ignoring all changes the last generation had brought and worked to re-establish the old-time Spanish absolutism.

The Spaniards revolted first. In 1820, a rising which began in the army forced Fernando to restore the constitution which Spain had already proclaimed in 1812 and which this reactionary king had later suppressed.

At that time, Beresford had left Lisbon for Rio to confer with João VI. The Portuguese straightway followed the Spanish example. An army mutiny, started in Oporto by Colonel Sebastião de Brito Cabreira, quickly spread to Lisbon and the two cities pooled forces to establish a provisional junta for governing the country. When Beresford returned to Lisbon the junta refused him permission to land. He went on to England, where his government decided not to intervene in Portuguese affairs.

Left to itself, the nation faced the hard task of preparing a new government with representative institutions. The country had no self-governing experience, and even the traditional aristocratic cortes had been a defunct body for generations. It was of course natural for the Portuguese to revive the old name, and so the junta decreed that an elected cortes should meet in Lisbon on January 6, 1821, for the purpose of drawing up a constitution. Elections should take place late in December and would follow the cumbersome process of elimination, moving up from the parishes to the districts and culminating in the provincial capitals.

When the cortes met, two weeks later than the scheduled time, the members had no common program beyond a general desire to put Brazil in its place. But they could orate fulsomely and seemed to believe that pious platitudes could take the place of knowledge of government. The Masonic Order was well represented in the cortes, which started by formally abolishing the Portuguese Inquisition, although this relic of a bygone era had amounted to little for years.

The conditions in Portugal brought João VI home in 1821. No one had talked seriously of deposing him, but the implied threat was there; so the reluctant monarch arrived, to find himself now largely regarded as a tool for the more radical party in the cortes. In Brazil, he left his eldest son Pedro as regent, and it is generally believed by Brazilians that the departing father advised the young man to place himself at the head of any future independence movement, since Portugal would be powerless to oppose it. Accompanying João and his wife, Carlota Joaquina, was their second son Miguel, of whom it is declared, perhaps maliciously, that he had not yet learned to read.

With the king home and installed, although by no means comfortably, in the royal palace of Queluz, the cortes proceeded with its work. An end was decreed to all remaining feudal rights and obligations in Portugal, and this brought a few repercussions which created the nucleus of a party for absolutist reaction, but for the moment this party had no chance of succeeding.

On turning to the affairs of Brazil, the cortes made its greatest mistakes and showed a lack of elementary common sense. With the Brazilian independence party growing daily stronger, the cortes members seemed to feel that, if they could bring Prince Pedro home, all resistance in the former colony would collapse. Through his subservient father they commanded Pedro to come, but Brazilian feeling was so strong that the prince could not have left Rio had he wished to do so. Meanwhile the cortes passed a series of decrees against Brazil, some serious and some merely irritating. A few Brazilians who had been sent to attend the sessions found themselves in an unpopular minority, jeered at and insulted. One Portuguese delegate, in the heat of debate, screamed at the Brazilians, "So they want to separate and go away with their

Brazil? Good, let them secede. Farewell, Senhor Brazil! We won't miss you in the least."

On September 7, 1822, Prince Pedro was making a horseback journey from Santos to Rio de Janeiro with an armed escort, and happened to be near the banks of the small Ypiranga River when a courier found him and handed over the latest dispatches from Lisbon. Pedro read these and found them impossible. Without hesitation he turned to his followers and in eloquent language proclaimed Brazil separated from Portugal. This was the famous *Grito do Ypiranga,* or Cry of the Ypiranga, the Brazilian equivalent of a declaration of independence.[3] Before the end of the year, Pedro became emperor of the new nation.

Portugal lacked any means of conquering the huge daughter country. A few Portuguese garrisons in Brazilian cities were easily overcome, and a Brazilian fleet, organized and commanded by the British Lord Cochrane, chased the Portuguese war vessels in Brazilian waters all the way to the Tagus. At first Portugal refused to recognize the independence of Brazil, but the United States did so in 1824; and it became evident that other countries would soon follow.

Meanwhile, in ignorance for the moment of the Brazilian secession, the cortes finished its work and produced a constitution, which João VI solemnly swore to maintain. It was in no way a remarkable or original document, but Portugal had nearly destroyed itself in giving birth to this commonplace child. Administration had become disorganized, and confusion reigned in many parts of the country.

A reaction of some sort was inevitable, but what came was no healthy reaction. Events in Spain again prepared the way when, in 1823, the French Duke of Angoulême led an army across the Pyrenees and restored Fernando VII as an absolute autocrat in the name of the Holy Alliance. Portuguese reactionaries took heart and began to clamor for a *Rei Absoluto.* This gave young Dom Miguel his chance. Ignorant and crude, he had but one ambition: to get rid of the constitution and restore absolutism. Abetted by his mother, he led a military revolt in May, 1823, ostensibly in his father's name, but more likely acting in what he considered

[3] Tobias Monteiro, *História do imperio: a elaboração da independencia* (F. Briguiet & Cia, Rio de Janeiro, 1927), p. 545.

his own interest. João VI, still largely the prisoner of the cortes, disclaimed any share in Miguel's scheme. At the first possible moment, however, he decamped to join his son and together they set up a new government at Vila Franca. The cortes capitulated and João promised to give the country a new and better constitution.

Next in 1824, Miguel tried a military *coup d'état* in order to establish a regime without taint of constitutionalism. João had brains enough to oppose this, and with the help of the diplomatic corps in Lisbon he got the upper hand. To rid Portugal of Miguel's troublesome presence, he next sent the prince traveling through Europe, on the pretense of giving him a much-needed education.

The last important act of João's reign was the recognition of Brazil in 1825. Negotiations had begun in London the previous year with the British minister Canning acting as mediator. The Portuguese negotiators tried delaying tactics and strove at all costs to avoid using the fatal word "independence." For one thing, they expected that João VI would not live long and that his death would bring Pedro of Brazil to the Portuguese throne. In this way, the two countries might be painlessly reunited. Meanwhile they proposed that, since the son ought not to have a higher title than the father, João should be the emperor and Pedro, though retaining freedom of action in Brazil, should be his vassal. The Brazilians contemptuously rejected this and the British then talked plainly to the Portuguese. They said that George IV would presently recognize Dom Pedro and that it would be a great face-saver for Portugal to do so first. On this the Portuguese yielded, although João insisted on "conceding" rather than "recognizing" Brazilian independence and used the meaningless title "emperor" for the rest of his days. Pedro agreed to pay Portugal the sum of £2,000,000 as Brazil's contribution to a debt contracted, theoretically in common, by the two kingdoms. This arrangement, though essentially fair, cost Pedro much popularity in Brazil and helped ultimately to cost him his throne. The treaty was signed in London in August, 1825.

João VI died early the next year. Although he had cut a rather pitiful figure in Europe, his record in Brazil had been better, and there at times he had showed himself a statesman of considerable stature.

His death raised a problem that Pedro feared to meet squarely. Much as the emperor wanted the Portuguese throne, which belonged to him by all law and precedent, his Brazilian subjects naturally viewed the prospect with alarm. They did not fancy a disguised re-annexation to Portugal after having so recently gone through a revolution for independence.

João, before dying, had signed a decree naming his daughter, Isabel Maria, as regent until his "legitimate heir" could make provisions for the government. Presumably this meant Pedro, and the old king evidently hoped in this way to pave the way for a reunion with Brazil. Portugal considered the Brazilian emperor its king and called him Pedro IV. But he knew he must straightway abdicate one of his two thrones and chose for the moment to keep Brazil and to name his seven-year-old daughter, Maria da Gloria, ruler of Portugal. According to Portuguese law a woman could reign, so Pedro set no startling precedent in proclaiming young Maria. But the child would need a man's help in governing, and therefore the emperor of Brazil, who did not quite know his brother Miguel's true character, decided that she should marry her twenty-four-year old uncle. Meanwhile he prepared and sent to Portugal a new constitution called the charter, which Miguel must accept and swear to maintain.

Miguel had been living at the French and Austrian courts during the past two years. He had not behaved himself well on his travels, and Louis XVIII of France had been very glad to see him leave Paris. In Vienna, Miguel came strongly under the influence of Metternich, who had small liking for the Portuguese prince but who, with his well-known hatred of liberalism, disapproved of the charter sent to Lisbon by Pedro. Metternich certainly helped plant in Miguel's commonplace brain the idea of upsetting the whole constitutional arrangement planned by Pedro, and of reigning alone, unencumbered by young Maria and her father's charter.

Even so, while in Vienna, Miguel went through a solemn ceremony of betrothal to Maria da Gloria and swore, in the presence of Pedro's emissaries, to abide by the charter. He then returned to Portugal by way of France and England, reaching Lisbon in February, 1828. On his arrival, he found the absolutists in control and he received a delirious demonstration of welcome. Cries of "long live Miguel I, absolute king" greeted his ears, accompanied by fierce calls for vengeance upon the constitutionalists. He surrounded himself at once with advisers who hated the charter and who favored the most reactionary policies. Although he repeated the ceremony of swearing to the charter, this time before a new Portuguese cortes, it is claimed that his partisans combined to make the occasion a farce. The Patriarch of Lisbon, who administered the oath, very likely substituted a vulgar book for the Scriptures. A tall nobleman stood between Miguel and the listeners, so that no one afterward could be sure just what the prince had sworn to or said. What is certain is that he appointed a reactionary ministry and that liberal leaders began emigrating from Portugal, going usually to England. Palmela, now ambassador in London, became the leader of this group and announced to the British government that he had severed all relations with Miguel and would henceforth serve as the envoy of Pedro. The Duke of Wellington, who had recently become British prime minister, recognized Maria as the legitimate ruler of Portugal but did not address her as queen. Other governments, including the papacy, Russia, France, Spain, and the United States, gave a sort of recognition to Miguel.

The higher Portuguese aristocrats generally sided with Pedro and Maria, either because of their growing liberalism or because of their fidelity to principles of birth and monarchial legitimacy. The lesser nobles or gentry tended to favor Miguel and absolutism, and had on their side most of the clergy and probably the bulk of the people. Though the church expected to gain from a Miguelist victory, the truth was that in the following civil war both sides plundered and confiscated ecclesiastical property with fine impartiality.[4]

Miguel seemed for the moment to have won. Portugal lay in his grasp and he even proclaimed an amnesty for the exiles, who could be restored to his good graces by appearing before his diplomatic agents and taking an oath of allegiance. Even so, he excepted many persons and few cared to test his promised liberality. The number of arrests and executions in Portugal revealed a bloodthirsty spirit, and Miguel's advisers mostly showed themselves a

[4] Fortunato de Almeida, *História de Portugal* (Coimbra, 1922-1929), VI, 100.

vindictive, shortsighted group of men, bent mainly on revenge and on paying off all their old grudges.

Young Maria's father, Pedro, had shipped the girl to Portugal before learning of his brother's breach of faith. Those in charge of the queen, now nine years old, learned in time that she must not go to Lisbon and so sent her to London instead. The British government gave Maria royal honors but no material help, and in 1829 she returned to Brazil.

Discouraging as prospects looked, the pro-Pedro party stood fast and even gained strength. Palmela did his best to help the émigrés who reached England. During the winter of 1828-29, a horde of them lived miserably in a large shed by the wharves of Plymouth. But a better refuge was soon provided. The governor of Terceira in the Azores pronounced in favor of Pedro and Maria, and the emperor of Brazil, acting from Rio de Janeiro, appointed a regency there. As soon as possible Palmela went to Terceira himself, and in the face of a certain British hostility helped his countrymen to go there from England.

The year of 1830 saw the prospects looking up for the Portuguese on Terceira, as the Belgians became independent of the Netherlands and the liberal Louis Philippe replaced the reactionary Charles X in France. And in 1831 Pedro returned to Europe, his position having become so precarious in Brazil that his abdication there had been necessary to prevent a revolution. Leaving his five-year-old son to reign as Pedro II, he now came to fight Maria's battles and to place her on the Portuguese throne. Without pausing at Terceira, the Duke of Bragança, as Pedro now called himself, went to England and then to France, where he gathered ships at Quiberon and Belle Isle and collected more anti-Miguelist Portuguese. He reached the Azores with this reinforcement in February, 1832.

Overmatched as he seemed by Miguel's overwhelming strength in continental Portugal, Pedro still had strong and able helpers. Besides Palmela the diplomat, he had on his side the two ablest Portuguese soldiers, João Carlos Saldanha and Antonio José de Sousa, Count of Vila-Flor. This military pair became the Dukes of Saldanha and Terceira, respectively, for their loyalty and distinguished services, and Palmela likewise received a dukedom. Of slightly lesser status at the time, but extremely valuable, was Bernardo de Sá Nogueira, presently Viscount Sá da Bandeira, who became one of Portugal's greatest nineteenth century statesmen.[5]

Helping Pedro in London was Juan Mendizábal, an interesting Spanish Jew attached to the cause of liberalism. Disgusted with conditions in his own country, he joined forces with the Portuguese constitutionalists and succeeded in floating a loan of £2,000,000 for them, though at enormous interest, in London and Paris.

Pedro remained in the Azores only long enough to make his final preparations. On June 27, 1832, he sailed for Oporto with a small fleet commanded by an English captain, George Sartorius, and a few thousand soldiers. The constitutionalists took the Miguelists completely by surprise and had no trouble seizing Oporto, where Pedro hoisted his daughter's flag. The partisans of Miguel later excused the fall of this important city to the small liberal army by saying that they wanted to get the whole force on shore and annihilate it along with Oporto, which was the chief radical hotbed in Portugal. If so, they nearly succeeded, for soon they besieged the city with overwhelming force, and nothing appeared likely to save Pedro. Such military authorities as the Duke of Wellington thought he had made a grave mistake in striking for Oporto instead of Lisbon and that he had thrust his head into a trap.[6]

But the months went by and Oporto refused to fall. Miguel's larger numbers kept Pedro penned up in the city, but cholera spread among the besiegers, who suffered from hunger almost as much as did the defenders.

The year 1833 came, and winter and spring passed, with the siege of Oporto still going on. In June, Pedro's headquarters decided to try a daring diversion. The Duke of Terceira was embarked with 2,500 men under convoy of a fleet now commanded by the Englishman Charles Napier. They sailed to the far south of Portugal, rounded Cape St. Vincent, and Terceira put his men ashore near Tavira. On his way back, Napier encountered the

---

[5] Violently pro-Pedro in tone is Felix Pereira de Magalhães, *Apontamentos para a história diplomatica de Portugal desde 1826 até 1834* (Imprensa de J. G. de Sousa Neves, Lisbon, 1871). Equally partisan from Miguel's point-of-view is João Ameal, *História de Portugal* (Livraria Tavares Martins, Oporto, 1940), pp. 640-677.

[6] These military events are well surveyed by William Bollaert, *The Wars of Succession in Portugal and Spain*, 2 vols. (E. Stauford, London, 1840).

Miguelist fleet off the cape and routed it, capturing two sail-of-the-line, two frigates, and a corvette. The rest escaped, but this defeat virtually ended Miguel's power on the sea. Lisbon now lay open to Napier's squadron; in the meantime Terceira was sweeping triumphantly toward the capital from the south. The victorious army and fleet reached the Tagus at almost the same time and the city fell to them easily. Dom Pedro slipped from Oporto to the capital to be the hero of a joyful reception on July 28. He gave the papal nuncio three days to leave the country, this Italian prelate having been a devoted partisan of Miguel. The Spanish representative went home without being asked.

Around Oporto, the besiegers made one final grand attack, which failed, and then drew off to Coimbra in the interior, after wantonly destroying all the property of value along the Douro. Miguel had the wild thought now of trying to besiege Pedro in Lisbon. He did reach the defenses of the city, only to be driven off by Saldanha, and once more he retired to the interior. Here he prolonged the war until May, 1834, when his generals forced him to make peace by accepting an amnesty from the government of young Maria, which had now been recognized by France and England. Miguel surrendered and Pedro awarded him the Concession of Évora-Monte, by which the beaten prince received permission to keep all his personal belongings and the right to collect an annual pension from the government. In return he must leave Portugal within fifteen days and promise never to return. Miguel's enemies protested this leniency, and some of them nearly mobbed Pedro as he emerged from a Lisbon theater the night after his brother's surrender. But Pedro stood firm, although many insisted that Miguel had forfeited his life. That thwarted young autocrat went into exile and, despite some bluster, did not trouble Portugal again. He long survived both Pedro and Maria, dying at the age of sixty-four in Germany in 1866.

Maria da Gloria, the girl queen, who had spent the recent years in Paris, arrived in Lisbon in September, 1834. Her father enthroned her at once, placing his charter in effect as the constitution of Portugal. The nation now hoped profoundly to enjoy years of peace.

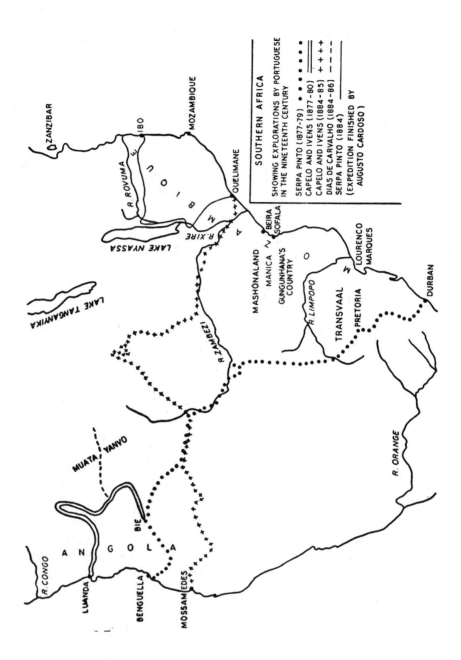

SOUTHERN AFRICA

SHOWING EXPLORATIONS BY PORTUGUESE
IN THE NINETEENTH CENTURY

SERPA PINTO (1877-79) • • • • •
CAPELO AND IVENS (1877-80)
CAPELO AND IVENS (1884-85) + + + +
DIAS DE CARVALHO (1884-86) – – – – –
SERPA PINTO (1884)
(EXPEDITION FINISHED BY
AUGUSTO CARDOSO)

Chapter XIV

THE LAST OF THE BRAGANÇAS

*H*AVING banished his brother Miguel and placed his daughter Maria da Gloria in unchallenged possession of the Portuguese throne, Pedro had accomplished the last mission of his adventurous life. Late in 1834 he died of an illness acquired during the siege of Oporto, leaving the fifteen-year-old Maria without a parent to guide her. Under the circumstances, the immature queen was bound to be heavily influenced by the four men who had cooperated most strongly with her father in placing the crown on her head. Two of these, the Dukes of Terceira and Saldanha, had shone principally as soldiers, Terceira having the greater honesty and popularity and Saldanha the loftier personal ambition. The Duke of Palmela was a veteran diplomat who knew the courts of Europe better than anyone then alive in Portugal. Viscount Sá da Bandeira was the most genuinely liberal of the four and possessed some of the instincts of an enlightened statesman.

So far nothing had been settled except the succession dispute. Portugal's real nineteenth-century problems—colonial administration, illiteracy and debt at home, the development of industry, and what to do about the church—as yet remained unsolved. In return for the loss of Brazil, Portugal had come through the civil war with a more or less constitutional monarchy and a colonial empire which, although profitless, was still considerable.

Queen Maria II made no great personal impression on the events of her time. Although pretty in a somewhat overweight way, and respected for her domestic virtues, she had no particular claim to intellect. Her first marriage, to a prince of Leuchtenberg, terminated in her widowhood within a few months. Her second, to Prince Ferdinand of Saxe-Coburg-Gotha, was extremely prolific, for it resulted in eleven children, of whom eight lived past infancy. The Portuguese could at least take satisfaction in comparing the respectable family atmosphere of their court with the different situation in Spain, where Maria's relative, Isabel II, set a much less edifying example.

Times remained very bad in Portugal. The debt piled up by the civil wars was staggering, and no one had any idea how to go about reducing it. National credit was almost extinct, and future revenues had been mortgaged. Much disorder still existed in the country, where the ghost of Miguelism had not been completely laid. And the political situation was definitely not stable. Portugal now had a cortes but, since there was no recent historical precedent for such a thing, the members did not know how to behave themselves and turned the parliamentary debates into a sterile farce. Ministries held power for very short periods, and then were replaced by others which showed an equal lack of courage and ability in tackling the nation's real problems. Portugal thus far had had two written constitutions: the first being the one so laboriously prepared by the cortes in 1822, and the second, known as the charter, having been dictated to the country by Pedro, when still emperor of Brazil in 1826. The charter, of course, went into effect at the beginning of Maria's reign. But rival political factions proceeded to make fetishes of these two unoriginal and rather inadequate instruments of government.

In 1834, while Pedro still lived, the government had tried to solve the church problem and recoup the treasury at one stroke, by abolishing the religious orders and confiscating all their property. The financial return proved altogether inadequate for the purpose and, at the same time, led to the alienation of a large part of the clergy and much of the rural population of Portugal, who were stoutly opposed to any changes.

Portugal had begun the constitutional movement in 1820, largely in imitation of Spain. This tendency to imitate continued through the decade of the thirties. When a Spanish army mutiny succeeded in placing the constitution of 1812 back in effect, a similar Portuguese rising took place in favor of the constitution of 1822 and accomplished its immediate aim, which was the overthrow of the government. Since this movement took place in September, 1836, its chief promoters, led by Sá da Bandeira, were called the Septembrists, as opposed to the Chartists, who were for sticking to Pedro's constitution. Sá da Bandeira quieted the fears of Queen Maria, who seems to have been on the verge of leaving Portugal, and assured her that both her throne and her person were safe. He then proceeded to share the ministry with two other men and to put through some reforms that he felt were urgently needed.

Although Sá da Bandeira's Septembrists did not hold together long, it is now possible to see that while they held power they accomplished some good. They made changes in the internal administrations of Portugal, adopted a new penal code, and began reforms in the Portuguese colonial empire. The most important decree prohibited the export and sale of slaves from any Portuguese colony in the future. Angola and Mozambique, the two largest possessions, protested at seeing their main source of income shut off, and for some years did not take Sá da Bandeira's laws very seriously. But this viscount, called the Portuguese Wilberforce, kept the problem very much in mind and was able to return to it some years later.

The short life of the Septembrist government, from 1836 to 1842, first was gravely threatened in 1837 by a revolt of the army leaders Terceira and Saldanha, who operated in the name of Pedro's charter. Although it was suppressed and the two dukes were forced into exile, the Septembrists proceeded to hasten their own downfall by quarreling among themselves and starting to disintegrate as a party. Thus they gave the Chartists time to reorganize, now under a new leader, Antonio Bernardo da Costa Cabral. The Duke of Terceira, who had meanwhile come back from exile, also joined the revolt which presently broke out, and he furnished the prestige that brought the abler but less known Costa Cabral into power. As the result of very complicated maneuvering early in 1842, Terceira took office as the head of a Chartist ministry, with Costa Cabral, whom the queen presently ennobled as the Marquis of Tomár, furnishing most of the real force and brains. But this administration had no better success than the others with the most pressing question of the day—the reduction of the debt, which in fact continued to increase all through the years of the Terceira-Tomár administration. By 1846 it had climbed to over 71,000 *contos*, or nearly 150,000,000 United States dollars, of which more than half was external debt—a staggering amount for a poverty-ridden little country.[1]

Costa Cabral deserves credit for some sincere efforts. But his reforms were too new fangled and outlandish to be understood or desired by the rural population of Portugal, especially the peasantry. One of his decrees, in the interest of public health and sanitation, forbade the burial of the dead in church yards and ordered them to be interred at some distance from the villages. This brought a revolt of peasants and priests in the province of Minho in 1846. Particularly did the women resist this decree, and the rebellion came to be known as the revolution of Maria da Fonte. Whether this Maria actually existed is not quite known; perhaps she was a collective name for the feminine resisters *en masse*. But certainly the movement swept the country, cheered on and assisted by the fallen Septembrists and the old supporters of Dom Miguel. It swept Costa Cabral out of office and out of the country. A government headed for a short time by the Duke of Palmela proved ineffective, and ultimately Saldanha came back to Portugal, where, with the permission and even the aid of the queen, he engineered a military *coup d'état* and seized power himself, ruling as a dictator. Saldanha still called himself a Chartist and brought many of the friends of Costa Cabral back to office and power.

This attempt to provide a radical cure for Portugal's ills accomplished nothing except to revive civil war. Sá da Bandeira and Saldanha, once old allies under Pedro, appeared in the field at the head of rival forces, still representing the Septembrists and Chartists, respectively. Neither side could obtain more than a dreary stalemate. Saldanha several times resigned from office and several times resumed it again. Costa Cabral made several more appearances in political life, each time in such a way as steadily to lessen his prestige. Portugal seemed to be dying a lingering death. The British government tried to arbitrate the sterile quarrel, and in

[1] H. V. Livermore, *A History of Portugal* (Cambridge University Press, Cambridge, England, 1947), p. 427.

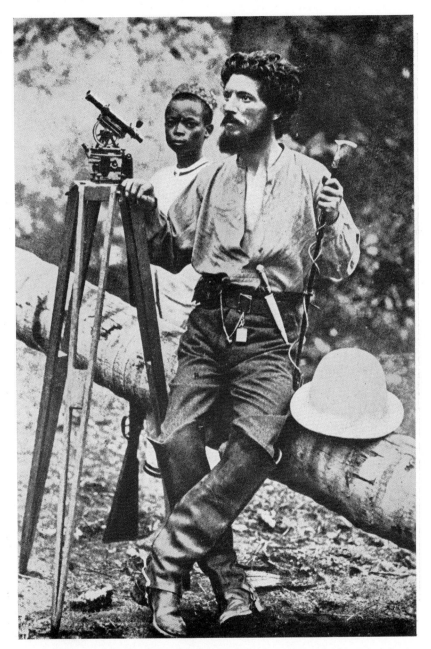

Serpa Pinto just after completing the crossing of Africa. From *História da expansão portuguesa no mundo*.

Monastery of the Jeronimos—The Westminster Abbey of Portugal. *Courtesy of Casa de Portugal, New York.*

1847 Spain actually did send an army of intervention into northern Portugal.[2]

Finally, in 1851, a turn came for the better. Saldanha, who had recently been out of office again, seized power by one of his usual *coups,* and then changed the name of his party from Chartist to Regenerator *(Regenerador).* At about the same time the Septembrists began to call themselves the Historic Party, but gradually dropped this in favor of the name Progressive. Weary of civil war and willing to try a change of technique, the Portuguese leaders abandoned violence for gentler political methods, and something akin to true parliamentarianism came into being. A modified form of the charter became the constitution and continued in force until the republic was proclaimed in 1910. The legislature consisted of two houses, the Peers and the Deputies. The House of Peers, at first an hereditary assembly, came to number 150 members, nominated by the sovereign for life, and including many besides the titled nobility, since some of the latter were left out. The House of Deputies, with a somewhat larger membership, was chosen by an electorate of male Portuguese able to meet a minimum property requirement. The ruler had a select advisory council of state, but the real ministry consisted of a cabinet and a prime minister governing by the support of the two houses and liable to fall when deprived of that support.

For the balance of Maria da Gloria's reign and for some years into the next one, Saldanha's Regenerator party continued as the government, with the Progressives acting as the opposition.

Queen Maria did not come of a long-lived family. Worn out by child-bearing and Portuguese politics, she died in 1853 at the age of thirty-four, while attempting to bring another prince into the world. Her eldest son, who ascended as Pedro V, was a minor, aged only sixteen. Therefore the king's father, Ferdinand, governed for a few years as regent. From this time onward, the royal line was technically the House of Coburg-Bragança, but the Portuguese generally preferred to use the old national name and exclude the German importation.

Any devoted Portuguese monarchist has reason to regret that Pedro V lived such a short life. Certainly he was one of the most promising young men who ever ascended a throne. His intelli-

[2] Fortunato de Almeida, *História de Portugal* (Coimbra, 1922-1929), VI, 312-315.

gence and the careful education he received prepared him to govern well. He had a passion for industry and for understanding all the problems with which he had to deal. As an enthusiastic advocate of the cultural and material improvement of Portugal, he easily ranks as the most attractive of the later Braganças. Had he lived even a normal span of years it is possible that he would have raised the prestige of the ruling house to the point where it could have withstood the shocks that laid it low within a few decades.[3]

Certainly few rulers have had more adversities to contend with than Pedro. His health was bad from the beginning, and a long life for him was plainly out of the question. He married Princess Stephanie of Hohenzollern-Sigmaringen in 1858 and was a widower within two months. Attacks of yellow fever and cholera ravaged Portugal during his reign and even nature took a hand, in the form of an earthquake which wrought heavy damage along the coast of the Algarve.

But there were a few bright spots in the picture. Portugal got its first railroad transportation in 1856 and its first telegraph line in the same year. Plans were made for an oceanic cable from Lisbon to the Azores and ultimately westward to the United States. The young king made a friend and unofficial adviser of the great historian and literary lion, Alexandre Herculano, and through his influence took effective steps to foster higher learning in Portugal. Popular education, however, continued to be retarded, and as late as 1910 four Portuguese out of five were classed as illiterate.

Saldanha's Regenerator ministry fell from power in 1856, being replaced by a Progressive government headed by the Marquis of Loulé and Sá da Bandeira. The latter, now definitely in the elder statesman class, took up the question of slavery in the colonies again. With the willing assistance of the young king, he sponsored a decree in 1858, ruling that in exactly twenty years' time all slaves in Portuguese territory should be freed.[4] This delay was decided upon in order to soften the blow to slave owners in Africa and to give them time to cushion themselves for the final

[3] Júlio de Vilhena, *D. Pedro V e o seu reinado*, 3 vols. (Imprensa da Universidade, Coimbra, 1921).
[4] *British and Foreign State Papers*, XLIX (1867), 1063.

shock. Everything went through as planned, though of course the final emancipation came in the reign of Pedro's brother Luís. Even after 1878 there were ugly rumors of slavery persisting in out-of-the-way parts of the Portuguese empire. The facts, as far as they can be learned, seem to be that Angola enforced the law fairly well, but that irregularities persisted for years in Mozambique.

The question of slavery, or rather slave traffic, caused Portugal to suffer a great diplomatic setback in the year 1858, which gave the nation every right to consider itself ill-used. A thinly disguised slave ship, the *Charles et Georges,* flying the French flag, had been taken by the Portuguese authorities off Mozambique late in 1857. She had on board a French official and a cargo of a hundred and ten Negroes. The captain of the *Charles et Georges* absurdly maintained that these were not slaves but voluntary colonists on their way to Reunion Island, a French possession. The Portuguese, having the word of the Negroes to the contrary, confiscated the ship and sentenced the captain to two years at hard labor. The news got to Lisbon, where Napoleon III's minister, the Marquis de Lisle, made a vigorous protest. This was backed by the French emperor, who evidently wished to show off for home consumption. After some hot diplomatic exchanges a French fleet anchored in the Tagus. The Portuguese appealed to their British ally, but England seemed indisposed toward any action. Portugal's prime minister, Loulé, did the only thing possible and handed over the *Charles et Georges,* which in the meantime had been brought to Lisbon. France still insisted on an indemnity, and the question of the amount was submitted to the arbitration of King William III of the Netherlands. He decided on the sum of 349,045 francs, which Portugal paid with bitterness, rightly feeling that it had been humiliated while trying to carry out a humanitarian program.[5]

Pedro V, always weak in body, died in 1861 at the age of twenty-four, being succeeded by his brother Luís. The new king, who was a year younger than Pedro, had not been educated for the throne but trained to follow the sea as an officer in the Portuguese navy. Thus his case was a little like that of William IV, the English "sailor king," a generation earlier. A high mortality rate was

[5] Fortunato de Almeida, *História de Portugal* (Coimbra, 1922-1929), VI, 362-378.

fast carrying off the numerous male progeny of Maria da Gloria, which made it desirable to make the new king a husband and father within as short a time as possible. So the year after his accession he espoused Maria Pia, daughter of Victor Emmanuel of the parvenu kingdom of Italy. The union was blessed by two sons.

Luís, unlike Pedro, did not aspire to much of a role in politics, and in general proved willing to let his Regenerator and Progressive statesmen fight out their parliamentary battles without his interference. In twenty-eight years of reigning, the king, to quote the words of Gilbert and Sullivan's *Iolanthe,* "did nothing in particular, and did it very well." He was what the Portuguese call an "apaixonado" for the arts, and he loved to entertain his court with amateur performances on the violoncello. In addition to this he made Shakespeare available to the Portuguese with translations of *Hamlet,* the *Merchant of Venice, Richard III,* and *Othello.*[6]

Although the monarch does not seem to have been of great importance in public life, the reign, which lasted until 1889, proved of considerable significance to Portugal. It was in these years that the country secured its main railway network and began to build tram lines for the larger cities. Several lines of track connected Lisbon and Oporto with Spain, and thence with the other countries of continental Europe. A submarine cable was built connecting Lisbon with Rio de Janeiro in Brazil. Foreign trade increased gradually, and Portuguese-owned steamships began to connect the capital with the Azores, the Madeiras, and various ports in Africa. Industry continued to be almost nonexistent, and such factories as there were in 1883, numbered only 1150, employed about 90,000 workers, and had a total output of scarcely over $30,000,000. Still, Portugal was distinctly wealthier than it had been a generation before, although the most pressing problem continued to be public finance and the debt. Regularly the budgets failed to balance by sums averaging 5,000 *contos,* but the governments felt that the public could not or would not stand increased taxation. These annual deficits were serious, but it is only fair to say that they did not indicate quite such a disastrous condition as in earlier decades. Since the national wealth and in-

[6] Fortunato de Almeida, *História de Portugal* (Coimbra, 1922-1929), VI, 412.

come had somewhat increased, this "red ink" at least represented comparatively smaller sums than previously.

Portugal had to hear once more from the Duke of Saldanha, before the fiery old marshal, revolutionist, and general free-lance, finally succumbed to senescence. He had been serving for some years as minister to France, but in 1869 he came back to Lisbon, now aged almost eighty. He alarmed the government by gathering about him all those military officers who were discontented with affairs in general and showed that he was still able to be the central figure in the country. He disliked the Loulé government, then in power, just as he had disliked many earlier ones. In May, 1870, he headed a military revolt and momentarily gained the ascendancy. The king had to send for the old marshal and consent to the dismissal of the entire Loulé ministry to be succeeded by a dictatorial one in which Saldanha held most of the important posts himself. Luís had evidently yielded just for the moment, knowing the old man to be a power in the country, but quietly worked with the main political parties to undo the damage as quickly as possible. Within a few months he induced Saldanha to accept the Portuguese Legation in London, and there the old firebrand lived the last six years of his life, while his country went back to constitutional forms.

The Saldanha *coup* had been connected with the problem of the succession to the Spanish throne, which had been vacant since 1868, when Marshal Prim, a Saldanha-esque character, had led a revolution and overthrown Isabel II. The Spaniards next shopped around for a ruler, and it was finally their offer of the throne to a Hohenzollern candidate that brought on the Franco-Prussian War of 1870. Prim himself would have preferred the father of King Luís, Ferdinand of Saxe-Coburg-Gotha, who was still in middle life, or, failing to get him, would have been glad to have Luís in person. Any such candidacy from Portugal was bound to involve complications and raise questions about the future independence of the country. Prim was known to have a Pan-Iberian program, which in plain words meant the ultimate absorption of Portugal by its larger and stronger neighbor. Saldanha appears to have been converted to Pan-Iberianism, and his intention after engineering his *coup* had been to push the candidacy of Ferdinand. The king's father did once go so far as to accept the Spanish offer, but only upon certain conditions that would insure Portugal an independent future. Prim would not agree to the terms, and in the meantime the Franco-Prussian War broke out and Amadeo of Savoy accepted the Spanish crown, which he was glad to abandon in less than three years. The Portuguese considered themselves well out of the whole affair, and Ferdinand had meanwhile disqualified himself from any more thrones by marrying his mistress, a German actress named Elisa Hensler.

The last quarter of the nineteenth century saw the major powers of Europe and some of the minor ones scrambling to take part in the partition of Africa, a continent where Portugal still had some important holdings. But as late as 1875, the present vast Portuguese empire in Africa existed mostly on paper. Aside from the Cape Verde Islands, it consisted of Portuguese Guinea, Angola, and Mozambique. The Guinea possession involved only a few population centers on the Atlantic. The larger colonies of Angola and Mozambique consisted of thin lines of settlements, also along the coast, with some attempted jurisdiction over the inland native tribes. But the jurisdiction grew nominal a few miles from the sea, and dwindled away to nothing in the real interior. Angola and Mozambique lie in approximately the same latitude, and Portugal had always claimed to rule from sea to sea. But in practice the claim meant nothing, and there is no record of any crossing of the continent at that point before 1801, when a Portuguese speaking Negro *Pombeiro*, as the Angola frontiersmen were called, attempted to find a route across. Ten years later he turned up at a Portuguese settlement on the Zambezi in Mozambique. He straightway started back and reappeared in Angola in 1814, having consumed a total of thirteen years in transit.[7]

Sporadic Portuguese exploration followed in the nineteenth century. Joaquim Rodrigues Graça, in the years 1846 to 1848, penetrated to the court of the curious Negro ruler called the Muata Yanvo, in the territory of the present Belgian Congo; and a few years later Francisco da Silva Porto, an Angola Portuguese, traveled eastward all the way to the headwaters of the Zambezi. But it was not until after the explorations by Livingstone and Stanley that the Portuguese government realized that Africa was

[7] Charles E. Nowell, "Portugal and the Partition of Africa," *Journal of Modern History*, XIX (1947), 2.

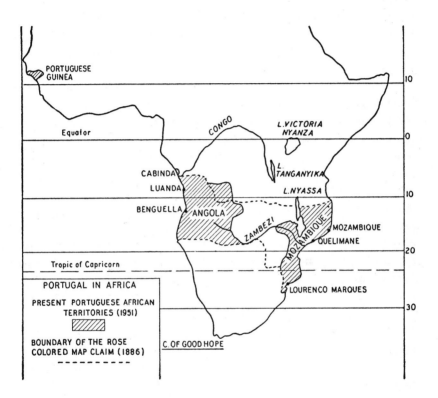

PORTUGUESE
GUINEA

CONGO

L.VICTORIA
NYANZA

Equator

CABINDA

LUANDA

BENGUELLA

ANGOLA

L.
TANGANYIKA

L.NYASSA

ZAMBEZI

MOZAMBIQUE

MOZAMBIQUE

QUELIMANE

Tropic of Capricorn

PORTUGAL IN AFRICA

PRESENT PORTUGUESE AFRICAN
   TERRITORIES (1951)

BOUNDARY OF THE ROSE
COLORED MAP CLAIM (1886)

LOURENCO MARQUES

C. OF GOOD HOPE

10

0

10

20

30

now very much in the foreground and that, if Portugal was not to be crowded out completely, there must be a revival of activity.

The opening gun in the race for Africa was fired by King Leopold II of Belgium in 1876, when he called an international conference of geographers at Brussels, where an association for exploring and civilizing Central Africa was formed under his presidency. From this nucleus grew the Congo Free State, which later became the Belgian Congo. By an odd oversight, Portugal had not been invited to send anyone to the Brussels meeting. The Lisbon Geographical Society, which had been formed the year before, urged the government of King Luís to take action for maintaining Portuguese rights in Africa. The society believed that the Portuguese, who had proved themselves good colonizers in the past, might be able to create in Africa a great dominion that would compensate them for the loss of Brazil half a century earlier.

Despite deficits, an empty treasury, and lack of a strong navy and merchant marine, the Portuguese government in some measure responded. Most of the original planning fell to João de Andrade Corvo, Minister of the Navy and the Colonies in the cabinet, to be carried on later by such statesmen as Manuel Pinheiro Chagas and Henrique de Barros Gomes. A well-equipped exploring expedition was prepared, headed by Alexandre de Serpa Pinto of the army and Hermenegildo de Brito Capelo and Roberto Ivens of the navy. The purpose was to explore the Angolan hinterland more thoroughly and to find a route across Africa and map the basins of the Congo and the Zambezi. Proceeding into the hinterland of Angola in 1877, the explorers divided their work, Brito Capelo and Ivens swinging northward through the *sertão,* or frontier wilderness,[8] and Serpa Pinto traveling through the continent. The three accomplished their mission well, even though Serpa Pinto, instead of proceeding straight eastward to Mozambique, was forced to drop gradually southward until he finally emerged at Pretoria in the Boer republic of the Transvaal.[9]

---

[8] Hermenegildo de Brito Capelo and Roberto Ivens, *From Benguella to the Territory of Yacca,* transl. Alfred Elwes, 2 vols. (S. Low, Marston, Searle, and Rivington, London, 1882).

[9] Alexandre de Serpa Pinto, *Como eu atravessei a Africa; do Atlantico ao mar Indico,* 2 vols. (S. Low, Marston, Searle, and Rivington, London, 1881).

In 1884, when Pinheiro Chagas was minister of the Navy and Colonies, Brito Capelo and Ivens were ordered to Africa again. Their mission this time was to link Angola definitely with Mozambique, in order that Portugal might place a chain of posts across the continent to assist travel and trade in the future. In a march of fifteen months, they gained the necessary geographical information, emerging on the east coast at the mouth of the Zambezi River in June, 1885.[10] In the meantime, Serpa Pinto had led a party through northern Mozambique as far as Lake Nyassa, where illness had forced him to abandon his enterprise, although the original plan had been for him to join forces with Brito Capelo and Ivens at the confluence of the Xiré (Shire) and the Zambezi.[11] At about the same time, Major Henrique de Carvalho had carried out another step in the ambitious Portuguese plan by heading a new expedition to the Muata Yanvo, where the intention was to establish a resident in the near future.[12]

Portugal had plenty of brave explorers, but its fatal weakness was the lack at home of adequate capital, merchant marine, and industry to back any solid colonial program. Some attempts were made, however, to carry through the ambitious plans in spite of these obvious handicaps. Major Paiva de Andrada, an enthusiast for Africa, formed the Mozambique Company with the assistance of the noted Portuguese historian Oliveira Martins, most of the capital being supplied from outside Portugal. Paiva de Andrada's earlier operations took place mostly in the neighborhood of the Pungwe River, where there was a magnificent natural harbor and where he built the thriving town of Beira. The principal interest of the company at first lay in mining, and Paiva de Andrada hoped to push inland to the Manica region, reported to be rich in minerals. Besides importing engineers and workmen to develop the coastal zone, Paiva de Andrada led important interior explorations himself. A galaxy of able explorers and administrators worked with him, including António Cardoso and Vitor Cordón. The story of their operations is too long and complicated for any detailed review, but the Mozambique Company ultimately grew into the largest colonizing enterprise in Portuguese Africa.

[10] Charles E. Nowell, *Journal of Modern History*, XIX, 11.
[11] *Ibid.*, p. 10.
[12] *Ibid.*, pp. 10-11.

The home government had meanwhile been using every diplomatic means to insure possession of the great corridor through Africa connecting its coastwise colonies. Portugal sent representatives to Berlin in 1884-85 to attend Bismarck's Africa Conference. They returned home with the assurance that the northern frontier of Angola would reach the Congo, and they also gained title to two small possessions just north of the river. In 1886, Portugal signed a treaty with France, settling the boundary between Portuguese Guinea and French West Africa, and by one of its clauses the French government recognized Portugal's right to the Angola-Mozambique corridor. A few months later, a treaty with Germany adjusted the boundaries between Angola and Mozambique and the adjoining German territories, with a similar guarantee regarding Portuguese rights to the hinterland.

The dream now seemed in a fair way to approach reality. Only the British had failed to endorse the program, and even they had given halfway approval to the idea by allowing an Anglo-Portuguese treaty regarding mutual navigation of the Zambezi to be worded so as to end English influence at the river. Although the treaty had not yet been ratified, Portugal counted the battle as good as won. So, when Minister Barros Gomes rose to explain some points to the cortes in 1886, he used the famous *mapa côr de rosa* (rose-colored map) to illustrate his speech.[13] This showed a giant Portuguese African empire which was rose-tinted. It took in both Angola and Mozambique and connected them by an enormous intervening area, including Northern and Southern Rhodesia and a good part of Nyassaland. It seemed to Barros Gomes and his listeners that the *mapa côr de rosa* had already become a geographical fact.

But they had reckoned without Cecil Rhodes and the British South Africa company, which he founded in 1889 with the dukes of Abercorn and Fife as more or less dummy directors. The company meant to push British control all the way from Bechuanaland to Tanganyika, which would of course mean confining Portuguese Mozambique to a strip along the coast. Rhodes hated the Portuguese and would have driven them out of Africa entirely if he could have had his way. Soon the Portuguese and English were waging an undeclared war for influence over the natives in Manica

[13] Charles E. Nowell, *Journal of Modern History,* XIX, 13.

and Mashonaland, being directed principally by Paiva de Andrada and Cecil Rhodes. It is worth noting that the British were not making notable headway in ousting the Portuguese until their government stepped in to exert its overwhelming power. With all these causes making for friction, a decisive collision could not be long in coming.

It came along the Xiré River of Nyassaland, late in 1889. Serpa Pinto had been sent there from East Africa to trace a route for a railway which the Portuguese intended to build. But the British anticipated him by sending an official to declare that the neighboring Makalolos were under Queen Victoria's protection and requesting Serpa Pinto to withdraw. The famous explorer declined to do so, and as quickly as the news got back to London and Lisbon the two governments took up the matter. After some preliminary parleying, Great Britain presented Portugal with a list of demands, on January 11, 1890, which amounted to an ultimatum. The Portuguese were required to retire their forces immediately from the Xiré and Mashonaland, and the penalty for refusal would be the withdrawal of the British Minister from Lisbon, which obviously meant war. The Portuguese government had to yield to the threat of superior force, but feeling ran so high in the country that the Barros Gomes government straightway fell from power. It was still hoped that the territorial disputes might be arbitrated, but Lord Salisbury, the British foreign minister, declined this. Later, Portugal had to accept a treaty which drew approximately the present boundary line between Mozambique and the British territory.

Portugal was naturally infuriated, because this ended the *mapa côr de rosa* dream forever. The nation, wounded in its pride, felt that the time-honored British ally had struck an unfair blow. But in spite of the national humiliation involved, the retreat forced by the ultimatum was probably a blessing in disguise. Portugal had grasped for more territory than could possibly be held or developed, and still retained more than enough in Africa to use up all spare capital and energy.

In the year 1895 Portugal had an opportunity to show the world that it could act effectively and decisively in a colonial crisis. A rebellion broke out in southern Mozambique, where the leading settlement, Lourenço Marques, almost fell into native hands. Heading the insurrection was Gungunhana, the powerful king of the Vatuas, a fighting people of Zulu stock who lived in Gazaland near the Limpopo. With Portuguese rule on the verge of collapse, the Lisbon government sent out its ablest colonial administrator, António Enes, to act as high commissioner for the duration of the crisis. Soon small Portuguese columns were setting out for the interior to attack Gungunhana, who in addition to his own people had the allegiance of many chiefs who reckoned his power superior to that of the Portuguese. Led by a group of fearless officers—Eduardo Galhardo, Paiva Couceiro, Caldas Xavier, and Mousinho de Albuquerque—the Portuguese showed that their heroic days were not entirely in the past. Time after time they smashed Vatua armies outnumbering them many to one, and their crowning victory came on November 6, 1895, at Lake Coolela, where Gungunhana's main forces were broken. Mousinho de Albuquerque then performed the most spectacular feat of the war when, with a small band of followers, he made a cross-country dash to the rebel king's *kraal* and captured him in the midst of his warriors. Mousinho brought Gungunhana down to the coast, and from there he was sent to Lisbon and later to the Azores to end his days in captivity. This broke the back of the rebellion, though several extra campaigns were necessary in Mozambique before the last resistance ended.[14]

The war gave the hero-loving Portuguese public a new idol in Mousinho de Albuquerque. He received the wildest ovations on returning home and was made tutor of the king's sons. It is sad to relate that this brave officer ended his life by suicide in a Lisbon railway carriage in 1902.

The complete subjection of the vast Angola territory allotted to Portugal in the African partition was a slow matter. It took the form of small-scale campaigns, waged year after year, in the Angolan hinterland. The pacification had not been completed by 1910, and the Portuguese republic finished what the monarchy had begun.

Even now, however, it is hard to say whether all this African territory was really a blessing for Portugal or merely another drain on the small, poverty-stricken nation. As early as 1898 Great Britain and Germany signed a treaty by which they agreed to a

[14] António Enes, *A guerra de África em 1895* (Typ. do "Dia," Lisbon, 1898).

partition of the colonies should Portugal default on a future loan. Before World War I, German forces from Southwest Africa were steadily encroaching on Angola, evidently with the feeling that the territory would soon be theirs. But circumstances kept intervening to spare Portugal the loss of its colonies, partly because England was never a very willing partner in the partition plan. For better or for worse, all Portuguese parties and factions are bent on retaining the empire regardless of cost, since it is one of the remaining sources of national pride and a reminder of the glorious past.

Republicanism grew steadily in Portugal during the last decade of the nineteenth century. King Luís died in 1889, and was succeeded by his son Carlos. The fact that the huge daughter state, Brazil, overthrew its Bragança emperor, Dom Pedro II, in that same year and established a republic had some effect on the Portuguese public. The British ultimatum, which followed almost immediately, weakened the royal house greatly in Portuguese estimation. The republicans began to say openly that the English alliance had never been anything but a private bargain with the Bragança family to keep the royal line enthroned and that it meant nothing to the people of Portugal. Carlos, the new king, was a man of energy and evidently of some ability, but he did little to win the nation's love, either for himself or for his dynasty. A yacht owner and a sportsman, he had expensive tastes and pleasures. It was rumored and later verified that he drew more money from the public treasury than the official accounts showed.[15] And in the meantime a section of the Portuguese had become convinced that a republic would furnish the solution to all their problems.

For years the Portuguese government had been an imitation of the British constitutional monarchy system. But, although the forms could be copied, the breath of life could not be injected into them. Regenerators and Progressives had none of the vitality of Conservatives and Liberals, and were, in fact, coteries of politicians who played a never-ending game, without solid backing from the country. Elections consisted of little more than the two parties bidding against each other to buy the votes of the public.

[15] E. J. Dillon, "Republican Portugal," *Contemporary Review* (November, 1910), p. 519.

By the twentieth century it was hard to tell in what respect one party differed from the other. *Caciqueism* flourished in Portugal, just as it did in Spain. This meant that in the towns and villages of the country, the parties' interests were handled by local bosses, known colloquially as *caciques,* an old West Indian word for "chiefs." The business of a *cacique* was to deliver, at all costs, the local vote in elections and to act as the distributor of local political favors. Under such conditions, the never-ending changes of government and ministerial shake-ups failed to interest the people greatly, especially as long experience had taught them that these changes would mean nothing.

An embryonic Portuguese republican party had made an appearance in the early seventies and in 1878 elected its first deputy, from an Oporto constituency. But the movement made small headway until 1890 and the British ultimatum, after which recruits to the republican cause came fast. Among the leaders were Dr. Teófilo Braga, professor of literature at the University of Coimbra, and the poet Guerra Junqueiro. In 1891, the year after the ultimatum, a republican uprising took place at Oporto. It was suppressed without much difficulty, but a larger number of republican deputies soon began to appear in the national cortes. Anticlericalism was of course a mainstay of the republican program. Teófilo Braga, while Portugal was still smarting from the 1890 ultimatum, said the four main causes of the country's decadence were the Inquisition, the Jesuits, the Braganças, and the English alliance. Although the Jesuits had been expelled by Pombal in 1759, and although there had been a wholesale suppression of monastic orders in 1834, the orders had returned later in the nineteenth century. From the politico-economic point of view, it probably no longer made much difference whether they left or remained. But they made a convenient scapegoat, since whatever influence they wielded was likely to be on the monarchist side.

As the two old monarchist parties degenerated, there remained few leaders with courage enough to risk anything in support of the throne. But the picture on the republican side was far from bright, as far as assurance for the nation's future was concerned. Some of the anti-monarchists were visionaries and dreamers like Teófilo Braga; others were politicians who looked upon the republic as the rising star and therefore decided to ingratiate themselves with the movement. Just before the fall of the monarchy, republicanism at its lowest level came to be represented by the Carbonaria Society, named in imitation of a much earlier revolutionary organization in Italy. The Carbonaria was distinctly a burrowing organization, which existed to sow revolutionary propaganda in the army and navy and among the civil service employees.

In the face of this growing republicanism, the Portuguese government could think of little to do except wait and hope for the best. It was, however, the worst that finally came. In 1906, Prime Minister Hintze Ribeiro informed King Carlos that in his opinion the only way to save the government was to proclaim an instant dictatorship. The king, after giving the matter brief consideration, declined to permit the dictatorship, saying that he felt such a move would disintegrate the monarchy rather than consolidate it, by alienating many people who up to then had been reasonably contented. "Woe betide those," said Carlos, "who can only rule in such a manner." [16]

In retrospect, the king's misgivings seem to have been based more on lack of confidence in Hintze Ribeiro than on distaste for dictatorship, because Carlos soon gave João Franco almost the same power that Hintze had asked for in vain. Franco was a wealthy, strong-willed man of the Regenerator party, the "last monarchist in Portugal." He hoped, by giving the country a "liberal monarchy" and an honest administration, to bring the royal house back into popular favor. There seems to be no question of his fundamental honesty and desire to serve both the king and the country well. Called at first by Carlos to head a ministry, he cut costs by abolishing sinecure offices and other wasteful expenses. The cortes began to hate him and to demand his resignation. The king now had to make a choice between his favorite minister and the old constitutional forms, and so entrusted Franco with full powers. For the moment Franco seemed to be the answer to all the country's needs, and the king spoke delightedly of his program for wiping out the deficit. The republicans hated the dictator, either because they feared his power or, possibly, as has been suggested, because they were afraid he would purify the

[16] V. de Bragança-Cunha, *Revolutionary Portugal, 1910-1936* (J. Clarke & Co., ltd., London, 1937), p. 76.

administration sufficiently to do actually what he intended—namely, restore monarchial prestige.

The dictatorship of Franco ended suddenly and drastically. On February 1, 1908, the royal family returned by boat to Lisbon from Vila Viçosa, where they had been staying. There had been disorders and violence in the city during the past few days, but the situation seemed quiet for the moment. Carlos had asked Franco if it would be safe for his family to ride through the streets, and the answer had been that they could do so with perfect security. As they entered their landau at the Terreiro do Paço, a crowd naturally gathered. They were proceeding toward the Necessidades palace when suddenly a young man leaped in back of the carriage and shot the king twice with a revolver, killing him instantly. A moment later another assassin fired and killed the heir to the throne, Prince Luís. Manuel, the second prince, received a wound in the arm which was not particularly serious.[17]

Franco fell from power at once, and the new king, Manuel II, a boy of less than nineteen, was left suddenly and helplessly at the helm. His father, at the time of his assassination, had been a vigorous man in the prime of life, and might normally have lived many years. Since Manuel had not been expected to inherit the throne, he had not only the handicap of youth but a lack of any training for the duties of kingship.

Although his "reign" lasted until October 4, 1910, it was merely a period of waiting until the republicans felt ready to take over control of the state. The Portuguese monarchy had effectively expired with King Carlos, for Manuel was "not an heir but an orphan." [18] Several ministries rose and fell during the brief marking-time period in which the last Bragança nominally ruled. No leader of any force or energy appeared to sustain the monarchy in its dying moments. The republican revolution was known to be in the offing, and by 1910 it was fairly certain that it would come before the end of the year. Foreign journalists even went to Portugal to witness the obsequies of monarchy.[19]

[17] Francis Gribble, *The Royal House of Portugal* (Eveleigh Nash, London, 1915), pp. 284-285.
[18] João Ameal, *História de Portugal* (Livraria Tavares Martins, Oporto, 1940), p. 752.
[19] E. J. Dillon, "The Portuguese Revolution," *Living Age* (December 3, 1910), p. 579.

A Residential Section of Lisbon—The Alvalade District. *Courtesy of Casa de Portugal, New York.*

Premier António de Oliveira Salazar of Portugal. *Courtesy of Wide World.*

Yet there is little evidence that the revolution came as any real expression of popular will. An election in the summer of 1910 returned only fourteen republican deputies to the cortes, eleven of them from Lisbon, which naturally showed the most radicalism. But the republicans were organized and eager; the monarchists, disheartened and apathetic.

The hour struck on October 4, 1910. Most of the risks were run by António Machado dos Santos, president of the Carbonaria Society, who directed a handful of followers. There was a little shooting and a little shelling of the royal palace from ships of the navy that had passed over to the republicans. The revolution triumphed not primarily because of its own strength but because almost no one lifted a hand to oppose. By the following day, the young king and his mother were on their way to Gibraltar aboard the royal yacht. From there they went to England, where Manuel spent most of his remaining days. A provisional government, headed by the elderly professor, Teófilo Braga, was set up in Lisbon and began to function immediately.

Portugal was a republic. A monarchy almost eight centuries old had gone down before a revolutionary faction. Events would soon prove that the republicans had little idea of what to do with the nation they had suddenly taken over.

Chapter XV

CULTURE IN THE NINETEENTH AND TWENTIETH CENTURIES

As the French Revolution approached, Portuguese literature was still in the Pseudo-classical stage, which meant that there was a great deal of imitation of French and Spanish writing. With illiteracy still so prevalent in the country, literary work was largely monopolized by a few cultured amateurs who had no idea of addressing a large public. Circles and clubs existed, in which the members heard and criticized each others' endeavors, which later on might or might not find their way into publication. Poetry and drama predominated, the plays usually dealing with historical themes and being composed according to the classical rules of unity. Since the Portuguese theater was virtually dead at that time, performance of a drama was rare, so the authors seldom worried about the stage possibilities of their work.

The Portuguese Royal Academy of History, formed by João V early in the century, was succeeded in 1780 by the Royal Academy of Sciences, which still exists with a name slightly altered since the republican revolution of 1910. From the beginning, the Academy of Sciences gave a liberal interpretation to its functions, because in addition to mathematics, physics, and medicine it took in most of the humanities and heavily emphasized historical studies. Soon it undertook the valuable work of editing and publishing important sources of Portuguese history. For the first time, thanks to the Academy, the history of the great overseas discoveries, which is the richest part of the national heritage, began to receive due attention. As time passed, this emphasis grew heavier, and Portuguese scholarship compensated for the earlier neglect by possibly overstressing the Age of Discovery.

Portugal produced no eminent poet between Camões, who died in 1580, and Barbosa du Bocage (1765-1805).[1] Although Bocage was a literary free lance, belonging to no particular school, it is easy to see the approach of the romantic movement, both in the literary forms he used and in the content of his poetry. Like Camões, he lived an intense and romantic life, exuding poetry at every pore. It is reported of him, perhaps apocryphally, that he once improvised a verse to recite to an armed bandit who held him up as he returned home late at night after a convivial evening spent in a tavern. Anecdotes like this told about Bocage were seized upon avidly by the general public, and the result has been to give him probably more of a reputation as a tavern brawler than he really deserved. The favorite theme of Bocage's writing was love, upon which he bestowed an exceedingly rich vocabulary and a verbal power suggestive of Poe and Baudelaire.

Portugal entered the romantic period in the fullest sense after the end of the Napoleonic wars and the beginning of the constitutional struggle. This was the era of Byron, Goethe, Chateaubriand, and Manzoni. In obscure countries like Portugal, the movement was bound to be somewhat imitative, but it is also true that here it played more than the normal role in public life and in the course of historical events. It is hard to say whether, in Portugal, literature became the handmaiden of politics or politics the handmaiden of literature. Many of the leading men took part in both activities. The literary production of the various nineteenth-century decades certainly well reflected the vicissitudes through which the nation was passing.

José de Almeida Garrett (1799-1854), a native of Oporto and a liberal constitutionalist of 1821, was several times exiled from Portugal because of his views. But whenever his friends were in power Garrett held government offices of some importance. His poem *Camões*, written in 1825, is commonly taken as the first great landmark of Portuguese literary romanticism. Garrett's *Camões* is both romantic and revolutionary, making its appeal to the glories of the Portuguese national past and having no strain of Greco-Roman classicism. To Garrett is also due a sustained

[1] Barbosa du Bocage, *Poesias*, ed. Guerreiro Murta (Sá da Costa, Lisbon, 1943).

effort to revive the Portuguese theater after centuries of the doldrums, naturally in the interest of romanticism. He not only worked hard as a dramatist, using national historical themes, but he encouraged others to do the same and personally promoted theatrical enterprises. He had success enough to make it possible to say that the revived Portuguese theater dates from him.[2]

Alexandre Herculano de Carvalho (1810-1877) is so well known as the pioneer in modern Portuguese historiography that his reputation rests mostly on his scholarly work. But it is well to remember that in his own time he was regarded as Portugal's most brilliant prose stylist whose fiction was more read than his history. Herculano, in the beginning, was another romantic liberal. Too young to have any share in the constitutional cortes movement of 1821, he later fought under Pedro of Brazil against Dom Miguel. After the victory he held government posts, none of them very important. He visited England but came more under the influence of France, where Augustin Thierry and others were finding an outlet for their talents by writing history. Deeming it disgraceful that Portuguese historiography should have sunk so low, Herculano determined to give his nation a true picture of its national past. His first volume, based on the best historical sources, appeared in 1846, and by 1853 he had completed the fourth, carrying the story to the reign of Afonso III in the thirteenth century. But as these volumes appeared they were attacked in the press and from the pulpit, largely by ignoramuses who accused Herculano of treason and atheism because he made light of the old fables and pious legends regarding the origins of Portugal. He proved somewhat thin skinned over this and, though he had friends and encouragers, decided not to finish the work. His own sarcastic statement was that if he had wished to be popular he should have declared that one Portuguese had always been a match for three Spaniards and two Frenchmen.

Herculano, although once fairly orthodox in faith, turned anticlerical because of the priestly reaction to his history. He ultimately revenged himself on the clergy by writing of the origin and establishment of the Inquisition in Portugal. Here the sources were much more recent than those for primitive Portugal and not

[2] Figueiredo, *Literatura portuguesa* (Editora a Noite, Rio de Janeiro, 1940), pp. 259-263.

at all doubtful as to meaning. In this way he scored a belated triumph, although the gain to scholarship would have been greater had he gone ahead with his early work. In the course of his life he also wrote many novels and short tales, invariably based on the historic past of Portugal or Spain—sometimes the remote past. Best known of his novels is *Euric the Presbyter,* in which the theme is the question of clerical celibacy, but to give it a setting Herculano goes all the way back to Visigothic times.

Herculano had a host of imitators who continued to pour out historical romances until almost the end of the century. Steadily the quality of the products declined until the whole movement was largely laughed out of existence by Eça de Queiroz, much as Cervantes once ridiculed the romances of chivalry. Eça had one of his literary characters write what might be called the romance to end all romances, and the plot, which he outlined with a great deal of care, was ridiculous enough to drive the point home.[3]

The only Miguelist intellectual of any distinction was the Viscount de Santarem (1790-1856). After the defeat of his party and the enthronement of Maria da Gloria, Santarem chose exile and thereafter lived in Paris. In the libraries of France, superior to those at home, he carried on learned studies that made him the founder of Portuguese historical geography. By tireless work with old maps and texts, the viscount, whose voluntary exile from his country did not lessen his love of it, stoutly maintained the primacy of the Portuguese as pioneers in navigation and overseas discovery. He was right in some of his contentions and mistaken in others, but the international reputation he won certainly gave Portuguese letters and scholarship an increased standing abroad at a time when little attention would have been paid to a scholar living in Lisbon or Oporto.[4]

A much younger romantic contemporary of Herculano was Julio Dinís (1839-1817). Since he lived in quieter times and was delicate in body, Dinís did not mingle much in politics. He was a doctor of medicine, but he practiced little, becoming instead a lecturer in the medical school of Oporto. His main works were

[3] Figueiredo, *Literatura portuguesa* (Editora a Noite, Rio de Janeiro, 1940), pp. 263-273.

[4] Of Santarem's numerous works, which include considerable editing of old documents, the best known is *Recherches sur la priorité de la découverte des pays situées sur la côte occidentale d'Afrique au-dela du Cap Bojador* (Paris, 1842).

all novels, which can be classified as romantic, but he did not seek inspiration in the past, laying all his plots in the Portugal of his own day. He was a sensitive soul who avoided writing on subjects that repelled him. Moreover, he became a literary spokesman for the middle class and the particular views on love and marriage that are commonly associated with that class. His novels therefore were always "respectable," breathing a note of cheerfulness and serenity. The heroes and heroines had their difficulties but always succeeded in overcoming them, to provide a happy ending. Perhaps the best known of the Dinís novels is *An English Family,* in which the setting is Oporto. The author died at the age of thirty-two, when his powers were still developing and when his best work should have been still ahead of him.[5]

Portugal's three best nineteenth-century poets were João de Deus (1830-1896), Antero de Quental (1842-1891), and Guerra Junqueiro (1850-1923), although it will be noted that the last of the three lived well into the twentieth century. Somewhat different as to type and style, they are all classed as realists.

João de Deus found the romantic Portuguese poetry that stemmed from Garrett's great *Camões* going sadly to seed. He started a reaction by replacing artificiality of form and language with simplicity and clarity. His entire poetic works, which are published in a collection called *Campo de Flores* (Field of Flowers), are most noted for their lyric qualities, and it is in that vein that João de Deus must be most highly esteemed as a poet.[6]

Antero de Quental, like many another Portuguese literary figure, was born in the Azores. When young he traveled widely in Europe and America and became a socialist. He finally ceased being a doctrinaire reformer, but never lost his social conscience. His private griefs and gloomy outlook for the future drove him to suicide before reaching the age of fifty. His verses have been published in four collections, one posthumously, and each represents a different stage in Antero's life and thought, with the tone growing steadily more pessimistic. The *Hymn of the Morning,* which is an ironic title, may be called his confession of faith, and is perhaps the extremist profession of pessimism in the Portuguese

[5] Figueiredo, *Literatura portuguesa* (Editora a Noíte, Rio de Janeiro, 1940), pp. 284-288.
[6] *Ibid.,* pp. 303-304.

language. From Camões to Antero de Quental, Portuguese poetry had traveled a long road indeed, even though Antero, in spite of his early departure from the Catholicism of his youth, continued to be intrigued occasionally by religious subjects.[7]

Guerra Junqueiro was interested in politics all his life. He joined the growing Portuguese republican party after the humiliating English ultimatum of 1890, and when the republic was proclaimed twenty years later he became its diplomatic representative in Switzerland. Being a social revolutionary poet, he turned to social themes, including disease, bad sanitation, and the sufferings of the poor; themes that Portuguese poets had been in the habit of neglecting. But for all his modernity, Junqueiro belongs essentially to the nineteenth century, and to him Victor Hugo was the beau ideal. Among his numerous poetic writings are a most unromantic version of the Don Juan legend, the *Hymn of Hate,* and the *Fatherland.* In the last-named piece, Junqueiro paints a most pessimistic picture of Portugal at the turn of the century, castigating the monarchy, clericalism, and Donjuanism as the main causes of the nation's ills.[8]

It is rather hard to assign Joaquim Oliveira Martins (1845-1894) a definite niche in Portuguese thought and literature, because he does not easily submit to classification. An engineer, railway director, and founder with Paiva de Andrada of the Mozambique Company, Oliveira Martins was chiefly a writer of history. But he had none of the romanticism of Herculano, nor is it solely as an interpreter of the past that he is remembered. He wrote voluminously, the subjects embracing anthropology, mythology, world history, and Portuguese history. His biographical studies included the sons of João I, as well as lives of Nuno Álvares and João II. His famous *History of Portugal* is primarily a series of brilliant sketches, picturing the country at various stages during its past. Like his contemporaries, Antero de Quental and Guerra Junqueiro, Oliveira Martins was essentially pessimistic. He felt that Portuguese history had taken the wrong turn centuries before when the country allowed itself to be drawn away from its rightful home mission in answer to the siren call of the East. Possibly because in his writings he went far beyond the history of his own

[7] *Ibid.,* pp. 304-309.
[8] *Ibid.,* pp. 309-317.

country, Oliveira Martins had the most distinct historical philosophy of any nineteenth-century Portuguese. Since his style was brilliant and his work always interesting, he was greatly read, and his ideas deeply penetrated the consciousness of the Portuguese people, at least the literate percentage. Although little is heard of republicanism on his part, he made his dissatisfaction with the government plain enough, and so had a share in bringing on the republic which came sixteen years after his death at the age of forty-nine.[9]

Of all Portuguese realistic novelists, José de Eça de Queiroz (1845-1900) is by far the most famous and doubtless the best. In earlier years he traveled widely in America, Europe, and the Near East. He belonged to a group of young literary men in Lisbon which included Antero de Quental, and for a time he directed a literary magazine called *Revista de Portugal*. In spite of a little early experimenting with other literary forms, he soon settled on the novel as his true vehicle. His keen powers of observation and understanding of human psychology made him a realist, while his irony and wit made him always entertaining even to readers who did not like what he had to say. Impossible though it is to go into any detailed account of Eça's novels, among those especially worth remembering are *The Crime of Father Amaro, The Relic,* and *The Illustrious House of Ramires.*

The first deals with that same problem of clerical celibacy that Herculano handled so romantically in his *Euric.* Eça substituted observation and knowledge of human nature for Herculano's romantic imagination and historical erudition. Naturally the fundamental tone of the novel is very different. *The Relic* is the rather comic story of a young Lisbon libertine who feigns virtue in order to sponge off a wealthy maiden aunt who is extremely pious and whose fortune he hopes to inherit. Persuading her to finance him in a "pilgrimage" to the Holy Land, he goes off and has interesting adventures during which he experiences a vision of the last days of Christ and the crucifixion. Not fundamentally altered by this, he returns to his aunt, but in presenting her with the souvenirs of his journey he makes a fatal mistake and is disinherited. This turns out to be a blessing in disguise, because it forces him to

[9] Fidelino de Figueiredo, *Literatura portuguesa* (Editora a Noite, Rio de Janeiro, 1940), pp. 327-332.

reform and become a successful man by hard work. *The Illustrious House of Ramires* is the story of a descendant of the bluest blooded *fidalgos* and his attempt to reconcile the ideals of his ancient, noble line with the realities of nineteenth-century Portugal.[10]

With Eça the century ends, and after that it is difficult to trace any pattern of Portuguese literature.[11] At the turn of the century the dean of Portuguese letters was Dr. Teófilo Braga (1843-1924), a professor at Coimbra who devoted himself to the study and revival of Portuguese literature of all eras. Dr. Braga studied and wrote voluminously and was responsible for the finding and reappearance of many treasures of the past. But with all this vast learning, Braga's mind was neither well ordered nor disciplined. Capable of boundless enthusiasms, it was nevertheless often careless and slipshod. Already it has been pointed out that Braga was an enthusiastic republican, and true to his doctrinaire notions he expected altogether too much from a Portuguese republic. However much or little his writing and preaching had to do with overthrowing the Braganças, the republicans recognized his services sufficiently to give him the provisional presidency of the republic. This "visionary from a medieval university," as one unfriendly critic wrote, would probably have done better to stay with his books. The position with respect to literature once held by Braga probably belongs today to Fidelino de Figueiredo (b. 1889), a much clearer and more penetrating critic, who is as well known in Brazil as in Portugal and who has several times traveled and lectured in the United States.

Portuguese literature in the twentieth century does not seem to have produced any masterpieces, but such novelists as Julio Brandão, Carlos Malheiro Dias, and Aquilino Ribeiro are worth mention.

In the other arts, there is little to be said for Portugal. No sculptor, painter, or composer of that country enjoys more than a local reputation. Although the Portuguese are music lovers their contributions to music are slight. Lisbon has its concert and opera seasons, but foreign works and artists usually have the preference just as is true in the United States.

[10] Clovis Ramalhete, *Eça de Queiroz* (Livraria Martins, São Paulo, 1942).
[11] Fidelino de Figueiredo, *Depois de Eça de Queiroz* (Editora Classico-Scientífica, São Paulo, 1943).

In Portuguese scholarship the humanities have always led the sciences. It is true that Garcia da Orta in the sixteenth century was one of the world's leading botanists and that, in the nineteenth, José de Anchieta, working in Angola, pioneered in tropical zoology. But in general the Portuguese scientists, though they do good work, are not among the world leaders. Exceptions might be made in geography and anthropology, both fields in which Portugal's large colonial empire creates an opportunity for original investigation. There are signs that the opportunity will be further exploited in the future.

Chapter XVI

THE REPUBLIC AND THE NEW STATE

*P*ORTUGAL began its republican history in a Europe that was still mainly monarchical. In Metternich's day the overthrow of Manuel II would have meant armed intervention and a quick Bragança restoration. But times had changed by 1910, and a republic, although still exceptional, had become respectable. No outside power showed a disposition to interfere, and there is no reason to believe that the deposed Manuel asked for foreign aid. In exile he had an opportunity to make friends with the existing Miguelist pretender, the self-styled Miguel II, son of the ruler cast out by Dom Pedro in 1834. The two men composed their differences and united their parties in support of Manuel. But the fallen king seemed to realize that his day had passed and took little part in restoration movements. He spent most of his remaining life in England; and, even though in 1913 he married a German princess, he died childless in 1932.

Some Portuguese royalists felt more hopeful than did their sovereign. A group of them gathered north of the frontier in Spanish Galicia under the lead of Henrique Paiva Couceiro, one of the heroes of the 1895 war against Gungunhana and later governor of Angola.[1] In October, 1911, about a year after the revolution, they crossed the border and took a few Portuguese towns before stronger government forces drove them back to Spain. The following July, Paiva Couceiro tried again with a larger number,

---

[1] For Paiva Couceiro's interesting career, see *Grande enciclopédia portuguesa e brasileira* (Editorial Enciclopédica Limitada, Lisbon, Rio de Janeiro), vol. XX.

including some of the Miguelist partisans. But the chances of success depended wholly on arousing a popular movement for a restored monarch, and the Portuguese people failed to respond in any measure to Paiva Couceiro's urging. Again the royalists fell back to Spain, with most of them now convinced that for the present they could do no more. A few years later their leader accepted an amnesty and temporarily made his peace with the republican regime.

That regime in the meantime had troubles aplenty. There was no great difficulty in gaining foreign recognition, Brazil being the first to grant it in November, 1910, and the main European powers and the United States following suit by the next summer.[2] But in other ways the republic found the going difficult. Not only did Paiva Couceiro's monarchists have to be reckoned with, but the republicans were forced to make some show of carrying out their pre-revolutionary promises. This ran them afoul of the church at once. Afonso Costa, the Minister of Justice in Braga's cabinet, revived the law of 1759 by which Pombal had driven the Jesuits from Portugal and the law of 1834, bearing the name of Dom Pedro's minister Joaquim António de Aguiar, which had outlawed all convents and religious orders. Costa followed these with the "family laws," which made marriage a civil contract, legalized divorce, provided aid for unmarried mothers, and protected illegitimate children. Some months later, church and state were formally separated in Portugal. Costa, as leader of the Democratic party, the most radical in the country, was an old line anti-clerical. When a number of bishops and priests protested such steps in a *Collective Pastoral,* punitive measures were taken against them.[3]

In the course of 1911, the republicans wrote a democratic constitution and prepared for an election. The new government consisted mainly of a president, a ministry, and a two-house legislature composed of a senate and a chamber of deputies. The president of the republic would be chosen by the combined votes of both houses for a four-year term and could not be re-elected. The Portuguese somewhat compromised between presidential and

[2] Marques Guedes, *A aliança inglêsa* (Editorial Enciclopédica, Lisbon, 1943)), pp. 475-476.
[3] "Afonso Costa," *Grande enciclopédia* (Editorial Enciclopédica Limitada, Lisbon, Rio de Janeiro), vol. VII.

ministerial government, leaning mostly in the presidential direction.

With the republic came a new coinage and currency, the *escudo* replacing the old *real* as the monetary unit. The *escudo* at first had a par value slightly greater than the American dollar, but within twenty years it had depreciated so far as to be a mere monetary symbol, useless for any commercial transactions. The Portuguese generally reckon money in *contos*, a *conto* being 1,000 *escudos*.[4]

Most Portuguese in 1911 expected the election of Bernardino Machado, who had been Minister of Foreign Affairs in the provisional government. To the general surprise, the presidency went to Manuel de Arriaga, an old man of Teófilo Braga's generation, who was a moderate. He had not greatly sought or desired the office, but now, as an elder statesman, tried to be a moderating influence.

In spite of Arriaga's wish for a peaceful administration, Portugal was in no peaceful mood just then. The new constitution permitted strikes, and a rash of them broke out. Each occasion was apt to be a violent one with riots and clashes between laborers and police. The headquarters of the *União operaria*, or workers union, in Lisbon was surrounded and closed with hundreds of people being taken into custody. "This is the bread the republic gives us to gnaw," screamed one plebeian woman showing an apronful of rocks, as the police dragged her away.[5] A ministry led by Augusto de Vasconcellos fell from power because of the labor troubles in July, 1912.

Afonso Costa became head of the ministry in January, 1913, and lasted a year in office. Even the many Portuguese who hated Costa admitted he had ability. As bitter an anti-clerical as ever, he declared himself able and ready to extinguish Roman Catholicism in Portugal within two generations. On the economic side he conducted government with great frugality and sponsored a constitutional amendment called the "Iron law." This was an attempt to cure the chronic deficit in Portuguese finances by requiring that after delivery of a proposed budget no project could be put forward to increase or reduce it. For a brief time Costa, with his

---

[4] "Moeda," *Grande enciclopédia* (Editorial Enciclopédica Limitada, Lisbon, Rio de Janeiro), vol. XVII.
[5] João Ameal, *História de Portugal* (Livraria Tavares Martins, Oporto, 1940), p. 765.

Spartan economies, gave at least the appearance of a balanced budget.

But no ministry could then last long in Portugal. More labor troubles and popular demonstration forced President Arriaga to dismiss Costa's ministry in February, 1914, and call upon Bernardino Machado to form another.

In August of that year World War I began. The Portuguese alliance with England still existed, for both countries had agreed when the republic was proclaimed that the venerable arrangement should stand. With the war certain to spread to part of Africa, Portugal felt great anxiety about the colonies. Teixeira Gomes, the minister in London, sounded the Foreign Office concerning British protection for Angola and Mozambique. Sir Edward Grey immediately guaranteed protection if necessary, but otherwise declared England would be satisfied if Portugal took no military action for the present and merely refrained from proclaiming neutrality.

As the month of August passed, however, the Germans attacked the Portuguese on the southern Angola frontier from Southwest Africa and likewise assaulted Mozambique from Tanganyika. Portugal sent heavy reinforcements to both colonies and protested to the Imperial German government, learning in reply that German colonial officials had been under the mistaken impression that Portugal had entered the war.

That very question of military involvement was being hotly debated in Lisbon. Afonso Costa wished from the beginning to fight on the British side. Soon requests began to come from the Allies for help. In October, England requested the loan of 20,000 small arms, which Portugal sent.[6] A destroyer was also loaned to the British navy early in the war. In the same month of October, with the Allies hard pressed on the Western Front, Grey asked Portugal to enter the war and send an artillery force to France. But this was a vain hope at the moment, because the Portuguese were in no way prepared to take part in a major struggle.

Even their home situation was unstable. The year 1915 began with a near revolution when General Pimenta de Castro took advantage of a moment when congress was not in session to compel old Arriaga to appoint him to a virtual dictatorship with a

[6] Marques Guedes, *A aliança inglêsa* (Editorial Enciclopédica, Lisbon, 1943), p. 491.

ministry composed of military officers. When the legislative politicians resumed their sessions, led by Afonso Costa and the radical Democrats, they refused any recognition of the Pimenta de Castro government and prepared a revolution which overthrew the dictator in May. These outbreaks proved too much for venerable President Arriaga, who resigned a few months before his term expired. Old Dr. Braga took the helm for the moment, until Bernardino Machado could be elected in August. Afonso Costa had recently suffered an accident which kept him out of politics for a few months, but on his recovery he became head of the ministry late in November.

At the end of 1915 England was feeling a shipping shortage, and Sir Edward Grey asked Portgual to seize the seventy-two German vessels interned in Lisbon and other ports, promising to award Portuguese firms the contracts for refitting them. In February, 1916, the council of ministers decided to comply with Grey's request, realizing that the step probably meant war. The ships were confiscated and Germany, after one futile protest, issued the declaration of war on March 9.[7] Austria-Hungary followed suit at once.

Portugal now faced no particular danger in Africa because, except for a few scattered bands of troops, German resistance had collapsed there. But the little country resolved to fight in Europe and offered to send forces to France. The Allies, then grateful for any help, accepted the proposal. An Anglo-French military commission visited Portugal and gave an optimistic report regarding the army.

Portuguese troops began to arrive in France at the beginning of 1917 and, by July, 40,000 had been sent under the command of General Tamagnini Abreu. These men seem to have had no adequate training and above all no psychological preparation for what they would face. The majority felt no personal interest in the war they had been sent to fight. The Methuen Treaty meant nothing to them, and Wellington's defense of the Torres Vedras lines, very little. Therefore, when the Germans suddenly struck their part of the Allied line at the Lys River on April 9, 1918, the result was a Portuguese rout. Only prompt and desperate action

[7] H. V. Livermore, *History of Portugal* (Cambridge University Press, Cambridge, England, 1947), p. 456.

by the Allies succeeded in plugging the gap. The Portuguese took no further conspicuous part in military operations.

Involvement in the war had the effect of staving off a threatened financial debacle in Portugal. Loans received from England largely financed both the war and the government, putting off an evil day of reckoning until the future.

Even while fighting Germany, Portugal could not enjoy internal unity. At the outset a coalition government had been formed consisting mainly of Costa's *Democraticos* and the more conservative *Evolucionistas*. But this did not last. High cost of living and war shortages brought national morale very low, and strikes created such havoc that in December, 1917, Major Sidónio Pais at the head of several military units drove out President Bernardino Machado and imprisoned Afonso Costa for four months. Pais, who seems to have acted for what he considered patriotic reasons, then assumed almost dictatorial control of Portugal for the rest of the war. He inspired more confidence among the Allies than had his predecessors, and the British and French showed him diplomatic favors. Pais made some progress in reorganizing the Portuguese army in France after the Lys disaster. At the same time he rapidly gained favor with the Lisbon crowds, and his government seemed verging in the totalitarian direction.

The dramatic career of Pais was suddenly cut short by assassination. Scarcely a month after the armistice, as he prepared to board a train from Lisbon to Oporto, a young fanatic shot him down. The succeeding government, with Vice Admiral João do Canto e Castro as provisional president, almost collapsed before a belated monarchist attack. Paiva Couceiro had not abandoned hopes of a Bragança restoration. Encouraged by the popularity of the conservative Sidónio Pais and by the general dismay at his death, he and his partisans made a final effort and in January, 1919, seized Oporto, Braga, Viseu, Coimbra, and Aveiro in northern Portugal. For a brief time he commanded thousands of followers, and officers of the regular army deserted to join him. In Lisbon, a portion of the garrison raised the monarchist flag. But the bulk of the army remained loyal to the republic, and a defeat suffered by the royalists at Monsanto near the capital turned the tide. The monarchist movement quickly collapsed, and, although many of the insurrectionist officers were captured, Paiva Couceiro again escaped.[8]

Afonso Costa had gone to France following his imprisonment by Sidónio Pais. In 1919, the Canto e Castro government named him head of the Portuguese delegation to the Versailles Peace Conference. Portugal played no conspicuous part in these grave deliberations but did gain a strip of former German territory in the Rovuma region along the northern frontier of Mozambique. Costa also won acknowledgment of Portuguese right to a small share of the indemnity levied on Germany. This same Portuguese radical, turned diplomat, spent his last years of public service as his country's representative in the League of Nations.

Canto e Castro, who followed Sidónio Pais in the presidency, took over only to finish the term originally started by Machado, which expired in October, 1919. He spent eight stormy months in office, most of the time engaged in suppressing rebellions and riots and in punishing insurgents. He tried to resign before October, but congress insisted that he wait for his constitutionally elected successor, António José de Almeida, who assumed the thankless burden of office at the appointed time.

Almeida became the first president of Portugal to serve a full term, but that was almost the only satisfaction connected with the turbulent years 1919-23. During 1920, the country had nine ministries, one of them lasting for twenty-four hours and another for six days. Crisis in government became almost the normal and accepted thing. Any attempt to recount the political history of Portugal in those months degenerates into a weary story of short-lived cabinets and their quick overthrow. During all this the *escudo* steadily dropped in value and the Portuguese burden of debt steadily mounted.

The year 1921 was particularly violent. António Granjo, a minister unpopular with certain officers of the army, was forced to resign when a revolutionary junta led by Colonel Manuel Coelho waited on President Almeida and coerced him into dispensing with Granjo. Coelho established a dictatorship and arrested Granjo with several other leaders of his party. Members

---

[8] The *Times* (London) for January 1919, *passim*. Paiva Couceiro ultimately returned to Portugal during the Salazar regime and died in Lisbon in 1944.

of the old Carbonaria Society received arms from the naval arsenal and were joined by sailors from two warships in the Tagus, *São Gabriel* and *Vasco da Gama*. The rioters captured Granjo, took him to the arsenal, and there murdered him. Several other prominent people were killed at this time. Colonel Coelho, the originator of the disturbance, meant to hold power, but the appearance of English, French, and Spanish warships before Lisbon persuaded him to resign. More respectable politicians again took over the government, but the ministries continued to be short-lived and frequently overthrown.

In 1922 the Brazilians celebrated the centenary of their independence. Portugal took notice of the celebration staged by the vast daughter nation and sent President Almeida to Rio de Janeiro on a visit. Any breach that had ever existed between the two countries had long since healed, and this good-will trip symbolized the cordiality prevailing between the old Portuguese speaking nation and the new. But the true sensation of the year was the airplane flight from Lisbon to Rio by the Portuguese aviator Sacadura Cabral, accompanied by Gago Coutinho (later admiral) of the navy, who served as navigator. Brazil greeted the flyers with enthusiasm, and, although theirs was not the first transatlantic flight, it was the first over that particular part of the ocean. Portuguese and Brazilians could not help remembering that Cabral bore the name of the discoverer of Brazil in 1500.

Home events in Portugal went on in their usual dreary way. No one dared punish Coelho and the others implicated in the murder of Granjo. Another revolutionary outbreak threatened the government in 1922, when President Almeida and his friends had to take refuge at Cascais several miles from Lisbon until enough troops could be brought from the provinces to restore order. The *escudo* in this year reached a new low, attaining an exchange value of approximately five cents in United States money.

Almeida was glad in 1923 to turn over the government to his elected successor, Teixeira Gomes, who had for many years been Portuguese ambassador in London. The new president, who had grown out of touch with the country, came home, in the words of Bragança-Cunha, "to mount a horse that had thrown six riders in thirteen years." [9] Teixeira Gomes, whatever his gifts as a diplomat, was not the man to ride the turbulent animal. He kept an unsteady seat in the saddle until December, 1925, his administration being a welter of strikes, street riots, mutinies in the army and navy, and ephemeral cabinets. He then resigned, and Bernardino Machado, who had been a two-year incumbent of the presidential chair before his overthrow by Pais in 1917, tried his luck for the second time.

President Machado entered office amid an aroma of financial scandal. A flood of bogus banknotes deluged the country, spread by the newly founded Angola Metropole Bank. These had been printed secretly in London and bore serial numbers duplicating notes already in circulation. The Bank of Portugal, on discovering the fraud, at once called in all the notes of the 500 *escudos* denomination, since the counterfeiters had limited themselves to these. Investigation showed that the English firm of Waterlow, which regularly printed for the Bank of Portugal, had been tricked into supplying the false notes by documents cleverly forged. The trickery even included the interception of a letter from Sir William Waterlow to the governor of the Bank of Portugal. Fortunately, the whole amount of *escudos* printed, totaling over £2,000,000, never got into circulation; and the police of several European countries found and confiscated large bundles of unused bogus notes. The Angola Metropole Bank was liquidated by the Portuguese government early in 1926, and it then developed that its board of directors contained several honorable men who had been deceived by their unscrupulous colleagues. Exposure of this fraud lowered the republic's prestige still further and proved humiliating to most Portuguese. [10]

The republican political game was almost played out in Portugal. The most revolution ridden Latin American state had never been more unstable than the Lusitanian republic between 1910 and 1926. Furthermore, during those years the situation showed no sign of mending but only grew worse as time passed; after sixteen years of republicanism the country was ready to try

[9] V. de Bragança-Cunha, *Revolutionary Portugal* (J. Clarke &Co., ltd., London, 1937), p. 213.
[10] For this large scale fraud, see Cecil H. Kisch, *The Portuguese Bank-Note Case* (Macmillan & Co., ltd., London, 1932).

something else. Inevitably, the army which stood always eager to mingle in politics would provide the leadership for the new movement.

General Manuel Gomes da Costa, commanding the garrison at Braga, proclaimed the revolt on May 28, 1926. His proclamation to the nation contained a curious mixture of sincerity and bombast: "Portuguese! For men of honor and dignity the situation of the country is inadmissible. Bent low by the action of a licentious minority, the shamed nation feels itself dying. As for me, I openly revolt. And let all men of courage and dignity come with me to conquer or die by my side. To arms, Portugal!" [11]

Proclaiming that the parliamentary system had outlived its day, Gomes da Costa led a march on Lisbon. No doubt he acted somewhat in imitation of Mussolini, who had overthrown the Italian government in 1922, and Primo de Rivera, who had seized control of Spain the following year. The Portuguese government capitulated as easily as that of Italy and a ruling triumvirate was set up, consisting of Gomes da Costa, General António Oscar de Fragoso Carmona, and Commander Mendes Cabeçadas, who had prepared the way for the revolution in Lisbon.

But it did not take the colleagues of Gomes da Costa long to realize that he would never do as a Messiah. Once in power he proved vain, blustering, and ignorant. Carmona, who possessed most of the real ability in the new government, managed suddenly to arrest Gomes da Costa on July 9 and ship him away as a prisoner to the Azores. The fallen leader, who had governed Portugal for a few weeks, remained in Ponta Delgada about a year, being promoted to Field Marshal in the meantime. By 1927, he was considered harmless enough to be allowed to return to Lisbon. From then, until his death in 1929, his only public appearance was in Rome, where he represented Portugal at the funeral of the Italian Marshal Diaz.

General Carmona had become undisputed head of the government, and although he called Portugal "a dictatorship without a dictator" he gave every appearance of filling the role himself. He and his new associates began to orate in the familiar fascistic fashion, to exalt jingoistic nationalism to the skies, and to talk of "Greater Portugal" and the divine mission their country was

[11] João Ameal, *História de Portugal* (Livraria Tavares Martins, Oporto, 1940), p. 784.

somehow called on to fulfill. But, although the generals in charge could discourse in stirring tones on the future greatness of the nation, there were some things they could not do without civilian help. They did not understand government, and above all they did not understand finance. Portugal staggered under a greater load of debt than ever, and Carmona and company had no ideas on the subject beyond a vague notion of a public subscription or, failing that, of borrowing more from abroad. General Sinel de Cordes, who was Minister of Finance, applied in 1927 to the League of Nations for a £12,000,000 loan to be used in carrying out financial reconstruction in Portugal. The League sent a committee to Lisbon in 1928 and this reported favorably on the loan, with the proviso, however, that satisfactory security should be provided and a foreign controller appointed. The Portuguese felt that their word of honor as gentlemen should be security enough and that to have an outside controller would be a national humiliation. These differences of opinion caused the whole plan to fall through.[12]

Carmona, meanwhile, was elected president of Portugal and took office in April, 1928. The financial situation of the country clearly loomed up as the gravest national danger, not only because bankruptcy threatened at home but because international talk had again started of depriving Portugal of the African colonies. Since before World War I, the successive governments had dealt largely with their financial problems by printing new issues of paper, despite an ever-dwindling gold reserve. By 1923, they had already gone far beyond the legal limit for paper money, and yet during 1924 the paper in circulation increased at the rate of 1,000 *contos* daily.

In 1928 the name of Professor António de Oliveira Salazar began to figure prominently in Portugal. Born in 1889, near Coimbra, he had studied at the university and at the age of twenty-seven had received the chair of economy there. He owed his reputation mainly to a thesis on the evolution of Portuguese currency. In 1921, he had his first introduction to practical politics when he was elected to the legislature. After one day in Lisbon, he returned to Coimbra, having already decided that party politics were essen-

[12] Leonard H. Leach, *Report on the Economic Conditions in Portugal* (H. M. Stationary Office, London, Department of Overseas Trade, 1928), pp. 12-13.

tially evil and not for him. Soon after the rise of Carmona to power, Salazar, following repeated urging, accepted the portfolio of finance in the cabinet. He resigned almost immediately but soon resumed the post. After May, 1928, he held office continuously. President Carmona accepted his ideas for financial reform, and the professor first became economic dictator of Portugal and finally political dictator as well. To think of Portuguese government today is to think of Salazar, although Carmona held the presidency without a break from 1928 until his death in 1951.[13]

Salazar began to balance the budget during his first year in office and even to obtain surpluses for reducing the floating debt, which he had wiped off the slate by the end of the fiscal year 1931-32. He also insisted that colonial budgets should balance, even though a few more years were required to make them do so. Angola in particular was in bad financial straits, because for development purposes the colony had been allowed to plunge heavily into debt. Further indiscretions of this sort were forbidden by the new colonial act passed in 1930, which cut down the autonomy of all the Portuguese possessions. Salazar regarded it as a triumph when the first balanced Angolan budget appeared, for the year 1935-36.

The principles of Salazar were summed up early in his regime by a decree which he published in 1928. His first point was insistence on budget unity, meaning that one total must be shown for all revenue, offset by another total for expenditure. Secondly, normal expenses of the state must be met out of normal revenues and could not be covered by loans. Thirdly, Salazar gave an exact definition of extraordinary expenditures, the only kind coverable by loans. In the fourth place, he prohibited financial assistance by the government to private concerns. For any department head who violated these rules, he provided severe punishment.

Salazar has kept the financial structure of Portugal closely geared to England's, and when in 1931 the British went off the gold standard the Portuguese did likewise.

Higher taxes had to be imposed to secure these balanced budgets and the upswing in national economy. It is difficult at present to answer the question of whether Salazar, to create a rich government, did so at the price of making the people poorer.

[13] The leading biography of Salazar to date is that of António Ferro, *Salazar: Portugal and her Leader* (Faber and Faber, ldt., London, 1939).

Nearly all who have written about him have been his enthusiastic friends or his bitter enemies, and the story varies greatly depending on who does the telling.

Portugal in 1933 received a new constitution by which it was proclaimed the "New State." The social theory on which the constitution rests places the "association" ahead of the individual. The smallest association is the family, and only heads of families vote, so that universal suffrage is abolished. The president is elected by direct suffrage for a term of seven years,* with the ministers appointed by him and entirely responsible to him. The legislature consists of the National Assembly, which is also selected by direct vote of the family heads. A corporative chamber also exists to pass on economic and social matters and is chosen through a system of guild or syndical representation.

Along with the constitution, Portugal in 1933 adopted the Statute of National Labor, which defined both the rights and duties of the workingman. Salazar has always abhorred socialism, and the Statute lays down the principle that individual enterprise is normal and state enterprise is exceptional. The worker has certain privileges, such as a rest day once in the week, an annual vacation with pay and health insurance. On the other hand, he is organized into national trade unions or syndicates which appear to be mainly agencies to keep him under control. These unions may not affiliate with international bodies, and a decree of 1934 makes strikes illegal. Businessmen are also organized, being grouped in guilds (grémios). They are obliged to work in harmony with the plans of the nation and to subordinate their own interests to those of the state.

Agriculture is still by far the most important occupation in Portugal, with at least sixty per cent of the people engaged in it. The climate being sunny and moist and most of the soil fertile, nearly the whole surface can be farmed. Steps have been taken by the government in recent years to improve the ancient farming methods, increase the productivity and put more soil under cultivation. The most important product is wheat, the bulk of which grows in the Alentejo region south of the Tagus. Other cereals widely grown are maize, rye, oats and barley. Portugal has become practically self-supporting in grain, and is the world's third largest

* Carmona was three times elected under this constitution; 1935, 1942, and 1949.

grower of olives, being surpassed only by Italy and Spain. The grape production of Portugal, used largely for wines, concentrates mainly along the Douro in the north and in the island of Madeira.

Portuguese exports have long consisted mostly of wine, sardines, fruit, cork, copper, salt, and textiles. The chief national industry is cloth, the greater part of which is for home consumption.

Portugal imports coal from England, cotton from the United States, and wheat from Argentina. Codfish comes from the Newfoundland banks, a great deal of it in the holds of Portuguese fishing boats. Petroleum is another valuable import coming from various parts of the world. Imports of iron and steel, railroad material, machinery and other engineering products now come largely from England, the United States, Belgium, and France, although in earlier years Germany provided a large share.

One of the campaigns vigorously waged by Salazar has been the fight against illiteracy. Before 1910, four Portuguese out of five could neither read nor write, and the early republic did not do much to improve the situation. With his mounting surpluses from the budget, Salazar could now devote funds to enlargement and improvement of the school system. By 1940, illiteracy had been cut to about fifty per cent of the total population, and, although exact figures since then are difficult to obtain, the literacy trend has been steadily upward.

Emigration was formerly considerable, with an average of 35,-000 persons annually leaving the country, mostly for Brazil and the United States. This migration has now been greatly cut down, largely because of restrictions passed by both the Brazilian and United States governments. Although Portugal, as a matter of policy, formerly disliked losing so many people, the new situation also has disadvantages. The remissions of money home by the emigrants, which used to be an invisible but important source of national revenue, have virtually ceased today.

Although the church has not been re-established in Salazar's Portugal, Roman Catholicism has flourished vigorously again. The dictator once studied for the priesthood and left the seminary for want of vocation, not for loss of faith. He is reported to be personally orthodox and believes in the church as a necessity for Portugal. Yet his elevation to power had no connection with his church sympathies, and, in the words of a biographer, he "is influenced by no sub-national interest." Freedom of worship exists, although there is very little Protestantism in Portugal. In Angola, on the other hand, there is a great deal, largely as the result of work by non-Portuguese missionaries.

When the Francisco Franco revolution broke out in Spain in the summer of 1936, Salazar and his government remained neutral but not indifferent to the outcome. They feared that a victory for the Loyalists would mean a Spain dominated by Soviet Russia and very likely converted to communism. Such a Spain would inevitably seek to annex Portugal. The old spectre of Pan-Iberianism thus rose to haunt Salazar and Carmona, and this time it seemed to wear a red garb. On October 23, Portugal severed relations with the Loyalist government and in December, 1937, gave *de facto* recognition to Franco, although at that time his victory was far from certain. There was some talk in England of terminating the old Portuguese alliance, but Salazar persisted in his course, privately saying that his nation had to think first of its own safety and that England needed Portugal as much as Portugal needed England. His contention was probably right because the re-armament program the British were then undergoing had deprived Portugal of many needed English products. In March, 1939, immediately following the Franco victory, there was signed in Lisbon a treaty of friendship and nonaggression between Portugal and Spain.[14]

In September, World War II began with the German invasion of Poland. England at once declared war on Germany but made no request for help from Portugal. Salazar therefore announced that the country would be neutral as long as its rights were respected. After the conquest of Denmark, Norway, the Netherlands, Belgium and France in the first half of 1940, Lisbon enjoyed a peculiar and rather dangerous importance which it retained for the remainder of the war. Being the one important free, neutral seaport on the Atlantic, it became the only feasible outlet between continental Europe and England and the New World. Horta, in the Azores, was the sole air stop between Europe and North America. Émigrés and refugees flocked to Portugal by the thousand, to

[14] Marques Guedes, *A aliança inglêsa* (Editorial Enciclopédica, Lisbon, 1943), pp. 521-522.

live expensively in Lisbon if they had money, or else to wait and
hope for some transportation to England or the Americas. Spies
and secret agents of all countries flocked there as well, to keep an
eye upon each other and to cause the Portuguese police endless
concern. Many people thought the neutrality of Portugal would
not be allowed to continue and predicted that the country would
ultimately be occupied by the Germans.

As Japan moved closer to war with the United States and the
British Empire, Portuguese territory in the Far East became a
matter of concern, particularly the island of Timor, which Portugal shared with the Netherlands. On November 4, 1941, the
British Foreign office asked the Portuguese ambassador what attitude his country would take if Japan attacked Timor and whether
Portugal would be disposed to accept English aid, suggesting a
plan of common action. Salazar at that moment considered a
Japanese attack unlikely, but answered that Portugal would resist
if it came and would most certainly accept British help.[15] He consented to discuss plans with the English, so arrangements were
made to send a Portuguese officer to Singapore and also to hold
joint conferences with the Dutch regarding East Indian defense.
While conversations of this sort went on, the Japanese struck their
first blows against the British and Americans. As they advanced
southward in the East Indies, the Dutch occupied the Portuguese
half of Timor. Portugal protested, but military events in the
Orient soon made such diplomatic gestures useless. Japan occupied the entire island in February, 1942, accompanying the
occupation with a note to Lisbon which explained the occurrence
on military grounds. Portugal protested to Tokyo, but by this
time the Japanese had small interest in continuing the discussions.

Portuguese Macau in China escaped an occupation. Although
Japanese forces held adjacent Chinese territory and British Hong
Kong until 1945, they evidently did not consider this small pos-
session important enough to molest.

Far more strategic than these minor oriental holdings were the
Azores. The British, and later the Americans, badly needed base
rights and facilities there to prevent a possible seizure by the Germans and to protect their own vast volume of shipping in the At-

[15] Marques Guedes, *A aliança inglesa* (Editorial Enciclopédica, Lisbon, 1943), pp.
521-522.

lantic from submarines. But not until October, 1943, did Portugal make the concession and allow Great Britain to use air and naval bases in the islands. Included in the agreement was the stipulation that the United States could use them as well. Portuguese sovereignty remained intact and the concession, which was not an occupation, did not affect the nation's neutrality in the war.

Allied bases in the Azores proved very valuable. They meant a great extension of the area protected by land based planes. The dangerous 1,000-mile gap between American and Mediterranean-North African ports was closed at last.

The Portuguese African colonies made some economic contributions to the Allied war effort and also helped to relieve wartime shortages in Portugal itself. The Diamond Corporation Ltd. of London bought up the entire Angolan diamond supply, most of it for industrial use. Angola also contributed fish and oranges to Portugal. The islands of Principe and São Tomé in the Gulf of Guinea greatly increased their cocoa output for Portugal and the Allies. Mozambique, with large mineral deposits, produced coal, chromium, and copper for war use, and shipped much of the South African supply through the port of Lourenço Marques.

Neutrality paid well, and the war meant prosperity for Portugal. When Germany definitely began to lose, profits fell off and certain classes within the country spoke more freely against Salazar than ever before. When the fighting entirely stopped, what was left of the wartime boom collapsed. The poorer classes and the wage earners found themselves losing the battle against high prices, since their pay increases were far slower than the increases in the cost of living. Strikes began to mount, and workers' demonstrations disturbed the serenity of Lisbon and Oporto as in the disorderly years of the early republic. The police dealt with these heavy handedly, but arresting agitators and exiling them to Portuguese colonies did nothing to improve the situation. By 1948, signs existed that the New State and Salazar's dictatorship might be approaching the end.

President Carmona's third term expired in 1949, and as an obvious concession to Anglo-American democratic sympathies, Salazar announced that, for the first time in over two decades, an absolutely free Portuguese election would be held. Carmona, now nearing eighty, would of course be one candidate. To oppose him there emerged another venerable army man, General José Mendes Ribeiro Norton de Mattos, who was even older than the president. This candidate was expected to provide only nominal opposition, and was slated to be the straw man whose overwhelming defeat would give the Salazar-Carmona regime a look of popularity.

But Norton de Mattos upset these calculations by taking the whole thing seriously. Despite his age he campaigned vigorously, using such catchwords as "democracy" and "freedom." The Portuguese Communist Party, although small, had a good organization and threw its full weight behind Norton de Mattos. Salazar, who had evidently permitted the existence of a rival ticket with the intention of creating a "loyal opposition," now found himself balked. Fearing that matters would get out of hand, he intervened so openly as to make the fact patent to all. His war minister, Lieutenant Colonel Santos Costa, mobilized troops and talked freely of how the army might take a hand in case the election went the wrong way. General Norton de Mattos claimed that every possible obstacle was placed in the way of his campaign. On February 10, 1949, three days before the scheduled election, the old general withdrew from the race, saying that the government had denied him the election privileges it gave Carmona. If the Communists had really stage-managed his candidacy as is charged, this was a shrewd move on their part and they had outwitted Salazar. Norton de Mattos could scarcely have won under any circumstances, and his extravagant display of disillusionment at the last moment gave the regime a very guilty look.

The New State had triumphed, but the opposition had scored. If Salazar had ever been popular in the country, and there is reason to think that he had once been very popular, he had now clearly passed his peak. Later in 1949, the dictator was reported to be thinking of a restoration of monarchy in the person of a boy prince of the Miguelist line, with himself as head of a regency council. Whatever truth lay in the report, no action had been taken in this direction by the opening of 1952.

On April 18, 1951, the aged Carmona increased Salazar's difficulties by dying. The old soldier-president had generally passed for a figurehead with the public outside Portugal; this, however, was not exactly the case. Carmona had always commanded respect and prestige, and he, after all, had been the true founder of the regime. It was by no means certain that the New State would endure tranquilly without him. Salazar had no desire for another election just then, and no desire to be president himself. Nevertheless the constitution compelled him to assume the office temporarily and also stated that an election must be held within sixty days.

Salazar rejected proposals that he become president and combine Carmona's former functions with his own. Aspirants to the office were allowed to announce their candidacy and meanwhile the Portuguese Supreme Court decided that sixty days were not enough for election purposes and announced that balloting would take place Sunday, July 22, 1951.

One candidate, Professor Ruy Gomes, had a reputation for strong leftist leanings and the Supreme Court, doubtless after consultation with Salazar, disbarred him as a Communist, despite his denial of Party membership. Admiral Manuel de Quintão Meireles, a distinguished soldier and a former cabinet minister, became the real standard bearer for the opposition. The government nominee was General Francisco Higino Craveiro Lopes, a man reported to be in full sympathy with the Salazar administration.

Admiral Meireles, like Norton de Mattos two years earlier, campaigned with some vigor. He had the support of some of Portugal's leading men, including officers of field rank in the army. Of doubtful value to his cause was the vociferous aid of the small Communist group, which shifted to him after the disqualification of the left-winger, Ruy Gomes. His repeated statements that he desired no Communist support failed to shake off the radicals. Specifically, the admiral advocated continuance of the main features of the existing regime with greater freedom for individuals and elimination of the official corruption which he declared existed.

The government political machine was still very strong, and it appears certain that General Lopes would have won, even if Admiral Meireles had not withdrawn from the race three days before the election. The admiral's sudden decision sounded like a repetition of Norton de Mattos's similar action in 1949. He declared that he was refused opportunity to present his case fairly to the public and that even the election tickets prepared for the polling were such as to intimidate his supporters.

When Meireles withdrew, on July 19, only General Lopes remained, and he was duly elected. Once again the New State had won, and once again in such a fashion as to arouse suspicion even among the most guileless. Whether the team of Lopes and Salazar will work as harmoniously as the old Carmona-Salazar combination remains to be seen. The new president is fifty-seven years old, hence some years younger than the dictator. The report is that while Lopes will not directly interfere in administration, neither will he be altogether a figurehead and may expect to make his influence felt.

Portugal, as 1952 opened, had not lost a foot of overseas territory, having received back its half of Timor and having seen the British and Americans depart from the Azores. But some changes seemed possible in the near future. With the British Empire in India now a thing of the past, the question arose of how long Portugal could hold Goa and the lesser Indian possessions with a nationalist government dominating the Indian scene. Macau furnished another large question mark because a Chinese Communist regime had come into power, definitely tied to Russia and hostile to the West. The African territories and the Atlantic islands appeared reasonably safe in the near future.

Portugal and its colonies had been important before; they might be important again. None but a rash prophet would have declared in the year 1952 that the Portuguese had played their last major role in world history.

SELECTED BIBLIOGRAPHY

Since no attempt has been made to provide this brief history with an elaborate apparatus of scholarship, the bibliography is not definitive. Preference has been given, wherever possible, to works in English, but these are too few to do justice to the subject and furthermore deal mostly with the era of discovery and empire building. Any serious writer of Portuguese history must lean heavily on the works of Portuguese historians. The following lists of authorities contain those titles in English and Portuguese, plus a few in French and Spanish, that have been found most useful in preparing the present work.

BIBLIOGRAPHY

Greenlee, William B., "A Descriptive Bibliography of the History of Portugal," *Hispanic American Historical Review*, XX, 1940.

PUBLISHED SOURCES

Alguns documentos do Archivo Nacional da Tôrre do Tombo ácerca das navegações e conquistas portuguezas, ed. by J. Ramos Coelho, Imprensa Nacional, Lisbon, 1892.

Collecção dos tratados, convenções, contratos e actos publicos desde 1640 até o presente, ed. by José Ferreira Borges de Castro, 30 vols., Imprensa Nacional, Lisbon, 1856-79.

Corpo Diplomatico Portuguez, contendo os actos e relações de Portugal com as demais potencias do mundo, 15(?) vols., Academia das Sciencias de Lisboa, Lisbon, 1862-1936.

Pina, Ruy de, *Chronica d'El Rei Dom João II*, Academia Real das Sciencias, Lisbon, 1792.

Quadro elementar das relações politicas e diplomaticas de Portugal com as diversas potencias do mundo, ed. by Viscount Santarem, 18 vols., J. P. Aillaud, Paris, 1842-76.

GENERAL HISTORIES

Almeida, Fortunato de, *História de Portugal*, 6 vols., Coimbra, 1922-1929.

Altamira, Rafael, *A History of Spain*, transl. by Muna Lee, D. Van Nostrand Co., Inc., New York, 1949.

Ameal, João, *História de Portugal*, Livraria Tavares Martins, Oporto, 1940.

Herculano de Carvalho, Alexandre, *História de Portugal desde o começo da monarchia até o fim do reinado de Affonso III*, 8th ed., 8 vols., Livraria Aillaud & Bertrand, Paris—Lisbon, n. d.

História de Portugal. Edição monumental commemorativa do 8° centenario

243

da fundação da nacionalidade, ed. Damião Peres, 7 vols., Portucalense editora, Barcelos, 1928-1935.

Livermore, H. V., *A History of Portugal*, Cambridge University Press, Cambridge, England, 1947.

McMurdo, E., *History of Portugal*, 2 vols., S. Low, Marston, Searle, & Rivington, London, 1888-1889.

Oliveira Martins, Joaquim Pedro de, *A History of Iberian Civilization*, transl. by Aubrey F. G. Bell, Oxford University Press, New York, 1930.

Stephens, Henry M., *Portugal*, G. P. Putnam's Sons, New York, and T. Fisher Unwin, London, 1891.

CHURCH HISTORY

Almeida, Fortunato de, *História da igreja em Portugal*, 4 vols., Imprensa Academica, Coimbra, 1910-22.

Herculano de Carvalho, Alexandre, *História da origem e estabelecimento da inquisição em Portugal*, 3 vols., Imprensa Nacional, Lisbon, 1854-59.

IMPERIAL HISTORY

História da colonização portuguesa do Brasil, ed. by Carlos Malheiro Dias, 3 vols., Litografia Nacional, Oporto, 1921-24.

História da expansão portuguesa no mundo, ed. by António Baião, Hernani Cidade, Manuel Múrias, 3 vols., Editorial Atica, Lisbon, 1937-1940.

Pires de Lima, Durval, *O oriente e a África desde a restauração a Pombal*, Agência Geral das Colónias, Lisbon, 1946.

THE ANGLO PORTUGUESE ALLIANCE

Guedes, Marques, *A aliança inglêsa*, Editorial Enciclopédica, Lisbon, 1943.

Osório de Andrade, Gilberto, *Os fundamentos da neutralidade portuguesa*, Ciclo Cultural Luso-Brasileíro, Recife, 1943.

Shillington, V. M., and Chapman, A. B. W., *The Commercial Relations of England and Portugal*, G. Routledge & Sons, ltd., London, and E. P. Dutton & Co., New York, 1907.

Sousa, Carlos Hermenegildo, *A aliança anglo-portuguesa*, Edições Marânus, Oporto, 1939.

PORTUGUESE ORIGINS

Gama Barros, H. de, *História da administração publica em Portugal nos séculos xii á xiv*, 3 vols., Imprensa Nacional, Lisbon, 1895-1914.

Bragança-Cunha, V. de, *Eight Centuries of Portuguese Monarchy*, S. Swift, London, 1911.

De Expugnatione Lyxbonensi (The Conquest of Lisbon), transl. and ed. by Charles Wendell David, Columbia University Press, New York, 1936.

Oliveira Martins, Joaquim Pedro de, *A vida de Nun'Álvares*, 6th ed., A. M. Pereira, Lisbon, 1944.

Peres, Damião, *Como nasceu Portugal*, Portucalense Editora, Oporto, 1942.

Prestage, Edgar, *Royal Power and the Cortes in Portugal*, Watford, 1927.

Watts, Henry E., *The Christian Recovery of Spain*, G. P. Putnam's Sons, New York, 1894.

PORTUGUESE DISCOVERY

Azurara, Gomes Eanes de, *The Chronicle of the Discovery and Conquest of Guinea*, transl. and ed. by C. R. Beazley and E. Prestage, 2 vols., Hakluyt Society, London, 1896-1899.

Azurara, Gomes Eanes de, *Crónica do descobrimento e conquista da Guiné*, ed. by José de Bragança, 2 vols., Lisbon, 1937.

Beazley, Charles R., *Prince Henry the Navigator*, G. P. Putnam's Sons, New York, 1895.

Beazley, Charles R., "Prince Henry of Portugal and his Political, Commercial and Colonizing Work," *American Historical Review*, XVII, 1912.

Beazley, Charles R., "Prince Henry of Portugal and the African Crusade of the Fifteenth Century," *American Historical Review*, XVI, 1911.

Blake, J. W., *European Beginnings in West Africa, 1454-1578*, Longmans Green & Co., London, New York, 1937.

Blake, J. W., *Europeans in West Africa*, 2 vols., Hakluyt Society, London, 1942.

Cordeiro, Luciano, "Diogo Cão," *Boletim da Sociedade de Geographia de Lisboa*, XI, 1892.

Cordeiro, Luciano, "Diogo de Azambuja," *Boletim da Sociedade de Geographia de Lisboa*, XI, 1892.

Cordier, Henri, "L'arrivée des portugais en Chine," *T'oung Pao*, XII, 1911.

Cortesão, Jaime, *Los portugueses*, Salvat Editores, Barcelona, 1947.

Cortesão, Jaime, *Teoria geral dos descobrimentos portugueses*, Seara Nova, Lisbon, 1940.

Denucé, Jean, *Magellan, la question des Moluques et la première circumnavigation du globe*, Brussels, 1908.

Ferrand Gabriel, "Le pilote arabe de Vasco da Gama et les instructions nautiques des arabes au xv° siècle," *Annales de Géographie*, XXX, 1922.

Ficalho, Conde de, *Viagens de Pedro de Covilhan*, A. M. Pereira, Lisbon, 1898.

First Voyage of Vasco da Gama, transl. and ed. by E. G. Ravenstein, Hakluyt Society, London, 1898.

Fontoura da Costa, *A marinharia dos descobrimentos*, Agencia Geral das Colonias, Lisbon, 1939.

Hart, Henry H., *Sea Road to the Indies*, The Macmillan Company, New York, 1950.

Kammerer, Albert, *Mer Rouge, l'Abyssinie et l'Arabie depuis l'antiquité*, 2 vols., Cairo, 1929-35.

Major, Richard H., *The Life of Prince Henry of Portugal, surnamed the Navigator*, A. Asher & Co., London, 1868.

Mees, Jules, *Histoire de la découverte des Iles Açores*, Librairie Vuylsteke, Ghent, 1901.

Morison, Samuel Eliot, *Portuguese Voyages to America in the Fifteenth Century*, Harvard University Press, Cambridge, Mass., 1940.

Nowell, Charles E., "Prince Henry the Navigator and his Brother Dom Pedro," *Hispanic American Historical Review*, XXVIII, 1948.

Nowell, Charles E., "The Rejection of Columbus by John of Portugal," *University of Michigan Historical Essays*, Ann Arbor, 1938.

Oliveira Martins, Joaquim Pedro de, *The Golden Age of Prince Henry the*

Navigator, transl. by J. J. Abraham and W. E. Reynolds, Chapman and Hall, London, 1914.

Peres, Damião, *História dos descobrimentos portugueses,* Portucalense Editora, Oporto, 1943.

Prestage, Edgar, *The Portuguese Pioneers,* A. C. Black, ltd., London, 1933.

Ravenstein, E. G., "The Voyages of Diogo Cão and Bartholomeu Dias," *Geographical Journal,* XVI, 1900.

Ross, L. Denison, "Prester John and the Empire of Ethiopia," *Travel and Travellers of the Middle Ages,* ed. by A. P. Newton, London, 1930.

Sanceau, Elaine, *Henry the Navigator,* W. W. Norton & Company, Inc., New York, 1947.

Taylor, E. G. R., "Pactolus: River of Gold," *Scottish Geographical Magazine,* XLIV, 1928.

Teixeira de Aragão, *Vasco da Gama e a Vidigueira,* Lisbon, 1898.

Voyage of Pedro Álvares Cabral to Brazil and India, transl. and ed. by William B. Greenlee, Hakluyt Society, London, 1937.

THE PORTUGUESE EMPIRE

Álvares, Francisco, *Verdadeira informação das terras do Preste João,* Agencia Geral das Colonias, Lisbon, 1943. First published in 1543.

Barros João de, *Da Asia,* continued by Diogo de Couto, 24 vols., Regina Officina Typografica, Lisbon, 1778-88.

Castanheda, Fernão Lopes de, *História do descobrimento e conquista da India pelos portuguezes,* 8 vols., Typographia Rollandiana, Lisbon, 1833.

Commentaries of the Great Affonso Dalboquerque, Second Vice-roy of India, transl. and ed. by Walter de Gray Birch, 4 vols., Hakluyt Society, London, 1875-84.

Correa, Gaspar, *Lendas da India,* 4 vols., Typ. da Academia Real das Sciencias, Lisbon, 1858-1864.

Danvers, F. C., *The Portuguese in India,* 2 vols., W. H. Allen & Co., ltd., London, 1894.

História quinhentista do segundo cêrco de Dio, ed. by António Baião, Coimbra, 1925.

Jayne, K. G., *Vasco da Gama and His Successors,* Methuen & Co., ltd., London, 1910.

Lane, Frederic Chapin, "Venetian Shipping during the Commercial Revolution," *American Historical Review,* XXXVIII, 1933.

Lybyer, Albert Howe, "The Ottoman Turks and the Routes of Oriental Trade," *English Historical Review,* XXX, 1915.

Marchant, Alexander, "Colonial Brazil as a Way Station of the Portuguese India Fleet," *Geographical Review,* XXXI, 1941.

Rey, Charles F., *The Romance of the Portuguese in Abyssinia,* H. F. & G. Witherby, London, 1929.

Summa Oriental of Tomé Pires, transl. and ed. Armando Cortesão, 2 vols., Hakluyt Society, London, 1944.

Travels of Ludovico de Varthema, transl. and ed. George P. Badger, Hakluyt Society, London, 1863.

Whiteway, R. S., *The Rise of the Portuguese Power in India,* A. Constable & Co., Westminster, 1899.

THE PORTUGUESE RENAISSANCE

Bell, Aubrey F. G., *Gil Vicente*, Oxford University Press, Oxford, 1921.
Bell, Aubrey F. G., *Portuguese Portraits*, B. H. Blackwell, Oxford, 1917.
Burton, Richard, *Camoëns, His Life and His Lusiads*, 2 vols., Bernard Quaritch, London, 1881.
Cortesão, Armando, *Cartografia e cartógrafos portugueses dos seculos xv e xvi*, 2 vols., Seara Nova, Lisbon, 1935.
Costa Cabral, F. A., *D. João II e a renascença portuguesa*, Livraria Ferin, Lisbon, 1914.
Ficalho, Conde de, *Garcia da Orta e seu tempo*, Imprensa Nacional, Lisbon, 1886.
Figueiredo, Fidelino de, *Literatura portuguesa*, Editora a Noite, Rio de Janeiro, 1940.
Figueiredo, José de, *O pintor Nuno Gonçalves*, Typ. do Annuario Commercial, Lisbon, 1910.
Pereira da Silva, Luciano, *A astronomia dos Lusiadas*, Imprensa da Universidade, Coimbra, 1915.
Pereira da Silva, Luciano, *Obras completas de Luciano Pereira da Silva*, Agencia Geral das Colonias, Lisbon, 1943.

THE PORTUGUESE DECLINE AND THE SPANISH PERIOD

D'Antas, Miguel Martins, *Les faux Don Sebastien*, A. Durand, Paris, 1886.
Ford, J. M., *Letters of the Court of John III, King of Portugal*, Harvard University Press, Cambridge, Mass., 1931.
Pimenta, Alfredo, *D. João III*, Livraria Tavares Martins, Oporto, 1936.
Queiroz Veloso, J. M. de, *Don Sebastián, 1554-1578*, transl. Ramón Garciasol, Madrid, 1943.
Sousa Viterbo, F. M. de, *O prior do Crato e a invasão hespanhola, de 1580*, Typographia Universal, Lisbon, 1897.

THE PORTUGUESE RESTORATION AND THE EIGHTEENTH CENTURY

Boxer, C. R., "Salvador Correia de Sá e Benevides and the Reconquest of Angola in 1648," *Hispanic American Historical Review*, XXVIII, 1948.
Boxer, C. R., "Padre António Vieira, S. J., and the Institution of the Brazil Company in 1649," *Hispanic American Historical Review*, XXIX, 1949.
Cheke, Marcus, *Dictator of Portugal* [Pombal], Sidgwick & Jackson, ltd., London, 1938.
Prestage, Edgar, *Diplomatic Relations of Portugal, 1640-1668*, Voss & Michael, ltd., Watford, England, 1925.
Rau, Virginia, *D. Catarina de Bragança*, Watford, England, 1925.
Rebello da Silva, L. A., *História de Portugal nos séculos xvii e xviii*, 5 vols., Imprensa Nacional, Lisbon, 1860-1871.
Smith, John, *The Life of the Marquis of Pombal*, 2 vols., Longman, Brown, Green, and Longmans, London, 1843.

PORTUGAL IN THE NINETEENTH CENTURY

Batalha-Reis, Jayme, "The Portuguese in Nyassaland," *Scottish Geographical Magazine,* V, 1889.

Bollaert, William, *The Wars of Succession in Spain and Portugal,* 2 vols., E. Stauford, London, 1843.

Brito Capello, H., and Ivens, R., *From Benguella to the Territory of Yacca,* transl. by Alfred Elwes, 2 vols., S. Low, Marston, Searle, and Rivington, London, 1882.

Cunha, Amadeu, *Serpa Pinto e o apelo de África,* Agencia das Colonias, Lisbon, 1946.

Enes, António, *A guerra de Africa em 1895,* Typ. do "Dia," Lisbon, 1898.

Gribble, Francis, *The Royal House of Portugal,* Eveleigh Nash, London, 1915.

Monteiro, Tobias, *História do imperio: a elaboração da independencia,* F. Briguiet & cia, Rio de Janeiro, 1927.

Nowell, Charles E., "Portugal and the Partition of Africa," *Journal of Modern History,* XIX, 1947.

Oliveira Lima, Manoel de, *D. Miguel no trono, 1828-1833,* Imprensa da Universidade, Coimbra, 1933.

Oliveira Martins, Joaquim Pedro de, *Portugal contemporaneo,* 2 vols., Parceria A. M. Pereira, Lisbon, 1925.

Pereira de Magalhães, Felix, *Apontamentos para a história diplomatica de Portugal desde 1826 até 1834,* Imprensa de J. G. Sousa Neves, Lisbon, 1871.

Queiroz Veloso, J. M. de, *Como perdemos Olivença,* Oficina "Ottosgráfica," ltda., Lisbon, 1933.

Serpa Pinto, Alexandre, *Como eu atravessei a África,* 2 vols., S. Low, Marston, Searle, and Rivington, London, 1881.

Serpa Pinto, Carlota, *A vida breve e ardente de Serpa Pinto,* Agência Geral das Colónias, Lisbon, 1937.

Smith, John, *Memoirs of Field-Marshal the Duke of Saldanha,* 2 vols., London, 1880.

Vaz de Carvalho, Maria Amália, *Vida do Duque de Palmela,* 3 vols., Imprensa Nacional, Lisbon, 1898-1903.

Vilhena, Júlio de, *D. Pedro V e o seu reinado,* 3 vols., Imprensa da Universidade, Coimbra, 1921.

RECENT PORTUGUESE CULTURE

Barbosa du Bocage, *Poesias,* ed. by Guerreiro Murta, Sá da Costa, Lisbon, 1943.

Figueiredo, Fidelino de, *Depois de Eça de Queiroz,* Editora Classico-Scientifica, São Paulo, 1943.

Ramalhete, Clovis, *Eça de Queiroz,* Livraria Martins, São Paulo, 1942.

Miscellaneous writings by José de Almeida Garret, Alexandre Herculano, Júlio Dinís, Viscount Santarem, João de Deus, Antero de Quental, Guerra Junqueiro, Eça de Queiroz, Teófilo Braga, and Fidelino de Figueiredo.

PORTUGAL SINCE 1910

Bragança-Cunha, V. de, *Revolutionary Portugal, 1910-1936,* J. Clarke & Co., ltd., London, 1937.

Derrick, Michael, *The Portugal of Salazar*, London, 1938.

Dillon, E. J., "Republican Portugal," *Contemporary Review*, November, 1910.

Dillon, E. J., "The Portuguese Revolution," *Living Age*, December 3, 1910.

Ferro, António, *Salazar: Portugal and her Leader*, Faber and Faber, ltd., London, 1939.

Kisch, Cecil H., *The Portuguese Bank-Note Case*, Macmillan & Co., ltd., London, 1932.

Leach, Leonard H., *Report on the Economic Conditions in Portugal*, H. M. Stationary Office, London, Department of Overseas Trade, 1928.

Various articles in the twenty-one completed volumes of *Grande enciclopédia portuguesa e brasileira*, Editorial Enciclopédica Limitada, Lisbon, Rio de Janeiro.

RULERS OF PORTUGAL

Afonso Henriques (count 1128-1143; king 1143-1185)	1128-1185
Sancho I	1185-1211
Afonso II	1211-1223
Sancho II	1223-1248
Afonso III	1248-1279
Dinís	1279-1325
Afonso IV	1325-1357
Pedro I	1357-1367
Fernando	1367-1383

INTERREGNUM OF TWO YEARS

João I	1385-1433
Duarte	1433-1438
Afonso V	1438-1481
João II	1481-1495
Manuel I	1495-1521
João III	1521-1557
Sebastião	1557-1578
Henrique	1578-1580

SPANISH PERIOD

Philip I (Philip II of Spain)	1581-1598
Philip II (Philip III of Spain)	1598-1621
Philip III (Philip IV of Spain)	1621-1640

PORTUGAL RESTORED

João IV	1640-1656
Afonso VI (effectively deposed 1668; died 1683)	1656-1668
Pedro II (governor from 1668; king from 1683)	1668-1706
João V	1706-1750
José	1750-1777
Maria (Maria's husband by courtesy known as Pedro III)	1777-1816
João VI	1816-1826
Pedro IV (Pedro I of Brazil)	1826-1828
Miguel	1828-1834

Maria II   1834-1853
Pedro V   1853-1861
Luís   1861-1889
Carlos   1889-1908
Manuel II   1908-1910

PRESIDENTS OF PORTUGAL

Teófilo Braga (provisional)   1910-1911
Manuel de Arriaga   1911-1915
Teófilo Braga (provisional)   1915-1915
Bernardino Machado   1915-1917
Sidónio Pais (dictator, 1917-1918; president 1918)   1917-1918
João do Canto e Castro   1918-1919
António José de Almeida   1919-1923
Manuel Teixeira Gomes   1923-1925
Bernardino Machado   1925-1926
Manuel de Oliveira Gomes da Costa (provisional)   1926-1926
António Oscar de Fragoso Carmona (provisional)   1926-1928
António Oscar de Fragoso Carmona   1928-1951
   (re-elected 1935, 1942, 1949)
Francisco Higino Craveiro Lopes   1951-

INDEX

252